T0293914

THE COAST TO COAST WALK

About the Author

Lancashire-born writer and photographer Dr Terry Marsh specialises in the outdoors and travel. He has been writing guidebooks since the mid-1980s, and is the author or revision author/editor of over 100 titles including the award-winning Cicerone guides to the *Coast to Coast Walk* (first published in 1993), *The Shropshire Way* (1999) and *Great Mountain Days in the Pennines* (2013).

Terry has a long-standing interest in Cumbria and the Lake District and the Yorkshire Dales. Academically, he is an historical geographer holding a Master of Arts degree with Distinction in Lake District Studies and a PhD in Historical Geography. He is a fellow of the Royal Geographical Society (FRGS) and a Life Member of the Outdoor Writers and Photographers Guild (www.owpg.org.uk).

Other Cicerone guides by the author

The Dales Way
Walking the Isle of Man
Walking the Isle of Skye
Walking on the Isle of Mull
The West Highland Way
The Severn Way
Walking in the Forest of Bowland and Pendle

Walking on the West Pennine Moors
Great Mountain Days in Snowdonia
Great Mountain Days in the Pennines
Geocaching in the UK

THE COAST TO COAST WALK

ST BEES TO ROBIN HOOD'S BAY

by Terry Marsh

JUNIPER HOUSE, MURLEY MOSS,
OXENHOLME ROAD, KENDAL, CUMBRIA LA9 7RL
www.cicerone.co.uk

© Terry Marsh 2017
Fourth edition 2017
ISBN-13: 978 1 85284 759 3
Reprinted 2020, 2021, 2023 (with updates)
Third edition 2006
Second edition 2003
First edition 1993

Printed in China on responsibly sourced paper on behalf of Latitude Press Ltd
A catalogue record for this book is available from the British Library.
All photographs are by the author unless otherwise stated.

1:100K route mapping by Lovell Johns www.lovelljohns.com
All photographs are by the author unless otherwise stated.
© Crown copyright 2017 OS PU100012932.
NASA relief data courtesy of ESRI.

The 1:25K map booklet contains Ordnance Survey data
© Crown copyright 2017 OS PU100012932.

Updates to this Guide

While every effort is made by our authors to ensure the accuracy of guidebooks as they go to print, changes can occur during the lifetime of an edition. Any updates that we know of for this guide will be on the Cicerone website (www.cicerone.co.uk/759/updates), so please check before planning your trip. We also advise that you check information about such things as transport, accommodation and shops locally. Even rights of way can be altered over time. We are always grateful for information about any discrepancies between a guidebook and the facts on the ground, sent by email to updates@cicerone.co.uk or by post to Cicerone, Juniper House, Murley Moss, Oxenholme Road, Kendal, LA9 7RL.

Register your book: To sign up to receive free updates, special offers and GPX files where available, create a Cicerone account and register your purchase via the 'My Account' tab at www.cicerone.co.uk.

Front cover: South-facing view along Haweswater to Speaking Crag (Stage 4)

CONTENTS

Symbols on the route maps

〜	route	♁ ✝	church/cathedral	
〜	low level route	■	building	
⌒	alternative route	◤◥	bridge	
Ⓢ	start point	⌇⌇⌇	crag/outcrop	
Ⓕ	finish point	⌂	castle	
ⓈⒻ	start/finish point	⌁	lighthouse	
>	direction of route	▲	youth hostel	

Route map relief

0 kilometres 1   2
0 miles   1
SCALE: 1:100,000

Contour lines are drawn at
50m intervals and labelled
at 100m intervals.

400m
300m
200m
100m

Features on the overview map

County/Unitary boundary

Urban area

National Park eg *Lake District*

Area of Outstanding Natural
Beauty eg *North Pennines*

Overview map relief

>800m
600m
400m
200m
75m
0m

See 1:25,000 map booklet for the key to the 1:25,000 maps

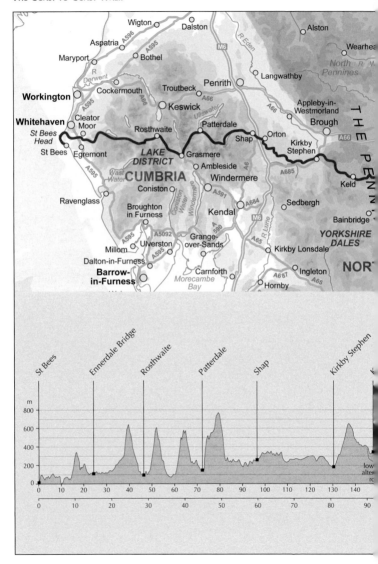

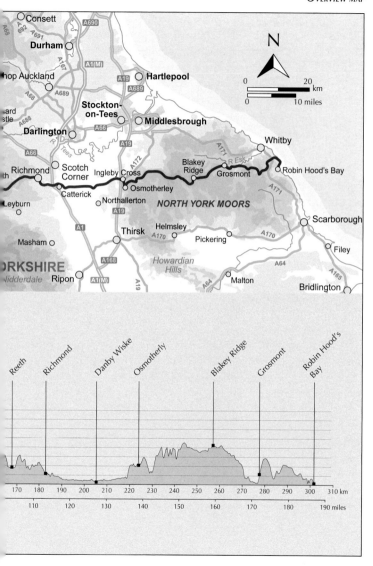

Coast to Coast Trek Planner

miles from St Bees

Location	miles from St Bees	miles from Robin Hood's Bay
ST BEES	0	188
Cleator	9	179
Ennerdale Bridge	15	173
Black Sail	24	164
Seatoller/Rosthwaite/Stonethwaite	29	159
Grasmere	37	141
Patterdale	45	133
Shap	60	128
Orton	68	120
Kirkby Stephen	81	107
Keld	92	96

miles from Robin Hood's Bay

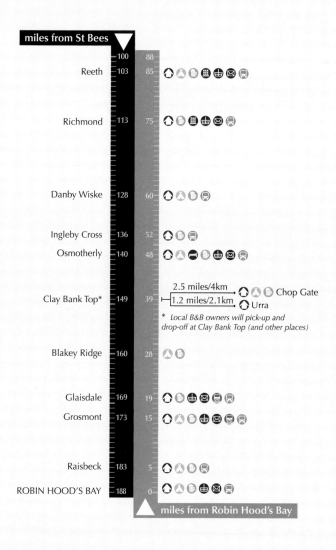

miles from St Bees ▼

	miles from St Bees	miles from Robin Hood's Bay	
Reeth	103	85	
Richmond	113	75	
Danby Wiske	128	60	
Ingleby Cross	136	52	
Osmotherly	140	48	
Clay Bank Top*	149	39	
Blakey Ridge	160	28	
Glaisdale	169	19	
Grosmont	173	15	
Raisbeck	183	5	
ROBIN HOOD'S BAY	188	0	

100

88

2.5 miles/4km 🔺🔺🔺 Chop Gate
1.2 miles/2.1km 🔺 Urra

Local B&B owners will pick-up and drop-off at Clay Bank Top (and other places)

▲ **miles from Robin Hood's Bay**

⬡ hotel/B&B ⬠ hostel/bunkhouse ⬠ camping ⬡ pub/inn
⬡ bank/ATM ⬡ food shop ⬡ post office ⬡ railway station ⬡ public transport

ROUTE SUMMARY TABLE

Stage no	Start/Finish	Distance miles (km)	Total Ascent ft (m)	Time hrs	Page
1	St Bees/Ennerdale Bridge	15 (23.9)	3625 (1105)	8	44
2	Ennerdale Bridge/ Rosthwaite	14½ (23.3)	2350 (715)	8	59
3	Rosthwaite/Patterdale	15½ (25)	4015 (1225)	9	72
4	Patterdale/Shap	15½ (25)	3685 (1123)	7–8	87
5	Shap/Kirkby Stephen	20¾ (32.9)	2030 (617)	10	105
6	Kirkby Stephen/Keld*	11 (17.5)	2115 (645)	5–6	130
7	Keld/Reeth**	11 (17.8)	2110 (643)	5–6	144
8	Reeth/Richmond	10½ (16.8)	1320 (402)	5	162
9	Richmond/Danby Wiske	14 (22.8)	575 (175)	7–8	171
10	Danby Wiske/ Osmotherley	12 (20)	862 (263)	5	183
11	Osmotherley/Blakey Ridge	20 (32)	3236 (986)	8	195
12	Blakey Ridge/Grosmont	13 (20.8)	937 (286)	5–6	212
13	Grosmont/Robin Hood's Bay	15 (24)	2275 (695)	6–7	222
		187¾ (302)	**29,135 (8880)**		

* following Blue Route (main route described)
** following high-level route (Stage 7A)

PREFACE TO THE FOURTH EDITION

Looking north-east to Roseberry Topping and the sea beyond (Stage 10) (J Williams)

In 2022 it was announced by Natural England that the Coast to Coast Walk was to be awarded National Trail status under section 51 of the National Parks and Access to the Countryside Act 1949. When completed, the route will be known as the 'Coast to Coast Path National Trail'. Work on upgrading the trail began in 2023 and is expected to be completed by 2025, when the new National Trail will be officially launched.

Work initially will focus on improvements to gates, stiles, signposting and waymarking to improve accessibility generally and for those with limited mobility, and developing opportunities and improved connectivity for horse riders and cyclists. Some realignments will be needed along with remedial work to sections of the route surface, and several new footpaths and bridleways will be created to ensure that the entirety of the path becomes a legal right-of-way.

Lyvennet Beck – a remote and lonely crossing on Crosby Ravensworth Fell (Stage 5)

INTRODUCTION

South-facing view along Haweswater to Speaking Crag (Stage 4)

When Wainwright devised a Coast to Coast walk across Northern England it was a masterpiece of inspiration, creating a tantalising and inspiring excursion that ranks among the best of the UK's long-distance trails. The walk is a firm favourite with generations of walkers who have followed its course up hill and down dale. In 2022 it was announced that the route was to become a National Trail having for so long had no official status.

Traversing the finest, many would say loveliest, ground in England, the route runs from the Irish Sea, lapping the pebbled western shores of Cumbria at St Bees, to where the waters of the North Sea flow into Robin Hood's Bay on the Yorkshire coast, a distance of just over 300km.

The route links three national parks and avoids urban development as much as possible. Up to a point it favours high ground over low and roughly comprises three distinct sections, separated by geology, history and culture.

In the west, the Lake District throws down a challenge that requires careful planning, while the stretch into and across the Yorkshire Dales, marginally easier, nevertheless injects a few of its own surprises, notably on Nine Standards Rigg. A glorious interlude then links the Dales with the North York Moors, across the Vale of

Striding Edge and Helvellyn from Grisedale (Stage 3)

Mowbray, feeding into the undulating Cleveland Hills before a happy scamper down to the sea.

This is certainly not the shortest way across England, nor a walk on which to cut one's trail-walking teeth – the Dales Way or the West Highland Way are better suited for that. But it is within the reach of any fit and well-prepared novice and one on which seasoned walkers will experience few difficulties.

AN UNMISSABLE EXPERIENCE

Across Lakeland

Usually tackled west to east, the Walk begins with an airy scamper above the cliffs of St Bees Head on the remote west coast of Cumbria (once described as 'the Odd Corner of England') and the first day, usually taken as far as Ennerdale Bridge, samples the delights of coastal walking before diving inland to the western fringes of Lakeland. The leg-wearying slopes of the minor summit, Dent Fell, particularly on a warm day, feel like Wainwright's idea of a joke, but beyond that the hidden Lakeland gems of Uldale and Nannycatch Beck are splendid compensation on the run in to Ennerdale.

With the exception of the sea cliffs and that ascent of Dent Fell, most of this section is pleasant and agreeable ambling, but largely unspectacular. If this were a day walk, it would be enjoyed and savoured at a leisurely pace, but the pressing engagement of limbs with the need to keep going can cause you to overlook an intrinsic beauty.

So, make the most of it now; there'll be no going back.

Ennerdale, however, marks your entry, to the Lake District proper, and penetrates far into the heart of steep-sided mountains that rise to the great summits of Pillar and Great Gable at the valley's head. From there, with a daunting flourish, the walk engages the short-lived wrath of Loft Beck as it hauls itself across the fells above Buttermere and into the head of Borrowdale, descending from Honister Pass into Seatoller, and then by a charming traverse to Rosthwaite. By now, in much-fêted Borrowdale, you are as firmly on the traditional Victorian tourist trail as you were off it at pedestrian-only Black Sail youth hostel in the deep and distant sanctum of Ennerdale.

By enterprising leaps, the walk then visits Langstrath, crosses the heights of Greenup Edge to Far Easedale and Grasmere, and then engages on a delightful journey to Patterdale by way of Grisedale Tarn, a haunting location on a misty day. Beyond Patterdale, the route clings as long as it can to high ground, before resigning itself to the inevitable and dropping to the shores of Haweswater, preparing to leave behind the embrace of Lakeland.

Understandably, for it was his greatest and first love, Wainwright was inclined to feel that once the Lake District was left, the finest had

At Ennerdale's edge – an open invitation (Stage 2)

gone, although he did not 'concede that the rest of the journey is in the nature of anti-climax'. If the truth is known, what lies ahead is every bit as enchanting, captivating, and spiritually reviving as Lakeland, qualities derived, if not from the ruggedness of the landscape, then from its sublime insinuation into our senses, its soft and outstandingly beautiful insistence on playing its part in this drama, with equal rights to top billing.

And quite rightly so! If you think all the beauty is in the Lake District, you are in for an agreeable surprise.

Into the Dales

The prehistoric and cultural importance of the landscape between Shap and Kirkby Stephen make for an inspirational passage, especially for those of a receptive mind. Once the delights of Kirkby Stephen are left behind, the way climbs by Faraday Gill onto Nine Standards Rigg, and then by Whitsundale to Keld at the head of Swaledale, arguably the finest of the dales. This stretch in its upper reaches, however, is problematic, bedevilled by high-quality peat bog – if you like that kind of thing – and few points of navigational aid in poor visibility. So, alternative routes have been devised, suitable for differing conditions, times of year and personal inclination.

Preferring a lofty traverse between Keld and Reeth, the original line makes what it can of the old mining routes that abound in this historically fascinating region, but for those who prefer a valley route, the superlative flower-laden meadows along the River Swale are an alternative option. Indeed, beyond the industrial

Wild Boar Fell from the Coast to Coast path, near Kirkby Stephen (Stage 6)

Heading for Hasty Bank (Stage 10)

archaeology, there is little to repay the effort of the climb onto the moors, and misty conditions often prevail to deny the walker any views.

Between Reeth and Richmond limestone scars, leafy lanes, woodland and rich pastures abound, while Richmond itself seems to remain aloof from the 21st century in many ways, retaining much of its great historical flavour, centred on its castle.

The ensuing Vale of Mowbray is quite simply delightful, forming a lengthy link between the Dales and the North York Moors, approaching marathon distance in length. There is for some a temptation to race across the vale, but that is to do it a considerable disservice. It is a quiet interlude, a lazy route linking farms and villages across a pastoral landscape.

The North York Moors

As the journey goes on, so the Cleveland Hills approach, and an unrivalled crossing of the North York Moors lies in wait. Superb views enliven the way, which here proves rather more undulating than might be expected. The landscape is perhaps not as dramatic as the Lake District, but the grandeur and scale of the North York Moors do provide a fitting conclusion. Not by chance is a good section of this magnificent upland also shared with two other walks of note, the Lyke Wake Walk, a gruelling 40-mile trek through the night against the clock, and the Cleveland Way, which in 1969 became Britain's second long-distance path, all 109 miles of it.

Beyond Clay Bank Top the walking is effortless, with only the pull on to Urra Moor demanding any head of steam, as the route ploughs on into the privately-owned Lord Stones Country Park. After that, leg-swinging freedom, partly along the line of a former mineral railway, is the order of the day, with expansive views across rolling moorland to cheer the spirit and prepare for the final stage of the journey.

The concluding stage is as fitting as the first, and finds its way along old toll roads, by way of ancient burial mounds, across tracts of heather moorland, through ancient, time-worn villages, delightful woodland, until, at the very end, the walker is faced, as he or she was in the beginning, with an exhilarating clifftop walk, this time to the beautiful Robin Hood's Bay.

The Coast to Coast Walk is, borrowing from Keats:

A thing of beauty...a joy for ever

Make sure you experience it.

The marker stone at the top of the first climb from Clay Bank Top (Stage 10) (J. Williams)

PLANNING YOUR WALK

Following the path onto the cliffs of St Bees Head South (Stage 1)

Walkers with other long-distance walks under their belts will find that the Coast to Coast Walk differs very little in terms of physical effort and organisation, but, as always, good forward planning and attention to detail can ensure a happy and rewarding endeavour.

For one thing, with so much of interest along the way, it is vital to allow time to explore and potter about, to paddle in the streams and rivers, to visit churches (and pubs) – to get something of a feel for the lifestyle that permeates the course of the walk and the history that has fashioned the land it traverses.

The first prerequisite is to be sure you are fit enough. Setting off to do around two weeks' worth of long walks back-to-back takes its toll, usually starting around Day 3. It is also important to plan days that you can realistically complete, and even then be prepared to abbreviate your intentions. Don't be drawn into joining other walkers you meet and inadvertently pressing on to do more than you feel comfortable with.

As a general guide, you will need about two weeks to do the entire walk, give or take a day or so, plus whatever time is needed to get to and from start and finish points.

The total distance as described here is 302km (187¾ miles), and involves an ascent (and descent) of more than 8,900m (29,000ft), no mean undertaking – a Himalayan peak, in fact.

SUGGESTED ITINERARIES

The walk must become what you want it to be. It is not a forced march, something you have to do in so many days. This is a walk to be enjoyed in a leisurely manner; something to take your time over and to use as a gateway to exploration of the countryside that lies to either side of it.

The Trek Planner at the front of this guide gives the distance between each of the principal halts, and shows what facilities are available at those locations. Using this, it should be possible to construct a walk that suits your abilities and preferences, but (if you have not done something similar before and so learned the lesson!) take care not to be over ambitious in planning a day's walk.

The whole route is divided into three geographical sections, loosely based on the three National Parks crossed along the way. Each section could form the basis of a splendid long weekend or short week's walking, with (limited) public transport available at either end for getting there and back. Within each of these sections, the day stages described all end at places where accommodation can be found (see Appendix B), although it may well be necessary to book ahead in some cases in high season. At the end of each of these stages, the route is also described in the reverse direction for those who choose to walk from east to west, rather than west to east.

Thousands of people every year tackle this route in one endeavour, and this is a commendable and logical challenge. But there is much to be said for doing it in instalments, and getting just as much fun out of it, and

Looking back over Shap Abbey to the distant fells (Stage 4)

in some cases rather more, because you can cut out and go home if the weather forecast is abysmal, or spend a little longer over lunch in one of the many country pubs along the route if you feel like lingering.

In this book the route is described in 13 stages, which gives you an average daily mileage of 14 miles (within a range of 11 miles to 20 miles) over widely varying terrain. If this seems too much like hard work, and you have more than two weeks' holiday to take, you can use the Trek Planner to plot a more comfortable itinerary. Two longer itineraries – of 15 days (averaging 12½ miles a day) and 19 days (10 miles a day) – are outlined below but these are only suggestions.

Some of the main decisions the walker needs to consider when adapting the itinerary to their needs and time available include:

• Whether to Stay at Black Sail Hostel at the head of Ennerdale. This needs booking well in advance, and leaves the walker with a short day up Ennerdale (unless they opted to stay the first night in Cleator Moor), followed by another short day to Rosthwaite in Borrowdale. It is feasible, although long, to get from Black Sail to Grasmere.

• Whether to stop at Grasmere or continue on to Patterdale. There is plenty to do and see in Grasmere, but this definitely needs an extra day as the onward stage after Patterdale to Shap is a long one.

• Whether to stop at Orton (a very short day) or tackle the full distance to Kirkby Stephen. Orton is a charming village and the walk to it across Ravenstonedale Moor an unexpected highlight after the Lake District section. Shap to Kirkby Stephen is nearly 21 miles (34km) and a long day, and many walkers would find this day's tally far too demanding, especially on a warm day.

• Whether to stay in Keld or continue on to one of the villages down valley. The stage to Keld looks fairly short but is tougher than the distance suggests.

• Whether to tackle the Vale of York from Richmond or Bolton-on-Swale as a single long day or break into two. This may be determined by the limited accommodation around Danby Wiske. Again it would make a long day, and your decision may reflect whether the lowland interlude appeals or you are impelled to reach the next high ground.

• Whether to stop at Clay Bank Top or press on to Blakey Ridge and the Lion Inn. The easy stretch from Clay Bank Top to the Lion along the old Rosedale railway is fast walking, and it is really a choice of which day you want to fit it in to. There are no options after Grosmont, and it may be better to get to this busy village as the final day is 15 miles/24km to Robin Hood's Bay.

COAST TO COAST IN 15 DAYS

1	St Bees to Ennerdale Bridge	(15 miles/24km)
2	Ennerdale Bridge to Rosthwaite	(14 miles/23km)
3	Rosthwaite to Grasmere	(8 miles/13km)
4	Grasmere to Patterdale	(8 miles/13km)
5	Patterdale to Shap	(15 miles/24km)
6	Shap to Kirkby Stephen	(21 miles/35km)
7	Kirkby Stephen to Keld	(11 miles/18km)
8	Keld to Reeth	(11 miles/17km)
9	Reeth to Richmond	(10 miles/17km)
10	Richmond to Danby Wiske	(15 miles/23km)
11	Danby Wiske to Ingleby Cross	(8 miles/14km)
12	Ingleby Cross to Clay Bank Top	(12 miles/18km)
13	Clay Bank Top to Blakey Ridge	(9 miles/15km)
14	Blakey Ridge to Grosmont	(13 miles/19km)
15	Grosmont to Robin Hood's Bay	(15 miles/24km)

COAST TO COAST IN 19 DAYS

1	St Bees to Cleator	(9 miles/14km)
2	Cleator to Ennerdale Bridge	(6 miles/10km)
3	Ennerdale Bridge to Black Sail Hut	(9 miles/14km)
4	Black Sail Hut to Rosthwaite	(5 miles/9km)
5	Rosthwaite to Grasmere	(8 miles/13km)
6	Grasmere to Patterdale	(8 miles/13km)
7	Patterdale to Shap	(15 miles/24km)
8	Shap to Orton	(8 miles/13km)
9	Orton to Kirkby Stephen	(13 miles/20km)
10	Kirkby Stephen to Keld	(11 miles/18km)
11	Keld to Reeth	(11 miles/17km)
12	Reeth to Richmond	(10 miles/17km)
13	Richmond to Bolton-on-Swale	(7 miles/11km)
14	Bolton-on-Swale to Danby Wiske	(7 miles/11km)
15	Danby Wiske to Ingleby Cross	(8 miles/14km)
16	Ingleby Cross to Clay Bank Top	(12 miles/18km)
17	Clay Bank Top to Glaisdale	(18 miles/29km)
18	Glaisdale to Grosmont	(4 miles/7km)
19	Grosmont to Robin Hood's Bay	(15 miles/24km)

However you structure your trek, be it for a fast crossing or a more leisurely exploration, plan your daily walk according to your own strengths and abilities.

WHEN TO GO

Some people, perhaps because of family or work commitments, may have little freedom over when they choose to tackle a long walk. But if possible there are certain times to be avoided, notably the main tourist months of July and August, although this is rarely the problem you might imagine.

It's a good idea, too, to avoid starting at weekends: if you can start mid-week, do so – it avoids congestion along the route. May and June, and September and October tend to produce settled weather, and these are the times of year that I would choose. Bear in mind that the days are noticeably shorter in April and October – a serious consideration if you are planning on walking up to ten hours a day.

A warning from personal experience: Having experienced the Coast to Coast and the abundance and variety of flowers in springtime several times, I would suggest that botanists doing the walk at that time of year might well be advised to keep the days short, add an extra week, and either travel alone or with very understanding and empathetic friends!

GETTING THERE AND BACK

St Bees
By rail: St Bees is served by the Cumbrian Coast Line, and St Bees is

Above the River Derwent, near Longthwaite youth hostel (Stage 2)

a mandatory stop. There is a railway station in the centre of the village with 22 trains a day between Preston/Lancaster/Barrow in the south, and Carlisle in the north. Local trains on the Cumbrian Coast Line are run by Northern Rail (www.northernrail.org) and times and fares are available from National Rail Enquiries (tel 03457 48 49 50, www.nationalrail.co.uk (which has a map of the whole rail network)).

There are no Sunday trains, but Whitehaven, just a short taxi ride away, has a Sunday service from Carlisle.

International travellers arriving by air will find Manchester the most convenient airport as it has a direct rail service to Preston, from where trains can be joined heading around the coast to St Bees.

By road: the village is on the B5345 just south of Whitehaven. If you are intending to leave your car at St Bees, then a number of hotels and B&Bs offer parking facilities, but getting back from Robin Hood's Bay to St Bees by rail to collect your car is quite a complex trip.

Robin Hood's Bay
By rail: The nearest railway station is at Whitby, served by the Esk Valley Railway (www.eskvalleyrailway.co.uk), which runs from Middlesbrough to Whitby.

By bus: Arriva run buses from Scarborough to Middlesbrough through Robin Hood's Bay and Whitby (www.arrivabus.co.uk).

Local bus services are operated by Arriva (www.arrivabus.co.uk) and Stagecoach (www.stagecoachbus.com). Moorsbus (www.moorsbus.org) is a service operated around the North York Moors by volunteers. Traveline (www.traveline.info) is an online service that covers all public transport. But bear in mind that bus services are structured to serve the needs of local people not those of transient visitors.

North Yorkshire Moors Railway (www.nymr.co.uk) is a heritage route from Pickering to Grosmont and Whitby.

FIRST AND LAST NIGHTS

St Bees
St Bees huddles in a valley near the sea, a grey village of antiquity and charm. The valley is that of Pow Beck, a direct link with the busy industrialisation of Whitehaven to the north. Approaching from the south, however, it is always with an element of surprise that the village springs into view; from a distance it possesses the quiet, unassuming air of a Scottish crofting community in the way the buildings seem to sit in harmony with the landscape with St Bees Head as the backdrop. On closer inspection the village turns out to be substantial and endowed with a history of considerable interest. The church is the oldest and finest in what was West

Cumberland and its grammar school (which sadly closed its doors in 2015) dated back to 1583.

St Bees has a modest range of facilities that will serve the needs of Coast to Coasters. There are no medical practices in St Bees; the nearest is in Egremont, three miles away, and there are several in Whitehaven, which is where you'll find the nearest hospital.

The beach at low tide is a wide expanse of red sand and rock pools, and in 2015 received an award for its cleanliness.

A map of the village and its facilities is available at www.stbees.org.uk.

Robin Hood's Bay

Robin Hood's Bay, located 5 miles (8km) south of Whitby, has a fishing heritage. Once a smuggling centre there is always something going on, and this village of narrow, steep streets has cafés and shops as well as regular music events and festivals. This is a far cry from the deckchair and fun fair seaside, but more elemental and rugged with the village spilling down to the water's edge. At high tide the sea runs into the village street, and comes in alarmingly quickly.

For more information visit: www.robin-hoods-bay.co.uk.

ACCOMMODATION

For a walk that spends a deal of its time away from civilisation, the Coast to Coast is supported with accommodation throughout much of its length. But it is not over-endowed, so don't

The end (or start) of the Coast to Coast at Robin Hood's Bay

take it for granted; book ahead – a day at a time may suffice at quiet times of the year. In the main tourist season, however, there is pressure on all the accommodation along the route, while in the quieter months some closes down altogether. It is vital to remember that if you choose accommodation that is 'off-route', then getting to and from it the next day is added distance to be included in your daily plan.

Appendix B contains list of accommodation providers along the route. There are also many up-to-date accommodation listings on the internet, notably on www.coasttocoast guides.co.uk..

If unsure, check with the appropriate tourist boards (see Appendix B) for information, as the situation is changing all the time.

FACILITIES EN ROUTE

The Trek Planner at the front of this guide outlines which places along the route offer which basic facilities, but the Coast to Coast Walk spends a good deal of time away from civilisation where such facilities are non-existent. Nor should it be expected that remote villages, even in the more populous Lake District, are well-endowed with shops and cafés that will still be open when you arrive, if they exist at all. Moreover, because local transport tends to serve the needs of local people it cannot be relied on to facilitate a quick trip to a supermarket or large town.

There are few sections of the walk where it is possible to get lunch during the day, so it is vital that you start each day well prepared and stocked. Have a good breakfast, carry plenty of liquid and daytime food, and make the most of your evening meal.

BAGGAGE TRANSFER

There is much to be said for not having to struggle along the Coast to Coast with 15 kilos of this and that on your back; all that sudden extra weight will be stressful on joints and feet in particular. Thankfully, a few companies specialise in baggage transfer services along the route, notably:
• Brigantes Walking Holidays and Baggage Couriers (www.brigantesenglishwalks.com)
• The Coast to Coast Packhorse (www.c2cpackhorse.co.uk)
• The Sherpa Van Project (www.coast2coast.co.uk).
See Appendix A for full contact details.

CASH MANAGEMENT

With few opportunities along the walk to get hold of cash, it becomes vitally important to estimate your money requirements in advance; you cannot rely on all accommodation providers accepting credit and debit card payments. For many B&Bs it is not worth their while to accept credit cards. If you cannot find a cash point, a cheque book and banker's card can usually be used to get cash from post

Flower fields at the edge of Greenup Gill (Stonethwaite) (Stage 3)

offices (often only open limited hours in rural areas) but only Kirkby Stephen and Richmond along the route have full banking facilities.

WHAT TO TAKE

All walkers have their own preferences in the matter of equipment and clothing. When extending day-walking into multiple-day walking much the same general items are needed, with the key concern being able to stay warm, dry (as much as possible) and comfortable in all weather conditions.

There is a saying – something of a cliché now – that there is no such thing as bad weather, just inadequate clothing. There is a lot of truth in this – so if you expect cold, wet and windy weather, and prepare for it, then anything else is a bonus. Approach the Coast to Coast in this frame of mind – equipped to cope with the worst – and then when you find beautiful days of perfect walking weather your joy will be unbounded.

The following list may be a useful reminder.

- comfortable, well-padded rucksack, appropriate to backpacking rather than day walking (unless you are using a baggage transfer service), and preferably one that you have already had some practice with
- boots
- socks (spare socks and more spare socks, which can also double as spare gloves)
- trousers (and shorts if you wish but not shorts alone)

- underclothes
- shirt
- mid-wear (eg fleece) and a spare
- wind- and waterproof jacket and over-trousers
- hat
- gloves
- maps
- compass
- torch (with spare battery and bulbs)
- whistle
- first aid kit including blister pads and knee supports
- survival bag or space blanket
- food and drink, and emergency supplies
- insect repellent
- washing kit, including half a roll of toilet tissue inside a separate plastic bag (for emergencies)
- small hand towel
- and, if you are using a GPS, then don't forget to carry spare batteries.

Given the proliferation of mobile phones, GPS devices and the like, all of which require batteries, there is also much to be said for carrying a solar-recharging device of some kind that can clip to the outside of a rucksack during the day; absence of sunlight doesn't mean it won't charge. You should also be able to recharge your devices overnight at your accommodation.

Campers will also need such additional weighty items as tent, sleeping bag, sleeping mat, and cooking equipment and utensils. Pedal-bin liners have a number of useful purposes – keeping wet clothes separate from dry in the sack; containing burst packets of food and rubbish until a suitable disposal point can be reached; and insulating dry socks from wet boots when walking.

Take a notebook and keep a personal record of your experiences, or a paperback book (in addition to this one!) to read.

PLANNING DAY BY DAY

Striding out across the moorland expanse of Crosby Ravensworth Fell (Stage 5)

USING THIS GUIDE

The main body of this guide is a step-by-step route description of the Coast to Coast Walk, split into three geographical sections and 13 day stages. Each stage description begins with a information box with key facts about the day's walking including where additional accommodation may be found along the route for those wishing to split the stage, a short introduction giving an overview of the route, and then the detailed route description, accompanied by a 1:100,000 route map and a height profile.

Aspects of the route shown on the route map are highlighted in bold in the text to help you use the map and the route description in tandem, alongside the 1:25,000 mapping booklet. Notes are also included throughout the route description of geological, historical, industrial, sociological and natural history interest.

At the end of each stage the route is described briefly from east to west for those wishing to walk in that direction. The reverse route description does not give the route data. This needs to be taken from the west-east description, and details of height gain, descent, terrain and accommodation reversed.

At the back of the guide are the appendices – a list of useful contacts, the accommodation listing and some suggestions for further reading.

Distances and total ascent

The figures given for distances and ascents are guidelines only. They were measured using a combination of digital and aerial mapping and in general relate more closely to the route on the ground, i.e. 'as walked', rather than as depicted on mapping.

Walking times

How long it might take to walk ten miles with a pack varies from individual to individual. Naismith's Rule (1 hour per 3 miles, plus 1 hour for each 2000 feet of ascent) is a popular rule of thumb which needs adjustment to suit each walker's personal abilities; not everyone can maintain Naismith's targets over an extended day and some will walk considerably faster.

For this reason, the walking times given are already an adjustment of Naismith's Rule based on the author's own experience; they are intended just to give an idea of how long you may need to be walking. These times are *walking times*, and therefore make no allowance for any kind of stopping – photographic, refreshment or otherwise.

MAPS

This guide comes complete with its own 1:25,000 OS map booklet, and individual 1:100,000 route maps, ideal for following the route.

Should you want to explore more widely, perhaps while taking a day off, the following maps may be needed.

Heading up Reigill towards Nine Standards Rigg (Stage 6)

1:50,000 Landranger maps
- 89 West Cumbria
- 90 Penrith and Keswick, Ambleside
- 91 Appleby-in-Westmorland area
- 92 Barnard Castle and surrounding area
- 93 Middlesbrough and Darlington area
- 94 Whitby and surrounding area
- 98 Wensleydale and Upper Wharfedale
- 99 Northallerton, Ripon and surrounding area

1:25,000 Explorer maps
Be sure to get current copies which show Access Land.
- 303 Whitehaven and Workington
- OL4 English Lakes, North West
- OL5 English Lake, North East
- OL7 English Lakes, South East
- OL19 Howgill Fells and Upper Eden Valley
- OL26 North York Moors, East
- OL27 North York Moors, West
- OL30 Yorkshire Dales, North and Central
- 302 Northallerton and Thirsk
- 304 Darlington and Richmond

Harvey maps
Harvey Maps also produce two maps covering the Coast to Coast Walk.

The whole of the Coast to Coast Walk is also available for the SatMap Active 10/12 GPS device (www.satmap.co.uk), which provides complete and accurate coverage of your progress along the Walk

using satellite technology. Other GPS mapping and tracking devices are available.

WEATHER

Britain is meteorologically sandwiched between moist maritime air and dry continental air, a combination that creates large temperature variations and atmospheric instability. As a result, many (and sometimes all) weather variations can be experienced in just one day. That said, there are often prolonged periods of stable weather that make recreational walking an utter joy.

Over the many years that I have been backpacking I have, at various times, encountered weather that has grilled my ears, and, at others, drenched me so thoroughly that it would have been simpler to walk with nothing on at all! Both extremes should be anticipated and prepared for by anyone contemplating the Coast to Coast Walk. Only those who don't think in terms of such weather conditions are likely to find themselves facing uncomfortable and (at the extreme) potentially dangerous conditions.

The Lake District in particular has a tendency to generate its own climate regardless of predicted weather forecasts. This is rather less the case on the rest of the walk, although high hills are never far distant, and these influence the weather patterns locally.

Weather forecasting is much improved in recent years, with the best forecasts on a day-to-day basis provided by regional television channels. The Met Office has a downloadable weather app (www.metoffice.gov.uk) in a new format introduced in 2016. It is available from iPhone's App Store (https://itunes.apple.com), and Android's Google Play Store (https://play.google.com/store/apps). The app is designed to work on iOS 8 and above, and Android 4.1 and above. 'Weather Live' is arguably the best of the non-Met Office apps, also available for iPhones and Androids.

WAYMARKING AND PATHS

As the Coast to Coast Walk moves to full national trail status, so waymarking and signposting will progressively improve as will conditions underfoot in the most eroded places. In the meantime, the route is rarely less than evident and follows good and long-established paths and tracks. Seasonal variants are available on the crossing of Nine Standards Rigg, where, at times, the path can become unhelpfully liquid. Generally, for the most part, there is firm footing.

EMERGENCIES

The police, fire service, ambulance or mountain rescue can be reached in an emergency by dialling 999 or 112. There are numerous mountain rescue teams operating in the regions covered by the Coast to Coast Walk; the appropriate one can be contacted on the above emergency numbers:

The **Lake District Search and Mountain Rescue Association** (LDSAMRA, www.ldsamra.org.uk) comprises 12 teams across Cumbria and the Lake District, including Cockermouth, Coniston, Duddon and Furness, Kendal, Keswick, Kirkby Stephen, Langdale, Ambleside, Patterdale, Penrith and Wasdale mountain rescue teams, plus the Cumbria Ore Mines Rescue Unit (COMRU), and the Lake District Mountain Rescue Search Dogs.

The **North East Search and Rescue Association** (NESRA, www.nesra.org.uk) covers the North East of England and comprises Cleveland, North of Tyne, Northumberland National Park, Scarborough and Rydale, Swaledale, Teesdale and Weardale and RAF Leeming mountain rescue teams.

PHONES AND WI-FI

Internet access via WiFi is increasingly available in cafés, pubs and hotels, but it is by no means universally available, and may not be available in some B&Bs and youth hostels.

Mobile phone signals are restricted and often erratic, especially away from urban centres. But the situation is constantly evolving and can be checked using www.signalchecker.co.uk/cumbria, which works best if you use a post code.

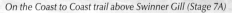
On the Coast to Coast trail above Swinner Gill (Stage 7A)

The reality is that you will not have a signal along many of the open stretches of the route. Yet surprisingly, signals from some distant transmitter can be picked up in the most unexpected locations.

Always ensure that your mobile phone is charged fully at every opportunity, and include among your kit one of the many portable mains and solar battery chargers available. Keep that topped up, too.

LANGUAGE

There are no regional languages spoken along the Coast to Coast. Dialect and vernacular terms, however, are another matter, and you may have many a happy hour in a pub trying to follow conversations between locals.

ALL ABOUT THE REGION

Great Gable and Green Gable from upper Ennerdale (Stage 2)

GEOGRAPHY AND GEOLOGY

There probably could not be a wider range of landscapes, all owing their characteristics to the underlying geology. Lakeland is a region of granite mountains, fashioned (as virtually all of the route is to varying degrees) by glacial and volcanic action. Slate developed from sediments in oceans, volcanoes erupted, limestone was formed by the deposition of dead crustaceans, and sandstone was created in desert conditions at a time when 'England' was much farther south than it is today. All of this was later shifted and shaped first by folding and uplifting and then by glaciers and water erosion. As a result, the topography of the Lake District features smooth U-shaped valleys below steep and sharp mountain ridges.

Between Shap and Richmond, sedimentary rocks are evident, set down largely during the Carboniferous period, 350 million years ago. The Vale of Mowbray is, by comparison, low lying and predominantly flat, before it gives way to the uplifts of the Cleveland Hills. Geological studies of the Cleveland Hills date them to the Middle Jurassic age, about 161–176 million years ago, although the North York Moors are formed on rocks from the Lower Jurassic, resulting in shale erosion along the north and west faces of the hills.

Rivers abound everywhere, following and enlarging the line of least resistance through whatever terrain they face, and they will be regular companions on the walk. Significant urban settlements are for the most part shunned. They cannot be ignored altogether, but will be encountered only at St Bees, Kirkby Stephen and Richmond, interspersed with small villages and linear developments.

WILDLIFE AND PLANTS

One of the intrinsic beauties of the Coast to Coast Walk is the way it, unavoidably, passes through a wide range of habitat from woodlands to moorland, hard rocky passes to limestone plateau, peat bog to beach, a diversity surpassed only by the flora and fauna they support. Hare, rabbit and possibly fox are the most likely mammal species to be encountered, although a bat, usually a pipistrelle, can often been seen flitting about around dusk. That unwelcome American import, the grey squirrel, is likely to be encountered everywhere, but the more precious and native red squirrel you may see only in the Lake District; likewise pine martens, which are rare in England having been almost wiped out in the 19th century. At any stage you may also encounter a stoat, and its smaller cousin the weasel, generally in daylight, although night-time brings a host of other creatures: badger, hedgehog, mouse, shrew and vole; even the otter is making a comeback, thanks to great conservation initiatives.

Nor is it uncommon to spot roe deer, a small native animal that favours woodlands, although they are also found grazing out in the open. Red deer are less well represented, and probably found only on the fringes of the Lake District.

Birdlife is abundant, and ornithologists will be able to tick off a goodly number of species from coastal birds like guillemot, razorbill, kittiwake, fulmar and gulls, to those that are more wide-ranging, such as buzzard, raven, kestrel and pheasant. A lucky few may spot a seasonal osprey – they nest in the Lake District, or can be spotted on passage – or an occasional peregrine falcon. Abundant throughout the walk are lapwing, curlew (occasionally whimbrel), redshank, snipe, ring ouzel and in such places as Crosby Ravensworth and Nine Standards such delightful rarities as dotterel and the piping golden plover.

The adder is the only snake likely to be encountered (most likely in the North York Moors on this route), notably in early spring as they come out of hibernation, although the non-venomous grass snake may also pop up from time to time.

Pass this way in spring, and anyone interested in wild flowers will be delighted whether traversing coastal meadows, where gorse, thrift and sea campion abound, or the woodlands, hedgerows and moorland that are a habitat for bluebell, anemone, primrose, celandine, campion, cranesbill, orchid and limestone-loving flowers like violet.

Blakeley Moss Stone Circle (Stage 1)

HISTORY AND PRE-HISTORY

People have lived in northern England for over 12,000 years, from the time, at the end of the last Ice Age, of roaming bands of hunter-gatherers, who only stopped their wanderings once they understood and developed the notion of farming. Their actions, on the move or static, did much to shape the landscape we see today. Around 7000 years ago most of the land was covered by trees. During the Neolithic, or New Stone Age, (4000–2000BCE) people learned how to produce their food rather than chase it, and began to grow crops, keep animals and set up more permanent homes in small clearings. This was the time of the wolf, bear, lynx, aurochs, wild boar and beaver, all long since disappeared from England's 'green and pleasant land'.

By the first century, the Romans had reached northern England and southern Scotland, effectively the frontier of the Roman Empire. To protect the borders and their supply routes they built roads and forts and the remains of some of these will be encountered on the walk, although much more, especially that which survives from the post-Roman period, lies concealed, quite conceivably beneath modern villages. For five hundred years, until the 10th century, there is little evidence of people in the landscape, although they were undoubtedly here. Then came the Vikings – the Norse people – some of whom came from Ireland, others by way of the North Sea. Much of the Lake District and parts of the Dales betray their presence in the way local place names end: –*thwaite* signifies a clearing in a forest and –*by* means a village or farmstead. Other names familiar to everyone convey Norse origin: beck (a stream), dale (a valley), fell (a hill) and gill (a ravine).

Although William the Conqueror came to England in 1066, it took almost another thirty years before his people penetrated northern England with any degree of permanence. The kings William I (1066–1087) and William II (1087–1100) doled out large tracts of northern England to their supporters to manage as 'forest', or hunting chases, and created large farms known as vaccaries. Monks established themselves widely, until Henry VIII dissolved the monasteries in the 16th century, and meanwhile packhorse trains evolved trade routes and embryonic road networks, many of which survive to this day. Other notable features encountered on the walk that date from this time are the large areas of land enclosed by walls, known as Parliamentary Enclosures; the building of their walls was often done by the very people who were then dispossessed from the land.

During the Industrial Revolution much of northern England was plundered for its mineral wealth, primarily in the form of slate, granite, sandstone, limestone, copper, lead, zinc and iron ore. Water was abundant, and was used to flush out mineral deposits, notably at the head of Gunnerside Gill in the Yorkshire Dales. Elsewhere, it fed water mills that generated power for a host of industries.

Then, from the 18th century, visitors began to see the landscape for its beauty and picturesque qualities, and in time this brought wealthy Georgian

Upper Swaledale and Swinner Gill (Stage 7B)

At the edge of Scarth Wood Moor (Stage 10)

and Victorian families north, especially following the introduction of railways in the mid-19th century, in search of the Sublime. Little did they realise that the landscape they gazed on was far from natural, having been denuded of trees by humans, mainly those in the monasteries, and grazed to oblivion by sheep.

It was the need to protect what remained that saw the introduction of National Parks: the Lake District in 1951, the North York Moors in 1952 and the Yorkshire Dales in 1954. In some places, Ennerdale for example, attempts are being made to withdraw from human interference with nature as far as possible, to 'rewild' the landscape and let it regenerate naturally. How successful this will be only time will tell.

THE COAST TO COAST WALK

First encounter with Ennerdale Water

ACROSS LAKELAND

To many seasoned walkers the Lake District will be the most familiar section of the Coast to Coast Walk and will need little by way of introduction. But traversing Cumbria as it does from the sandstone cliffs of the west coast at St Bees to the limestone fringes at Shap, this stretch also includes many less well-known delights. One such is the excellent little Dent Fell scaled on Stage 1, offering one of the finest panoramas in Lakeland, and another the peaceful valley of Uldale just beyond it. Stage 2 takes you right into Lakeland proper, through the ever-wilder valley of Ennerdale and up past the iconic Black Sail Hut youth hostel nestling as it does in splendid isolation under some of the highest peaks in England. Leaving the summit-bagging for another day, the Walk presses on, skirting round Brandreth and Grey Knotts to the top of Honister Pass and on down into the tangled landscape of craggy precipices, verdant woodlands and vivid green pasturelands that is Borrowdale.

You'll find it hard to tear yourself away from Borrowdale (unless, perhaps, it's competing once again to retain the title of 'wettest place in England') but more highlights of the central Lakes await on Stage 3. These could be savoured longer by splitting

Views across Ennerdale Water from the northern shore (Stage 2)

Kidsty Pike from the foot of Riggindale (Stage 4)

the stage at Grasmere if your schedule allows. Otherwise it's a day of two high passes and two long, scenic descents – first over the epic Greenup Edge from the Stonethwaite Valley and into gentle Easedale and then over Grisedale Hause, on the shoulder of Fairfield, and down through Grisedale to Patterdale. And if that isn't enough there's an option here to add in a quick ascent of the rocky ridge of Helm Crag on your way down into Grasmere.

Stage 4 is your farewell to the Lake District but the hard work isn't over until it's over. This stage includes the official high point of the Coast to Coast Walk in the form of Kidsty Pike, a distinctive outlier of Rampsgill Head high above Haweswater at 2560ft (780m); but once you've left Riggindale and the Far Easterns you've a pretty gentle afternoon in prospect along the reservoir and across the fields to Shap Abbey and into Shap.

STAGE 1
St Bees to Ennerdale Bridge

Start	St Bees shoreline (NX 961 116)
Finish	Ennerdale Bridge crossroads (NY 070 158)
Distance	15 miles (23.9km)
Total ascent	3625ft (1105m)
Total descent	3295ft (1005m)
Walking time	8hr
Terrain	Once you've managed the initial climb onto St Bees Head, the rest of the way to Cleator is easy by comparison and an exhilarating start to the walk, largely on good paths, tracks and lanes across. The walk through Uldale and Nannycatch to Ennerdale Bridge is a delight and easy enough, involving some road walking towards the end. But you have to get there first, and Dent Fell stands in the way. The view from its summit is truly grand in all directions, but the plod up from Cleator is wearisome, while the descent to Uldale is very steep.
Accommodation	St Bees, Whitehaven (off-route), Sandwith, Cleator, Ennerdale Bridge

Buttressed by so much of interest and antiquity on the one hand and the swelling Irish Sea on the other, St Bees is both a fitting and inspiring overture to the walk. The first section of the walk is across sandstone clifftops, rare in Cumbria, a fine elevated introduction on which to attune legs, lungs and mind. Farther north lies the mess of Whitehaven's industry, passed quickly enough before the relaxed agricultural landscape around Cleator that does nothing to herald the high fells and deep valleys of Lakeland.

The walk then hastens to leave Cleator behind, and between its sad reminder of times gone by and the approaches to the lake at Ennerdale, it travels a fascinating route that only a few and the curious will know. The dome of Dent is an excellent little fell of great stature on which to rev up for things to come. Dent's panorama is one of the finest in Lakeland, and its summit a perfect resting place, while beyond lies the quiet valley of Uldale and the secret meeting place of three sparkling, softly murmuring streams. This is Nannycatch Gate, a hidden gem beneath the dark frown of Raven Crag that is sure to call you back when the walk is done.

Half a mile or so from the village centre, the beach at St Bees is the recognised starting point for the Coast to Coast Walk. Here tourism has invaded the scene – tea room, car parks, toilets and a caravan site straggle the coastal frontage – and suddenly for the walker escape becomes a priority. But before you go there, take a moment to visit the church.

THE CHURCH OF ST MARY AND ST BEGA

The greatest glory of this exquisite place is the west doorway, a deeply recessed, richly columned and decorative portal dating from about 1160, and a splendid example of late Norman work. The church contains a number of late Norman coffin slabs, while in the transept is a beautifully incised effigy of Lady Johanna Lucy, who died in 1369. In the churchyard rest two mutilated 13th-century knights, one bearing a shield with the arms of Ireby upon it. Of more recent times, there is a touching monument of a child of four on a tomb under a recess, a disquieting little figure as she lies asleep, a spray of lilies in her hand.

The earliest record of St Bega is to be found in the *Life and Miracles of St Bega the Virgin*, dating from the 12th century and now preserved in the British Museum. Material for this work comes, the author claims, from the narrative of reliable men, a significant comment in the light of latter-day claims that she never really existed.

Bega was the daughter of an Irish king, and determined to remain a lifelong virgin, a decision reinforced by a dream in which she received from a stranger an arm-ring bearing the sign of the holy cross. Bega's father, however, was equally determined she should marry a Norwegian prince, a proposition so abhorrent to Bega that she fled across the sea with a company of nuns seeking peace and solitude, and landed in a wooded region, near present-day St Bees. Here there probably existed a primitive Christian community, for the name Preston, 'priest town', was given by Anglians to land between what is now St Bees and Whitehaven. Later, this land was granted to the Priory of St Mary and the Virgin Bega at its foundation in 1120. Bega and her nuns established a nunnery on the site of the present priory church which survived two centuries before being plundered by Danish raiders. Much later, after its foundation, the Priory Church of St Mary suffered a similar fate at the hands of Scottish raiders, in due course ending its days in much the same manner as numerous other monastic buildings, under the dissolution decree of Henry VIII in the 16th century.

Although it is claimed by some that Bega was a mythical character arising from the pagan Nordic custom, in vogue in the 9th century, of swearing oaths on a sacred arm-ring, the 'bracelet of the blessed Virgin Bega, kept in the priory church' on which oaths were taken is mentioned in no less than six charters recorded in the early 13th century. The *Life and Miracles* does not mention that Bega was shipwrecked on the Cumberland coast, or that a nunnery was founded, these details apparently being added in the 17th century by one Edmund Sandford. Sandford also wrote: 'There was a pious religious Lady Abbess and some of her sisters driven in by storm at Whitehaven and ship cast away i'the harbour.' The Abbess begged assistance from the Lady of Egremont, whose lord promised the nuns as much land as snow fell upon the next morning 'bein midsumerday'. In pre-global warming days, snow did indeed often remain as late as mid-summer, but all the same he must have been a little taken aback the next day when he saw the land for three miles to the sea covered with snow 'and thereupon builded this St Bees Abbie and gave the land was snowen unto it and the town and haven of Whitehaven' with other dues and further lands. Obviously, a man of his word.

The sea walls, built to protect St Bees from the worst ravages of the sea, end abruptly in a downfall of boulders and debris from the ever-crumbling cliffs, soon to be encountered. This is where the walk starts, and it is a tradition either to dip your boots in the sea, or pick up a pebble to transport to the east coast...or both – it depends how far out the tide is.

Cross Rottington Beck and the journey begins, leaving the beach behind and climbing by a flight of wooden steps alongside the RSPB St Bees Head Nature Reserve.

Height is gained rapidly, and with it, on a clear day, a widening **panorama** of far horizons. To the south, beyond the towers of Sellafield, rise the whaleback summits of Black Combe and its acolytes, to the east the first tantalising glimpse of high Lakeland fells, while far out to sea, 50km (30+ miles) distant, the blue-purple form of the Isle of Man looms hazily from a shimmering sea.

Still ascending by a prominent path, the walk soon reaches the remains of a coastguard lookout post, where the suddenness of the drop to the shore impresses itself noticeably.

The beach at St Bees: the westerly starting point of the Coast to Coast Walk

The whole of **St Bees Head** is formed from shales and sandstone, and dates from comparatively recent times in the geological evolution of the Lake District, between 135 and 225 million years ago. This is the only stretch of Heritage Coast on the English coastline between the Welsh and Scottish borders, and as such stands as a Site of Special Scientific Interest (SSSI). The true geographical head is North Head, the most westerly point of northern England and the site of St Bees lighthouse. The South Head is known locally as 'Tomlin' and it dominates the long sandy St Bees beach.

This whole coastal uplift is by far the most impressive feature on the Cumbrian coast, unless you have a particular penchant for the nuclear power plant at Sellafield!

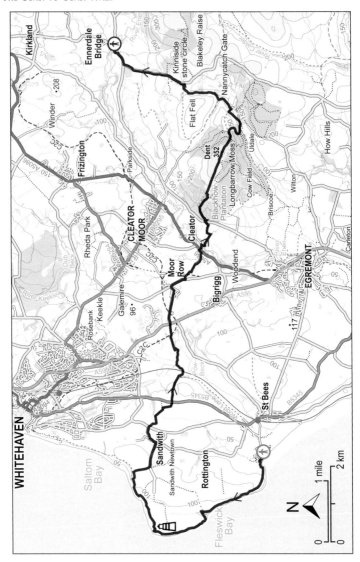

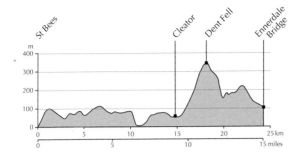

At a stile, the path moves away from the clifftop for a short while to follow the bottom edge of steeply sloping pastures, an easy stroll on flowery turf beside a fence. Here, the openness of the view, the wheeling, swooping company of countless sea birds and flitting butterflies, arouse sensations of well-being and contentment, a perfect mental conditioning for what is to follow on the journey eastwards. ▶

For the moment, however, the route lies northwards, easing downwards to **Fleswick Bay**. Out to sea is the Isle of Man, like some large vessel, suddenly becalmed.

Fleswick Bay cuts sharply into St Bees Head, forcing a return almost to sea level. A brief halt would not be unwelcome or unjustified here, even so early in the walk, for the bay is a most beautiful part of the headland, a shingle beach on a wave-cut platform, famed for attractive pebbles, hanging terraces of wild flowers, caves, colourful, weathered rocks, and intimate views of towering sea cliffs.

A direct return may be made to the path above Fleswick Bay, without having to retreat inland to the main stile, by locating a series of holds in the rocks ascending to a hurdle/stile. Heavily laden walkers still trying to find their backpacking legs might wisely opt, however, for rejoining the walk at the inland crossing point.

Along the way a number of protected arenas have been constructed for observation of the sea birds, which include gannet, kittiwake, fulmar, guillemot, razorbill, puffin and black-backed gulls.

49

For a few minutes, narrow paths slope across the hillside, leading upwards once more. Soon the St Bees **lighthouse** comes into view, but is never quite reached (without a diversion), the path passing beneath it to another lookout post. Here, cross a stile and continue ahead with the headland swinging now to the right, and, far away, Criffel and the hazy hills of Galloway easing into view. Ahead, too, across the wide sweep of Saltom Bay, Whitehaven and its suburbs appear, unavoidably drawing the eye.

The great mound of land south of Whitehaven, technically known as **Preston Isle**, has had enormous influence on the prosperity of the town and its people. Beneath the surface have been found not only extensive coal measures, now largely worked out, but large quantities of anhydrite, or calcium sulphate, which, suitably processed, can be used to manufacture sulphuric acid and cement. This 'buried treasure' has brought up to 2000 jobs to the area, and the importance of this, in a district that has known more than its fair share of unemployment, cannot be overestimated.

A **lighthouse** on St Bees Head was first operated in 1718. In 1822, it was the last coal-powered lighthouse in Britain, when it was destroyed by a fire in which the keeper's wife and his five children perished. The present structure, its light more than 100m above the sea, was erected in 1866. During the Second World War a radar station was operated from here.

Finally, the route starts to creep round to the east, the direction of the ultimate destination, Robin Hood's Bay. At a stile at the end of a wall a more prominent path is gained, fenced on the right, and delineated on the left by a sharp drop to a level green pasture suspended halfway down to the seashore. Soon, however, a clifftop path is reached once more, heading towards Whitehaven until, dramatically, it ends at a gate at the very edge of Birkham quarry, from which, it is said, sandstone was used as ballast in ships that took the first pilgrims to Americas.

Go round the quarry to the end of a lane, near cottages, and here turn right (waymark and signpost 'To Sandwith'), following the lane to its meeting with a metalled minor roadway leading, left, down to Sandwith (pronounced 'sannith').

> As the road descends easily to the village, the immense spread of **Lakeland fells** across the horizon beyond the bald pate of Dent Fell presents a tantalising backdrop – Grasmoor, High Stile, Pillar, Steeple, Red Pike and the Scafells separated by the conspicuous gash of Mickledore.

A convenient bench at the road junction in **Sandwith** is temptation for a brief respite, especially with the possibility of refreshments nearby, but first-day enthusiasm will soon have feet treading the road again, left through the village, round by the Dog and Partridge, and up to the junction at Lanehead. Cross the minor road (Byerstead Road) and onto a superb green lane leading to Demesne Farm.

At the farm, keep left in front of the buildings, and then turn right on a farm access track signposted 'Coast to Coast'. Soon the **B5345** is crossed to gain a metalled access track leading down towards Bell House farm. Keep on past the farm to cross a cattle-grid, with a splendid view ahead of Stanley Pond in front of an intricate pattern of fields rising far into the distant folds of flowing fells.

Shortly after the cattle-grid take a right fork (waymarked) and descend to a gate, beyond which a less pronounced path descends left (also waymarked), keeping on down the field side to a railway underpass.

> Between Sandwith and Cleator the route threads a tapestry of patterned fields and **flower-decked lanes** belying the nearby urban developments, and in spring and early summer are sure to have botanists dawdling along the paths.

Once through the underpass, bear half-left across a meadow to a group of trees, and then follow a hedge-row away to a field corner, with Stanley Pond concealed nearby. Follow a fence on the left, the corner of the field proving boggy after rain, to a gate. Keep with the ensuing fence (now on the right) for a while, until the path breaks away to cross the field it borders. More fields follow as the path leads unerringly to another underpass beneath the defunct Cleator Moor to Whitehaven mineral railway.

Press on beneath the underpass and ascend easily to a gated access onto the **A595** near Scalegill Hall. Keep ahead across the A595 and head for **Moor Row** along a metalled roadway, and at a T-junction near the post office, turn right.

To **keep off the tarmac** for a while here, you could choose to make use of the trackbed of the old railway and course of the C2C cycle route. Immediately after the underpass go up steps on the right to gain the trackbed of the old railway and follow this as it passes beneath both the A595 and then Scalegill Road to the outskirts of Moor Row at Moor Road, and there turn right again into Dalzell Street. Walk down the street to rejoin the main route at a road junction.

Moor Row is a small industrial village of grey Victorian terraces, in its heyday a busy railway meeting point, operating passenger and mineral lines, now merely a forlorn reminder of past glories.

Now leave the village, climbing steadily. Shortly, over a brow, depart the lane at a kissing-gate (NY 007 139) on the left giving access to a field. Keep ahead, passing through a succession of gates and crossing the old railway line again, until you meet the edge of **Cleator** at its cricket ground, from where a metalled roadway leads into the main street. ◄

In the distance, a little nearer than the main Lakeland fells, a rounded grassy dome has been looming ever larger. This is Dent Fell, a Lakeland 'appetiser', all too soon to be encountered.

CLEATOR

Cleator, alas, is like so many of the villages that in this part of Lakeland were dependent on mining for their well-being and prosperity, and has clearly seen better days. The growth of the iron-ore industry, and the rapid building of simple, unattractive terraced houses to meet the demands of miners, destroyed much of the village's former charm and character.

Other nearby villages – Frizington, Arlecdon and Cleator Moor – also grew, as between 1840 and 1880 they bore the weight of an increase in population from 835 to 17,651, with the number of miners rising from 60 to over 6000. These statistics tell little of the real story that afflicted this proud and beautiful region, a story of overcrowding and deprivation, of hard, drinking men, who brought to West Cumberland – from Ireland, Scotland, Cornwall, Northumberland, Lancashire and Yorkshire – a social atmosphere akin to the Klondike, albeit before that phenomenon had reached North America.

Now all that remains to delay passers-by, apart from the Three Tuns pub, is Cleator's church, dedicated to St Leonard, built from red sandstone. Though modern in style, the church has elements of Norman handiwork in its chancel walls, and one of the windows depicts the Lady of Egremont and her husband meeting (St) Bega at the castle gate.

Unlikely to feature high on tourist itineraries, Cleator is nevertheless very much a gateway to Lakeland. Nearby flows the River Ehen, and that, before long, marks the boundary of the Lake District National Park.

On reaching the main street in Cleator turn left for a short distance, leaving it, right, into Kiln Brow. Descend until a signpost ('Fell Road via Nook Farm') directs you right to the River Ehen and Black How Bridge. Cross the bridge and, having made but the briefest of acquaintances with the **River Ehen**, turn left on the access road leading to Black How Farm. A signed path leads between the farm buildings, to a track, right, for Dent, soon to join a metalled roadway. ▶

Cross the road to a gate giving into **Blackhow Plantation**, taking to a broad, gravel track rising into woodland. When you reach a junction, turn left for Dent Fell, now following a narrow path along the edge of a larch plantation. After about 100m, the path swings to the right, and climbs through a firebreak towards **Dent Fell**.

If the weather is truly bad, this road, going north, can be used to bypass Dent and get round to Ennerdale Bridge, crossing the River Ehen at Wath Bridge.

On the summit of Dent Fell

At the top of the plantation, cross a track, and go forward beside a fence, maintaining this direction onto the highest part of the fell. The prominent cairn you see ahead is a shelter, with the very modest cairn that marks the summit another 550m distant across a grassy plateau.

Wainwright commented that **Dent Fell**, 'impels the...urge to linger awhile'. This a masterpiece of understatement – only the fittest of the fit will feel that lingering is anything other than essential for survival. Mere mortals will be obliged to remain collapsed in a heap for some time before taking in the wonders of its vast panorama – laid out like a map of towns and villages, fields and furrows, blue, swelling sea and misty isles, far-off mountains and richly green valleys – while onward beckon the fells.

Just a few strides beyond the cairn, the path starts to descend. Cross a stile, and continue down through an area of cleared plantation to intercept a forest trail at a signpost. ▶ Turn right, and shortly meet another track. Cross this and go down along the edge of plantation, with more cleared areas to the right. The descending track is steep in places, and requires care, but you get lovely cameos of Uldale framed by trees to take your mind off aching knees.

Eventually, the track merges with another running out from **Uldale**. Go forward along this to another junction, and here turn left, almost immediately leaving the broad trail for a bridleway on the left, passing through a gate, and then following a lovely route through a simple dale, crossing and re-crossing a stream in the process.

Follow the path until it reaches a gate and stile (known as **Nannycatch Gate**), beyond which the path divides. Turn right, keeping east of **Flat Fell**, and when, just after crossing a small stream, the path divides, bear right past a low hillock. The path climbs towards the moorland road, but when it forks bear sharp right to go up to the road. **Kinniside stone circle** lies a short distance to the left, on the other side of the road.

The original line of the route went left here, but the descent is very steep, and anyone laden with a heavy pack could have difficulty.

The Coast to Coast path through Nannycatch

Kinniside is a small stone circle on the road that runs between Calder Bridge and Ennerdale Bridge. It also goes by the name Blakeley Raise stone circle, but it is not an original prehistoric monument, just a 1925 creation of 11 stones arranged in a circle with an 18m diameter. The original circle was apparently dismantled in the 18th century by a farmer who used the stones for gate-posts. In 1925, Doctor Quine of Frizington restored the circle, setting the stones in concrete, but whether he erected the stones in their original stone holes is unclear, and it is almost certain that few, if any, of the re-erected stones came from the original circle.

On reaching the fell road, turn left, pass the stone circle and take to a roadside footpath descending to a T-junction. Turn right into the village of **Ennerdale Bridge**.

Things have changed in **Ennerdale Bridge** since one traveller described the pub as 'small, dirty, and filled with roaring tipplers' – and that at nine in the morning! The village now sees few visitors, its general inaccessibility ensuring that the throngs don't inadvertently stumble upon it, and the pub is an excellent community-run venture. Thankfully, it remains a quiet farming and forestry retreat, well known and loved by local people, but never likely to figure highly on tourist itineraries. In prehistoric times, iron was smelted here, and much later haematite was mined along the valley of Ennerdale. There were also a number of small industries here related to weaving, and Ennerdale Bridge grew as a result.

The Church of St Mary was built between 1856 and 1858 on the site of a medieval chapel, and enlarged in 1885.

EAST TO WEST: ENNERDALE BRIDGE TO ST BEES

Leave Ennerdale Bridge heading west, and at a junction go left up a fell road for about a mile (1.5km) to a track on the right. Turn onto the track, but soon leave it to go left into a sheltered valley through which flows Nannycatch Beck – this ultimately runs into the valley of Uldale, a truly quiet corner of Lakeland, and a place to be savoured for what comes next is hard work.

Follow the obvious path to a gate below **Flat Fell** (**Nannycatch Gate**). Turn left here, following the path for a short distance until, on the far side of Raven Crag a very steep path rockets upwards on the right to a stile leading into forest. Go left along a forest trail and shortly branch right into **Uldale**, climbing less steeply in zigzags through the forest to emerge not far from the top of **Dent Fell**.

Continue across Dent's two tops, and down the other side, following clear paths for a time through plantation, to reach a surfaced lane near Black How Farm. Cross the lane and take a track that leads around the farm buildings, and on to another track weaving a way round to Blackhow Bridge (NY 016 133), spanning the **River Ehen**.

Cross the bridge and go ahead until you can turn left up Kiln Brow, to reach the main street of **Cleator**. Go left for a short distance and then take the first road on the right.

Follow the road as far as the cricket ground and then go round it, passing through a succession of gates and pastures, and crossing the trackbed of a former railway in the process. Finally, you emerge onto another road. Turn right and walk down to the village of **Moor Row**. When you reach the post office you have a minor choice of routes.

Either turn left and follow the road out of Moor Row, across the **A595** and then along an enclosed track passing beneath a disused railway line. Or continue ahead up Dalzell Street until you reach the old railway trackbed, and turn down onto it, going left and following this traffic-free route until you reach the same point.

The on-going path swings left along the northern edge of woodland to a gate. Through this, follow the field boundary, right, to a stile in a corner, near Stanley Pond. Cross the ensuing field, diagonally left, to reach a railway underpass. On the other side, climb the field ahead to a track leading to Bell House Farm and on to the **B5345**. Cross the road and follow an access track round to Demesne Farm, and there turn left to pursue a delightful lane running out to Lane Head. Keep ahead, following the road round to **Sandwith**. At the southern edge of the village turn right on a narrow,

View of the cliffs of St Bees Head

enclosed road, until it branches right to head for a cliff-edge quarry where Whitehaven springs suddenly into view.

Keep left on reaching the quarry and follow an obvious path around North and South Head, two component parts of **St Bees Head**. These are separated by **Fleswick Bay**, a short incursion into the cliffs, preceded by a coastguard lookout station and St Bees **lighthouse**.

The path runs on in a lovely manner before finally descending dramatically to the seashore at **St Bees**.

Ennerdale Bridge to Borrowdale

Start	Ennerdale Bridge (NY 070 158)
Finish	Rosthwaite (NY 258 149)
Distance	(1) via Ennerdale Water south 15 miles (24km) (2) via Ennerdale Water north coast variant 14½ miles (23.3km)
Total ascent	(1) 2253ft (687m) (2) 2100ft (640m)
Walking time	8hr
Terrain	A straightforward walk through Ennerdale along the south shore of Ennerdale Water, later joining a broad forest trail to Black Sail Hostel. A variant makes use of the forest trail along the north shore of the lake. From Black Sail a steep ascent rises beside Loft Beck onto fell upland to a disused quarry tramway to Honister Hause. Then following an old toll road down to Seatoller and on beside the River Derwent to Rosthwaite village.
Accommodation	Ennerdale Bridge; hostels along Ennerdale and at Honister and Seatoller; hotels and B&Bs in Seatoller and Rosthwaite.

The first stretch of today's walk ventures into the long recess of Ennerdale, going along the southern shores of the lake until forced to the northern flank for comparatively easy progress to the isolated Black Sail youth hostel. Most walkers starting from Ennerdale Bridge will find this too short a day, and opt to push on to Seatoller or Rosthwaite. Walkers with relatively little experience of long-distance walking may, however, detect the wisdom in electing to inject a couple of short days (the next day, too, to Rosthwaite or Langstrath would be short) into the proceedings at this early stage to allow body and soul to acclimatise, instead of slogging onwards remorselessly.

Black Sail youth hostel, surely, lies in one of the most dramatic and awe-inspiring locations in the Lake District, a perfect base for mountain adventurers wanting to cut their teeth on the ring of craggy, challenging summits that surround it (as well as a scenic stop for a coffee and slice of homemade cake if you pass by in the afternoon). Well-established routes leave the youth hostel for the heights, though none of the principal lines is used by the Coast to Coast Walk, which prefers the crumbly confines of Loft

Beck before swinging high across the flanks of Brandreth and Grey Knotts to the top of Honister Pass.

For walkers this is the first moment of real challenge, the first opportunity to come to grips with the mountain uplands of Lakeland, and not a place to linger if the weather is turning for the worse.

Leave Ennerdale Bridge along the minor road for Croasdale, soon leaving it at Lily Hall (NY 072 158) for a gravel path on the right that parallels the road, finally emerging near the road junction that runs down towards Ennerdale lake. Rather than take the road, go forward into Broadmoor Woodland. The path eases through a pleasant pine and birch spread to emerge on a broad trail (NY 084 157). Turn left, ignoring a branching path that soon appears, and keep forward to arrive at the western end of **Ennerdale Water** at NY 090 157.

Here bear left to take the alternative north shore route (see below), or right to continue with the main line, soon entering light woodland cover before crossing the bridge at the outflow of the lake. Keep forward to cross a bridge that gives onto a good path running along the south shore.

The start of the walk into Ennerdale

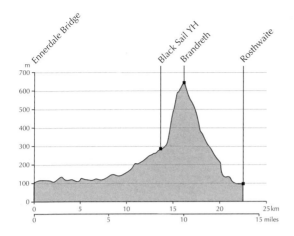

ENNERDALE NATIONAL NATURE RESERVE

Ennerdale has long been a Site of Special Scientific Interest, a highly important area in Lakeland history, home to some of England's most vibrant natural environments and one of the longest running ecological restoration projects in the UK. In 2022, some 3000 hectares of water, forests and mountains were designated the Wild Ennerdale National Nature Reserve, a Super NNR, recognised for its landscape-scale approach to partnership working (the Wild Ennerdale Partnership, www.wildennerdale.co.uk), in this instance the combined efforts of Forestry England, the National Trust, United Utilities and Natural England. The partnership began 20 years ago and has a vision to allow natural processes to shape the ecology and landscapes within the valley. Wild Ennerdale is a diverse and varied landscape that supports some of our most unique and precious wildlife, including red squirrels, freshwater pearl mussels that dwell in the River Ehen and which can live for 100 years, and the Arctic charr – a fish that has survived in the valley since the last Ice Age.

The chance discovery in 1947 of the site of a Neolithic axe factory in Langdale, from which items have been carbon-dated to between 2700 and 2500BCE, and the finding of finished artefacts in Ireland, Scotland and southern England, has led to speculation that Ennerdale, reached via Aaron Slack and Windy Gap (between Great and Green Gable), was the route prehistoric man took to reach the coast.

Much later, the area, especially around upper Ennerdale, was a medieval deer forest under the control of the monks at St Bees, while from 1810 comes the tale of 'T'girt Dog of Ennerdale', something of a cross between a mastiff and a greyhound and weighing eight stone. For months it ranged from Cockermouth to Ravenglass, St Bees to Wasdale Head, defying all attempts to capture and kill it, and savaged hundreds of sheep, often wantonly destroying seven or eight sheep in one night before finally it was slain.

There is no denying the beauty of Ennerdale. Edwin Waugh, a notable Lancashire poet, and at his best when revelling in the wild and stormy side of nature, wrote a most evocative description of the lake in moonlight in his *Rambles in the Lake Country*:

In this sheltered corner little eddies of shimmering silver flit about –
the dainty Ariels of moonlit water; there, is a burnished islet of stirless
brilliance, in which even the moon smiles to see herself look so passing
fair; and, out beyond, the wide waters are in a tremulous fever of delight
with her sweet influence… If there be magic in the world, it is this!

Nor did Cumberland's own poet, Wordsworth, neglect the place, remote though it was from his Grasmere home. In *The Brothers* he cast a spell over Ennerdale and the monolith of Pillar Rock, writing:You see yon precipice; it wears the shape

Of a vast building made of many crags,
And in the midst is one particular rock
That rises like a column from the vale,
Whence by our shepherds it is called the Pillar.

Ennerdale Water is Lakeland's most westerly lake, a glacial lake with a maximum depth of 45 metres; it has had a few identity issues over the years being known variously as Brodewater (1576), Brodwater (1695), Broad Water (1760), Ennerdale Water (1784) and Ennerdale Lake in Jonathan Otley's guide – *A Concise Description of the English Lakes and adjacent Mountains* (1823).

The sudden impact of Ennerdale's lake as you reach its edge is awesome, a wonderful and dramatic moment. A good path traces its southern shore, within stepping distance of the water, and continues uneventfully until its encounter with the cliffs of **Angler's Crag**. Here you need to clamber through the crag's fractured base to regain a solid path on the far side. ▶

Energetic souls may opt for a steeply ascending path, encountered a little before Angler's Crag, crossing the top of the crag, a splendid viewpoint, before descending steeply on the other side.

Not far along the southern shore a small headland juts out into the lake. This is known as **Robin Hood's Chair**, a fanciful connection, perhaps, but of interest to Coast to Coasters, linking as it does with the final destination, and, for that matter, with his alleged grave, encountered on the crossing of Crosby Ravensworth Fell a few days hence, and, of course, the final destination.

Once beyond the hiatus of Angler's Crag the path (intermittently paved) continues into an area of stunted woodland and moss- and lichen-covered boulders. Beyond, sectioned by streams and little waterfalls, the path presses on without incident to the head of the lake, following a track sweeping round to join the broad forest trail on the northern side of the valley at **Irish Bridge** (not named on OS maps), beneath the minor wooded summit of Latterbarrow and not far from Ennerdale (Gillerthwaite) **youth hostel**.

The route now follows a simple and direct route, first by metalled roadway and then by forest trail, to a gate leading finally from the forest along the final few metres to Black Sail **youth hostel**. En route, Low Gillerthwaite is encountered, a field centre, and then High Gillerthwaite, a traditional 16th-century barn, now a camping barn.

North shore alternative

A more accessible route follows the north shore of Ennerdale Water. On reaching the lake turn left (north-east) following a clear path round the end of the lake then south-east to the Bowness car park, there joining a broad forest trail that continues until it rejoins the main route at Char Dub (NY 130 142).

This alternative is marginally shorter and offers a splendid view down the length of the lake to the dominant peak of **Pillar** and the isolated **Pillar Rock**.

Pillar rises above the southern flank of Ennerdale

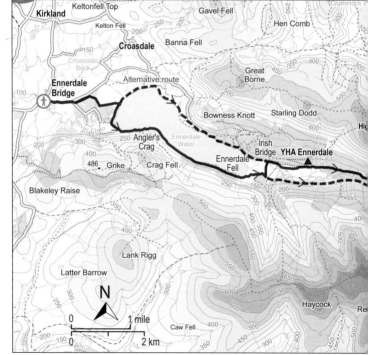

Quieter approach to Black Sail

For the adventurous, from the Irish Bridge end of
Ennerdale Water there is an alternative to the forest trail
in the form of a clear path along the true left bank (south
side) of the **River Liza** that runs all the way to a ford (NY
191 122) not far from Black Sail youth hostel. If the river
is swollen there is a footbridge (NY 197 120) you can
take a little farther on at the northern base of **Kirk Fell**,
where the path descends from Black Sail Pass.

This alternative adds little to the overall distance,
and is generally much quieter than the main forest trail,
and with a better chance of seeing wildlife. But this
way doesn't offer a view of the magnificent ridge that

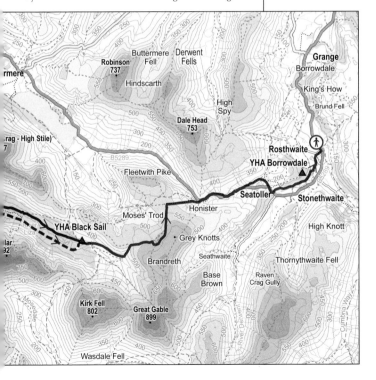

forms the southern wall of Ennerdale, along which **Pillar** stands proud.

> **Pillar Rock**, thankfully you might say, is not on the route of the Coast to Coast Walk, but its presence draws the eye for quite a while as the way ventures deeper and deeper into the valley. This, the only significant Lakeland summit that cannot be achieved by walking alone, has been prominent in men's imagination for centuries, and although the undertaking had undoubtedly been accomplished hundreds if not thousands of times before, it was John Atkinson, an Ennerdale shepherd, who inched his way onto the top of Pillar Rock in 1826, thus effecting the first recorded rock climb, as reported in *The Cumberland Paquet* on 25 July 1826.
>
> Its parent mountain, Pillar, is a '...mighty mass of natural Gothic architecture', a monument to nature's creation.
>
> Beyond Ennerdale Water is the **River Liza**, its name thought to have derived from the Icelandic river Lysá, meaning 'the bright water', and suggestive of the area having been settled by Norsemen. The tumbling waters of the Liza, half-hidden among ferns and trees, are a bold contrast with the high fells that look down on it.

On a warm day the beck is something of a heat trap, but the retrospective views are adequate justification for taking the climb easy.

The ongoing route from Black Sail hostel to the foot of Loft Beck can be confusing in mist. Immediately on leaving the hostel, avoid the more pronounced path that descends to the bridge spanning Liza Beck and, instead, look for a higher path striking east, rising away from the River Liza that leads to the foot of Loft Beck. Cross the beck and follow it up on the far side to begin the steep pull to the shoulder of the fell above. ◄

At the top of Loft Beck, a line of cairns directs the path to easier ground, with the summits of **Brandreth** and **Grey Knotts** ahead. If you intend staying at Honister, or even Seatoller, you may want to consider bagging this pair of fairly easy summits.

The route keeps west of these outliers of the Gables, following a more prominent path. This is **Moses' Trod**, a long-established trail from Honister to Wasdale and beyond. Away to the left, a delightful view of the Buttermere valley opens up, framed between the heights of the High Stile range and Fleetwith Pike.

> **Moses' Trod**, or more correctly, Moses' Sledgate, is an old slate road across which Honister slate was transported to Wasdale and out to Ravenglass on the coast. Fragments of green Honister slate may still be found along its length.
>
> Rather more romantically, it is said to have been named after an illicit whisky distiller who had his still concealed among the surrounding crags. Whether there ever was a still remains uncertain, for there is a theory that Moses was a quarryman at Honister who smuggled plumbago (graphite) as a side-line, perhaps distilling whisky after his day's work. During the 18th century, Borrowdale plumbago was very much at a premium, and smuggling likely to have been a profitable business. Either way the trod serves a useful and convenient purpose for Coast to Coasters bound for Honister, and the name of Moses, for his sins or otherwise, lives on, remembered by every walker who places foot on Moses' Trod.

The route collides with the trod at a large cairn, and continues an easy descent northwards (left) to the remains of the tramway and Drum House that served the Dubs Quarry. Here turn right, descending even more steeply for a while to reach the defunct slate quarry buildings at the top of one of Lakeland's better known motor passes, **Honister**.

HONISTER SLATE MINE

Honister Slate Mine (www.honister.com) is still being worked, producing high-quality Honister slate. If you have time, you could join one of the guided visits as this is now a major tourist attraction.

Working conditions at the quarry used to be extremely harsh and dangerous. Slate was brought down to the knapping sheds on hurdles, or trail-barrows, which had two inclining handles ('stangs') at the front between which the man would position himself, going, like a horse, before the weight. These contraptions weighed as much as 80lb empty, and it took the men half an hour of laborious effort to carry them back to the quarries in the honeycomb of tunnels above. The subsequent laden descent, unbelievably, was only a matter of minutes, depending on skill, dexterity and good fortune.

Remarkable tales are found of men who worked in the quarries in the 19th century: Samuel Trimmer once made 15 journeys in a day for a bottle of rum and a small percentage of the slate he sledged, and Joseph Clarke of Stonethwaite, who made 17 journeys, bringing down each time 640lb of slate, a total of 10,880lb in one day. 'His greatest day's work,' writes Harriet Martineau, 'was bringing 11,771 pounds; in how many journeys it is not remembered: but in fewer than seventeen.' This highly dangerous method of obtaining slate was ended in 1881, when a gravitational railway was introduced.

Quarry workers, like drystone wallers, often lived during the week in small huts on the hillsides, going home only from Saturday night until Monday morning, and while away, communicating with their wives by carrier pigeon.

Now from Honister thoughts turn to Borrowdale, one of the most loved and popular of Lakeland's valleys.

From the summit of the pass follow the descending motor road until a former highway, now abandoned, branches off on the left. This was a toll road, and for the most part provides a traffic-free descent to **Seatoller**, reaching the tiny village through walled enclosures.

Descend through the village and turn left into the car park, leaving it by a stile at its far end to follow a track branching right (ignore the ascending track at this point). The track runs above the **River Derwent** below Johnny Wood towards Borrowdale **youth hostel**. But before getting that far there is an interesting but brief interlude where, just beyond a kissing-gate and amid light

River Derwent near Rosthwaite

woodland, the path crosses smooth rocks across which a piece of cable has been fixed to aid walkers, although few are likely to need its aid.

> It is not immediately obvious to those sensibly concerned with the placement of their feet, but just at this point, on the other side of the river, the ragged end of a **glacial moraine** is clearly exposed as a bank of earth studded with small rocks and boulders.

A clear path runs on to pass the youth hostel (refreshments available), and soon follow an access road over a humpback bridge spanning the Derwent.

Follow the road beyond for a short distance to a footpath on the left. Continue past a number of small cottages and through another gate to enter a pasture of low scrub, following a fence and then a wall to a gate. Once through the gate turn right to a metalled road, and then left to follow the road round until the main road through the valley is reached. The centre of **Rosthwaite** lies just to the right.

> **Rosthwaite**, the 'capital' of Borrowdale, is a small, peaceful community flanking the roadside. Unwittingly, however, Sir Hugh Walpole in writing his *Herries Chronicles*, planted the seeds of discord,

for at least three houses claim to be the 'original' of Rogue Herries' Farm.

The landscape around Rosthwaite is geologically fascinating. Apart from a very large and obvious *roche moutonnées* – huge outcrops of rock shaped by glacial erosion – there is also evidence of glacial lakes having been formed here, although exactly what actually occurred awaits academic study: for an enterprising geology student there's a good PhD in there waiting to get out.

At a more prosaic level, Rosthwaite is a fine end to a day, a good spot to prepare for the next day and a rare chance to sleep in glacial embrace.

BORROWDALE

Borrowdale lies at the very heart of Lakeland, its great length probing far into the 'turbulent chaos of mountain behind mountain, rolled in confusion' that greeted Thomas Gray when, the day after his arrival at Keswick on 2 October 1769, he 'rose at seven, and walked out under the conduct of [his] landlord to Borrowdale'.

It is the most beautiful of valleys. Journalist Bernard Levin once observed, during his trek *In Hannibal's Footsteps*, that any 'varied landscape, provided it is not marred by hideous…manmade objects…is beautiful', commenting how this suggested that 'the harmonies of nature are so powerful that no matter what instruments they are played on, in what combinations and at what relative strengths, the result will be pleasing.' He noted, too, that 'if the manmade objects…are not ugly and do blend well…nature absorbs them into the picture and they actually enhance its beauty'. Nowhere is that perception better exemplified than in Borrowdale.

EAST TO WEST: ROSTHWAITE TO ENNERDALE BRIDGE

From the centre of the village, follow the road south past charming cottages, and keeping left near a barn café. Go past more cottages and look for a path between cottages on the right that leads along field boundaries to a humpback bridge spanning the **River Derwent**. Immediately go left to reach the **youth hostel**.

From the youth hostel, press on into the edge of Johnny Wood, never far from the Derwent, negotiating a short section of rock to which a cable for assistance has been attached, and then through a kissing-gate following a route linked by more gates that eventually emerges into the edge of the car park at **Seatoller**.

Go across the car park to the road and turn right through the village, and just after Dalehead Barn go right at a gate, at first heading away from Honister, before doubling back to follow the course of an old toll road to rejoin the surfaced road near the top of the **pass**.

By a gate, enter the grounds of the Honister Slate Quarry. Go beyond the buildings, and in a short distance follow a path that climbs steeply to gain the line of an old tramway used by the quarry. Follow this until, as the gradient levels, you encounter an obvious path going left. Turn onto this, climbing gently until at a large cairn another track branches right (**Moses' Trod**).

Take the right branch and start gradually descending to the top of Loft Beck, a steep and friable gully that speeds you down to the head of Ennerdale, not far from Black Sail **youth hostel**.

Keep an eye out for wildlife as you pass through Ennerdale, the chances of an encounter with which could be improved by opting from Black Sail to cross the **River Liza**, either by a footbridge (NY 197 120) or ford (NY 191 122), and taking a less-trodden path along the river's true left bank, and eventually re-joining the main line.

If you opt for the north size of the Liza, head along a broad track into Ennerdale Forest (some of which has been cleared in recent times). Press on to High Gillerthwaite and then Low Gillerthwaite, a short distance beyond which a path swings left to cross **Irish Bridge** (not named on maps) and follow a delightful path along the southern shore of **Ennerdale Water**, grappling with **Angler's Crag** and maybe taking a break on Robin Hood's Chair, before finally arriving at the western end of the lake.

Cross the outflow of the lake, going forward into light woodland cover and walking as far as a bench on the left at a path junction (NY 090 157). Turn left here, taking to a pleasant path, and ignoring a branching path to continue to an old gate post (NY 084 157). Here, turn into Broadmoor Woodland, following a gravel path looping through the trees to emerge at a road junction. Cross the junction, towards the main road, to locate a path on the left running parallel with the road as far as Lily Hall (NY 072 158), there taking to the road for a short stretch into **Ennerdale Bridge**.

STAGE 3

Borrowdale to Patterdale

Start	Rosthwaite road junction (NY 258 149)
Finish	Patterdale, junction with access to Side Farm (NY 394 160)
Distance	15½ miles (25km)
Total ascent	4015ft (1225m)
Total descent	3825ft (1165m)
Walking time	9hr
Terrain	An easy start into the steep-sided Stonethwaite valley, following the course of Stonethwaite Beck leads to the confluence between Langstrath Beck and Greenup Gill, from where the route climbs steadily across steep craggy fellsides to the watershed at Greenup Edge, beyond which everything is downhill on a clear and improving track that plunges into Far Easedale and down to Grasmere. Another steady climb across open fellside from Grasmere, nowhere unduly steep, leads to a narrow link – Grisedale Hause – between Fairfield and Seat Sandal, beyond which the path drops to Grisedale Tarn. An easy but stony descent follows all the way into Patterdale.
Accommodation	Stonethwaite and Grasmere

If you wish to savour the central Lakes a little longer, Grasmere would be the ideal place to break this stage. If you need to press on, bear in mind that the climb up to Greenup Edge, although largely a constructed affair these days, is quite steep in places, and tiring late in a long day's walking. Whatever choice you make, there is beauty throughout, and joy with every stride – well, at least the downhill ones.

The area between Borrowdale and Grasmere is a rugged enclave that leads weekend walkers onto High Raise, or north onto rarely visited Ullscarf and Coldbarrow Fell. On the way down to Grasmere, a fine variant makes use of the long ridge leading to Helm Crag, descending from there to the village. This will add time, and finishes with a steep descent, but it is a magnificent alternative for other than weary legs.

Between Grasmere and Patterdale there is little to tax walkers who have accomplished the crossing thus far without difficulty – a simple, high-level mountain pass lies in wait, beyond which a long and invigorating descent leads to the valley of Patterdale. When leaving Grasmere, it is perfectly straightforward to walk up the main A591, there turning left to stroll up to Mill Bridge. But the quiet back road from Goody Bridge offers comparatively greater safety as well as charm and fine prospect of the onward route. The choice is yours.

Leave Rosthwaite as if heading north to Keswick, but in only a few strides, at the edge of the village, turn right at the entrance to Hazel Bank Hotel on a public bridleway (signposted 'Stonethwaite' and 'Watendlath'). The path leads to a sturdy, arched footbridge spanning Stonethwaite Beck; beyond which you turn right on a signposted footpath to Stonethwaite. An intermittently enclosed path now runs alongside the beck for a while, later becoming a field path leading to Stonethwaite Bridge.

From the high point of the path the view ahead to **Eagle Crag** opens up, while to the right you may be able to pick out the summits of Base Brown, Green Gable and

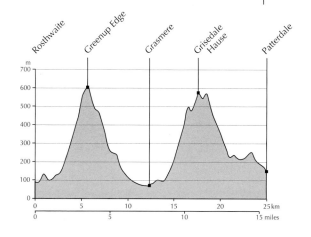

73

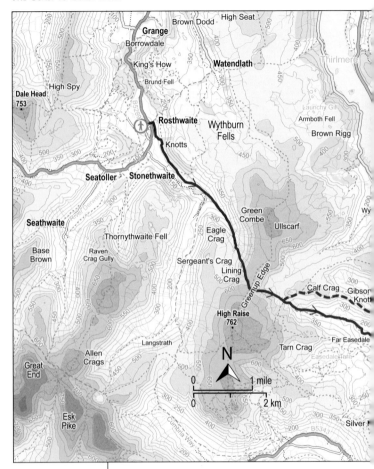

Lingmell, the latter rising directly behind the great white mare's tail of Taylorgill Force.

At Stonethwaite Bridge, the path continues ahead (signposted 'Grasmere via Greenup Edge') to the source of Stonethwaite Beck, lavish product of Greenup Gill and Langstrath Beck.

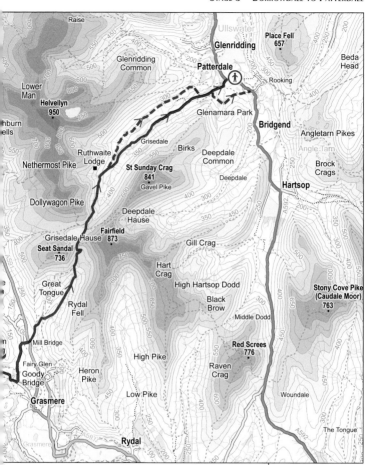

Cascades here form delightful company, notably
Galleny Force just below the confluence, while the
encompassing scenery is so extravagantly beautiful and inspiring you could almost believe nature
is showing off! This is Lakeland at its best. With the
show of cascades beyond the dark frown of Eagle

In the upper Stonethwaite valley

Crag increasing with every step, the landscape becomes more austere.

The sounds of waterfalls are left behind, and the path springs upon an unsuspected corrie, a hanging valley, a vast green and delightful bowl carved by glaciers and filled with moraine, hidden high in the hills, beneath the summit of **High Raise**. Nearby, glacier-smoothed Lining Crag stands sentinel over this lonely spot, and is approached on a steepening path, and then passed on a steep, constructed path to its left (as you look at it), which must have shed a gallon or two of perspiration in the making, just as it does now in the walking, especially on a hot day. In the event, the top of **Lining Crag** is a lovely resting point – what Victorian walkers might call a 'belvedere', although whether any but the hardiest of them made it this far is doubtful.

Once above Lining Crag most of the uphill work is done. An indistinct path leads across frequently boggy ground to traverse **Greenup Edge** (old fence posts) to the head of Wyth Burn. This is confusing in mist, so don't just go charging into it. Get your compass out and keep ESE. Otherwise there is a temptation, most keenly to be avoided, of being drawn into the upper **Wythburn** valley; this will take you far off route.

From Greenup Edge, a descending path traverses a boggy shelf above the infant Flour Gill and other streams, before rising to meet the grassy col of Far Easedale head at a redundant fence line marked by two fence posts.

The ensuing descent into **Far Easedale** is the main route and the best choice if supplies of time or energy are in doubt and you are going all the way to Patterdale or if the weather is uncooperative. The route is never in doubt – it begins from an old fence post as a stepped descent initially bearing right, into the head of the dale, and working a lovely way down to a footbridge spanning Far Easedale Gill at Stythwaite Steps – Stythwaite being the old name for the lower part of Far Easedale. This is a rough and pleasant walk largely in the company of Far Easedale Gill, and leads to the head of a surfaced lane at Little Parrock cottage.

> Over on the right-hand side of the dale, small farm cottages sit tight against the fells for protection. Some were once the home of the **Greene family**, far-from-affluent farmers, two of whom died in a snow storm while returning from a sale in Langdale. Unable to find their way home, the parents lived out their final moments in the storm. Meanwhile, their eldest daughter, Sally, no more than a child herself, took charge of her siblings, tended the fire, milked the cows and pressed on with the work of their farm until the storm abated. Once the alarm was raised, the dead parents were soon found on the ridge above Blindtarn Moss.

Keep along the lane as it crosses a wide stretch of meadowland, and then continues to the outskirts of Grasmere at Goody Bridge.

Walkers continuing to **Grasmere** should simply fol-low the road ahead from Goody Bridge, entering the village centre directly. Those continuing to Patterdale without visiting Grasmere village, turn left at this point.

> The beauty of this narrow and scenic **road**, in preference to walking up the A591 from Grasmere, lies in its elevation above the Vale of Grasmere, and the view it affords of the western flanks of the Fairfield Horseshoe, Seat Sandal, and the waterfalls just below Grisedale Hause that flag the onward route.

Variant over Helm Crag

From the head of the dale, a more attractive alternative for those with enough time and animal vigour is available in the form of the long ridge on the north side of Far Easedale, passing over Gibson Knott to the summit of Helm Crag.

A prominent, narrow path runs out from the fence post at Far Easedale head (NY 295 102) to pass first round **Calf Crag** before continuing in entertaining fashion to **Gibson Knott** and, beyond the dip to Bracken Hause, a final steep flourish to the chaotic topknot of **Helm Crag**. The clear path does not always visit the various minor summits, but simply presses on its determined and enterprising way, keen to gaze down on the beauty that is the Vale of Grasmere.

> The summit rocks of **Helm Crag** are an amazing array of pinnacles and tilted rock slabs, many of which, over the years, have attracted names. Indeed, the profile of the summit of Helm Crag is probably the best known of all the Lakeland summits, instantly identified by everyone who crosses Dunmail Raise. One of its formations, viewed from the vicinity of Grasmere, is immediately recognisable and universally known as the 'Lion and the Lamb', truly one of the most distinguished of Lakeland tops. Also named is the summit rock itself, known, for obvious reasons when seen at close quarters, as the 'Howitzer'.

I would encourage anyone who wants to claim to have 'conquered' Helm Crag at least to touch its very top, but discourage everyone, including the most hare-brained, from actually attempting to stand on it!

Much less striking when you're standing next to them, the Lion and the Lamb are passed by as the summit is left. Keep on along a clear path, soon descending quite steeply and requiring careful placing of feet. Lower down, a broad grassy path appears on the right, and this is the way to go. It appears to be going the wrong way, heading back into **Far Easedale**. But it is correct, and later sweeps round to the left to face towards **Grasmere**.

Keep following this down (and up at one point!), and eventually it drops to meet a wall in the valley bottom. Go right for a short distance, as far as a clear walled gap on the left. Pass through this and soon join the main valley route, bearing left to a gate and out to the cottage at Little Parrock. Now simply follow the surfaced lane all the way to Goody Bridge. ▶ Turn left here, along the side road signed for Thorney How hostel. This is a narrow road and care should be taken against approaching traffic.

Those bound for Grasmere need simply keep ahead at Goody Bridge.

GRASMERE

Approaching from Dunmail Raise, Thomas Gray wrote of Grasmere, 'The bosom of the mountains, spreading here into a broad bason [sic], discover in the midst Grasmere-water; its margin is hollowed into small bays with iminences; some of rock, some of soft turf, that half conceal and vary the figure of the little lake they command…a little unsuspected Paradise.'

Thirty years later it was William Wordsworth who came this way, concluding that one day this place, 'Must be his home, this valley be his world'. Poet Samuel Taylor Coleridge also spent time at Dove Cottage (originally an inn known as the Dove and Olive Bough), where the Wordsworths first lived, and often wandered the fells. Sir Walter Scott was a frequent visitor to The Swan (on the main road), a 17th-century inn and later a coaching inn that serviced the coach trade between the rail-head at Windermere and Keswick. Of more recent renown the husband-and-wife artists William Heaton Cooper, a landscape painter, and Ophelia Gordon Bell, a sculptor, lived, and were buried, in Grasmere.

After some days 'in the wilderness', Grasmere comes as a shock to the system. Anyone looking for accommodation in Grasmere would do well to avoid late August when the Grasmere Sports are held, as they have been since 1852. Less energetic is the annual rush-bearing ceremony which centres on St Oswald's church in mid-July.

Valiantly, the village struggles to retain its dignity and charm above the rising tide of visitors, teased in by holiday brochures and coach tour operators to find pleasure and enjoyment in crowded streets, amid jostling throngs, and souvenirs galore. Only in winter, when the last of the day-trippers has gone, does any semblance return of how life might have seemed in Gray's and Wordsworth's time, the still pall of wood smoke lying frozen above an ice-held lake, sunlight filtering through icy, crystal fingers, black ravens winging business-like above the bracken-brown fells.

From Goody Bridge the road leads to Low Mill Bridge, spanning the River Rothay. Turn right at a T-junction to cross the bridge and ascend to the main valley road at **Mill Bridge**. Cross the busy road and take a bridleway opposite (signposted 'Patterdale') running alongside attractive cottages, becoming enclosed between walls and climbing to a gate.

Beyond the gate the path continues to climb for a while, then levels as it approaches a group of sheep enclosures at the tip of **Great Tongue**. Here, cross Little Tongue Gill first, by a footbridge or a ford, and then Tongue Gill itself, rising then in easy stages. Gradually the path approaches the waterfalls near the head of the gill and arrives at a rock step, climbed by a series of ledges and a rough path. This is quite exhilarating stuff, in a modest kind of way. ◄

Throughout much of this ascent there is an ever-improving retrospective view to Crinkle Crags and the Langdale Pikes, Wetherlam and the Old Man of Coniston.

Cross the stream ahead, and climb a constructed pathway across rough ground to a false col, beyond which lies a shallow hollow that probably once held a lake. Continue rockily around its left edge and climb easily to **Grisedale Hause**.

At **Grisedale Hause** a vastly different prospect opens up. Hitherto the views have all been retrospective, but now it is time to look forward across the great bowl that houses Grisedale Tarn to what lies ahead, as we slowly (there is no hurry just yet!) start to leave behind the great rugged heights of central Lakeland and head for the sublime traverse of limestone country and the dales of Yorkshire.

Grisedale Tarn is an ideal place for a pause, deep set beneath the fell sides of Dollywaggon Pike, Fairfield and Seat Sandal, a setting wild and grand, with a true mountain atmosphere, though none of the surrounding heights presents its best profile to the lonely lake. TS Tschiffeley, in his *Bridle Paths Through England*, said that Grisedale Tarn 'brought back memories of the highlands of Bolivia and Peru'. It is a fine jewel in a fine crown, on a still evening faithfully mirroring the surrounding hills.

There is a legend that Duvenald (corrupted to Dunmail), King of Strathclyde, of which north Cumbria was then a part, cast his crown into

Ascending Tongue Gill from Grasmere to Grisedale Hause

Grisedale Tarn, thereby ceremonially rejecting his insignia of royalty before taking to the pilgrim's staff. Some claim that Dunmail lies buried, slain by Saxons, beneath the cairn at the head of the nearby pass that bears his name. Alas, the records show that he died peacefully in his sleep in Rome. Undeterred, Graham Sutton, author of a number of novels about Lakeland, has spun a chilling short story around this myth entitled 'Dusk below Helvellyn'.

From Grisedale Hause descend a stony path, shortly to cross the outflow of the tarn and maintain the same direction to begin the descent into the long reaches of Grisedale.

A number of paths lead away from the outflow of the tarn to a large cairn at the start of the descent. Make for this and then pursue the downward trail, rocky underfoot but never in doubt, as far as **Ruthwaite Lodge**.

After only a few minutes' descent it is possible to deviate right for a moment to visit '**Brothers' Parting**', where one of Wordsworth's poems is carved in a rock tablet (all but illegible now). It commemorates the parting from his brother John in September 1800. John Wordsworth was captain of the Earl of Abergavenny, a ship of the East

Ruthwaite Lodge, Grisedale

India Company, which sank off Portland in 1805, taking more than 200 lives, including his own. The Wordsworth family were very close, and the occasion of the poem was not the last time they were to meet. But the tragedy that cost John his life was something that haunted William for many years.

Ruthwaite Lodge, once a shooting hut and later the property of the Sheffield University Climbing Club, for a long time lay in fire-razed ruins on a sheltered plateau beneath Nethermost Cove. Now, however, it has been restored and dedicated to the memory of two instructors from Outward Bound Ullswater, who perished on the slopes of Mount Cook in New Zealand in 1988.

Press on beyond the lodge, descending a little abruptly for a while until the path forks. Either path will now take you to **Grisedale**. Take the one on the right for the speedier route down the valley at the end of a long day, although it sometimes suffers from the gloom cast upon it by the towering bulk of **St Sunday Crag**. The path heads down to cross Grisedale Beck, beyond which a clear, and later, broad track leads all the way down the valley.

Variant along the north of the valley

If you go left at the fork and across a wooden bridge spanning the stream flowing from Ruthwaite Cove instead, a more satisfying descent may be made keeping to the north side of the valley, twisting and turning, and undulating from time to time until, finally, the path intercepts one descending (on the left) from Striding Edge on **Helvellyn**, at a wall corner. Take the right-hand gate of two, dropping across a steep pasture to another gate, beyond which an access track leads to a bridge spanning Grisedale Beck, and the main valley route.

Here a metalled road is followed easily to meet the **A592** at Grisedale Bridge, there turning right into Patterdale village.

Variant through Glenamara Park

Part way down the metalled road a gate and footpath sign on the right mark a minor variant finish to **Patterdale** village, through delightful Glenamara Park. Go up through the gate to a step-stile above, and over it bear left on a clear path that curves round to cross Hag Beck. Beyond, the path continues clearly to a kissing-gate at the edge of a small birch woodland, after which it divides. Branch right through the woodland, and finally go right again at the rear of properties in **Patterdale** to emerge on the valley road near the White Horse pub.

PATTERDALE

Patterdale is said to be named after St Patrick, one of the missionaries believed by some to have travelled in this region on evangelical missions during the early years of the 5th century.

The story goes that Patrick, born in the Solway region around the year 389, had the misfortune at the age of 16, along with 'male and female slaves of his father's house', to be captured by Irish pirates. He was taken to Ireland where he was obliged to work as a cattle herd. After six years of slavery, he experienced visions and heard angelic voices urging him to return to his own country to spread the word of Christ, a calling which on his escape he dutifully obeyed, travelling far into the Cumbrian mountains to convert the natives. Patterdale, St Patrick's Dale, is known to have been an area of a well-established, if scattered, British settlement, and would have been an obvious target for the young man's task although some say he never came near the place!

In later years, many of these remote villages were often presided over by one family. The Mounseys were known as the 'kings' of Patterdale and lived at Patterdale Hall, now extensively rebuilt, but dating from around 1677. Dorothy Wordsworth, in her journal for 21 December 1801, gives a little insight into life there: 'When we were at Thomas Ashburner's on Sunday Peggy talked about the Queen of Patterdale. She had been brought to drinking by her husband's unkindness and avarice...She said that her husband used to be out all night with other women and she used to hear him come in the morning, for they never slept together'.

The modern village is described in Baddeley's *Guide to the English Lake District* as 'one of the most charmingly situated in Britain, and in itself clean and comely'. Unspoilt by the livelier atmosphere that draws day-trippers to nearby Glenridding – a place extensively damaged by flooding in late 2015 – Patterdale has changed little over the years. Encircled by rugged heights and at the southern end of one of the Lake District's finest lakes, the village pursues life placidly.

EAST TO WEST: PATTERDALE TO ROSTHWAITE

There are two ways into Grisedale from Patterdale village. The main route leaves Patterdale heading for Glenridding and passes the church. At the next bend, leave the main road and go left on a minor road passing Patterdale Hall and climbing steadily. Keep forward to a gate (ignore the broad track descending to the right) and go ahead, through the gate, to be joined by the alternative route from the White Lion.

Alternative start: Opposite the White Lion turn onto a signed path climbing past public toilets. At the rear of an isolated building, leave the track by turning left onto a signposted grassy path through bracken and heather. This leads to a gate giving onto open fell side. A path climbs rockily for a short while before descending to a kissing-gate to the left of two other gates. Through this, follow the on-going wall, then climb to a horizontal path before descending gently to cross Hag Beck on stepping stones. The path continues easily, crossing the slopes of Glenamara Park and the steeper slopes below Thornhow End. Follow the path as it runs alongside a wall bounding a pine plantation, and then maintain a level course as the wall drops away to the right. A short way on, the path re-joins a wall and leads to a gate. Through this, continue descending beside a wall to a couple of semi-circular sheepfolds, and turn right through a gate, going down-field, past a barn to a surfaced track. Here the alternative escape from Patterdale is met. Turn left and follow the track up-valley.

Now simply press on up the valley. When the track swings round to access Braesteads Farm, keep ahead onto a graded track to Elmhow Farm. After the farm, the path becomes increasingly rugged, as the route penetrates to the heart of the high fells and into a harsher, mountain landscape.

Below Nethermostcove Beck, a footbridge crosses Grisedale Beck. Continue beyond on a rough path that leads on to join a path descending from nearby **Ruthwaite Lodge**. Climb up to the lodge, beyond which a clear path leads on, eventually to achieve the lip of the mountain hollow housing **Grisedale Tarn**.

Keep to the left of the tarn, crossing its outflow and heading up to the obvious col on the left of **Grisedale Hause**. Cross the collapsed wall on the hause and, on the ensuing descent, as the path forks, go right, following Little Tongue Gill to the foot of the **Great Tongue**. Cross the stream near the confluence of the two gills, and pass through a sheep enclosure to reach a broad path descending to reach the main road at Mill Bridge.

Cross the road with care and go into the descending lane opposite, passing the Old Mill Cottage and continuing to Low Mill Bridge, a small, humpbacked bridge spanning the River Rothay. Here turn left, still following a narrow lane, one that eventually leads past the turning to Thorney How youth hostel, and in due course meets a T-junction at Goody Bridge. *Walkers bound for Grasmere need to turn left at the T-junction and walk down into the village, retracing this short section the next day.* Turn right at the T-junction to pass Goody Bridge Farm.

Keep following the road into Easedale, passing the footbridge that takes walkers to Easedale Tarn. Stay along the road (signed for Far Easedale), which soon bends left and crosses a wide, open area of grassland.

Continue past Little Parrock cottage and, when the lane forks, branch right onto a bridleway, a stony track. A short way further on, when this forks, branch left, soon joining the company of Far Easedale Gill. A clear path now leads on into the dale to reach a footbridge at Stythwaite Steps – Stythwaite being the old name for the lower part of the valley. Over the footbridge and a short way further, ignore a tempting waymark above (which leads up to Easedale Tarn), and instead branch right onto a narrow path that continues the route up the valley.

The path now rises steadily, at varying distances from the gill, until, near the head of the dale, it climbs more steeply, following a constructed path to reach the remains of an old fence line on a col, which marks the parish boundary. Beyond lies the grassy gulf of upper **Wythburn**, and a narrow route across to Greenup Edge.

Descend from the old fencepost at the head of **Far Easedale** on a boggy path that cuts across the head of Wyth Burn and climbs to **Greenup Edge**. Once across a clear path descends to the top of **Lining Crag**, from where there is a spectacular view down the length of the valley that awaits. The descending route is never in doubt, and continues past the confluence with Langstrathdale to head for **Rosthwaite**.

STAGE 4
Patterdale to Shap

Start	Patterdale, junction with access to Side Farm (NY 394 160)
Finish	Shap village centre car park (NY 563 150)
Distance	15½ miles (25km)
Total ascent	3685ft (1123m)
Total descent	3330ft (1015m)
Walking time	7–8hr
Terrain	A high-level and demanding farewell to the fells of Lakeland, starting with a steady climb across the southern slopes of Place Fell, then by an undulating landscape of tarns and peaks before climbing onto Kidsty Pike. Some respite comes on the long descent to Mardale and the walk out alongside Haweswater to Burnbanks. Largely agricultural landscapes follow, bound for the abbey at Shap, and then onward along minor roads to Shap itself.
Accommodation	Bampton (off-route)

The great upland mass of the High Street range stands between Patterdale and the end of the next day at Shap, a kind of 'sleeping policeman' before the Lake District finally releases its hold and allows the walk to head for Yorkshire. Obligingly, this section puts all the hard work into the first half, allowing a less demanding conclusion in which to appreciate the gradual change of scenery that heralds the approach to Shap and the margins of limestone country.

From the George Starkey Memorial Hut take the broad track signposted 'Howtown' and 'Boredale', and leads to a bridge spanning Goldrill Beck, beyond which it continues to Side Farm. Once past the farm turn right on a broad path (slate signpost 'Angle Tarn' and 'Boredale Hause') and start to climb a little, heading for the scattered farm buildings and cottages of **Rooking**.

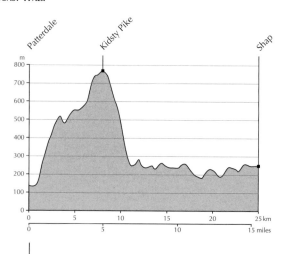

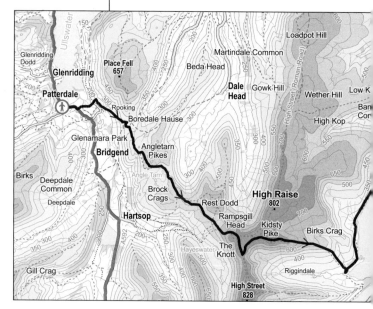

The path now climbs steeply, right, for a short while to a fork. Both the ensuing paths lead with minimal effort to Boredale Hause, with nothing to choose between them, except that the left fork leads to an old iron bench (dated 1897) from which to take in the green loveliness of the valley below and the rugged heights just traversed of Striding Edge and Helvellyn, Nethermost Pike and Dollywaggon Pike. As the route approaches **Boredale Hause** this retrospective view, by no means yet finished with, is particularly inspiring.

Overlooked by the broad spread of nearby Place Fell, **Boredale Hause** shelters the remains of a chapel, these days looking very much like a ruined sheepfold. **Take care here not to wander off along the wrong track, especially that descending to Martindale.**

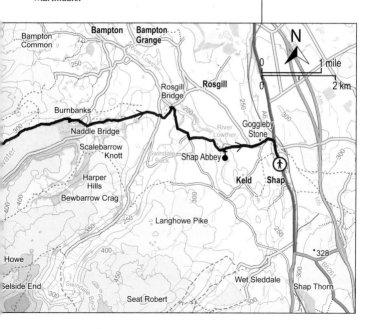

At the hause, cross a small beck, right, onto a prominent path. By a series of twists, turns and undulations, the path works steadfastly in and out of hollows and around grassy hillocks until, as Angletarn Pikes first come into view, there is a splendid framed view down to Brotherswater, and beyond to the sinuous line of Kirkstone Pass. The path continues easily, passes beneath **Angletarn Pikes**, and then rounds a corner to spring dramatically upon **Angle Tarn** itself. Away to the right the great spread of the Fairfield and Helvellyn massifs sweeps round in a craggy arc.

The path descends easily to the tarn, following its edge to climb again with ever-wider views westwards to a level stretch of ground approaching Satura Crag. ◄ Go through a gate and pass beneath Satura Crag, where the broad expanse of the fells still to be climbed rolls across the horizon. Beyond Satura Crag, muddy ground and an undulating path (improved by the use of stone slabs), crossing Prison Gill and Sulphury Gill, lead to the final ascent to **The Knott**, merging with a path ascending from Hartsop and Hayeswater just below the summit at a wall corner.

In good visibility it is a simple and rewarding prospect to cross the top of **Rampsgill Head** before heading for Kidsty Pike. This minor deviation would rob Kidsty Pike of the distinction of being the highest point crossed by the walk, but provides a stunning view northwards down the length of Ramps Gill.

Stay with the path passing round The Knott (a slight diversion is needed if you want to add the summit to the walk) and continue towards a depression known as the Straits of Riggindale. Just before the lowest point, turn abruptly left on a good path skirting the rim of the steep drop to Riggindale.

The path curves uneventfully above **Riggindale** to the sharp summit of **Kidsty Pike**, a profile recognisable from as far away as the M6 motorway, but on closer inspection

Thornthwaite Crag is the conspicuous summit directly ahead, viewed end on.

HIGH STREET

The highest fell in this area is High Street, bold in its architecture, with sweeping fell sides dropping to the valley below, and the arrow-straight thrust of Rough Crag on the right opposed by Kidsty Pike's flanks of crag and scree. Across this narrow strait the Roman legions threaded a lofty highway, reaching almost 830m on the whaleback summit that now bears its name. The road linked forts at Galava, Ambleside, and Brocavum (Brougham) at the confluence of the Lowther and Eamont rivers, built, it has been suggested, to prevent the people of Hartsop, Deepdale, Glencoyndale and Bannerdale from joining forces with the tribesmen in Mardale, Bampton and Askham to attack the fort at Brougham. Whether that is so remains unclear – indeed, there is some doubt the Romans were even the original route-finders. A Langdale axe found near Troutbeck suggests a prehistoric route across the mountains to the Neolithic and Bronze Age settlements among the limestone hills of east Westmorland.

Many similar axes from Langdale have been found along the River Humber – in fact Humberside has the greatest concentration of Langdale axe finds in Britain. This all suggests that a 'trade route' was pioneered across these fells more than 2000 years before the Romans. Whatever the truth, the Roman High Street remains as a lasting memorial to the skill and endurance of the Roman engineers and 'navvies' who, far from the comforts of home, built and patrolled it in all weathers.

a sham in terms of independent grandeur as a mountain, for in reality it is no more than a bump on the shoulder of Rampsgill Head. No such falsehood for its setting, however – nothing could be finer, a perfect place to rest awhile after the exertions of the pull from Patterdale.

Silent and observant walkers may be privileged to spot here some of the **deer** that roam freely upwards across the fells from their sanctuary in Martindale, or the hardy, half-wild **fell ponies** that wander through even the most bitter of winters. Rough **fell sheep** scrounge scraps of food and nuzzle into your sac (if you let them), and, from time to time, the lone, furtive shape of a fox skulks along beneath the crags. For a while there was even a pair of golden

Heading for Burnbanks along the north shore of Haweswater, Mardale

eagles to be seen from the RSPB observation post in Riggindale but the female died in 2004 and the male has not been seen, presumed dead, in 2016.

As the walk crosses from Patterdale to Mardale, Kidsty Pike offers one last lingering look back to the central stronghold of Lakeland.

◀ With a final glance of farewell descend the long east ridge of Kidsty Pike. The going is simple, and the line more distinct now than it used to be. After a brief skirmish with the rocky upthrust of Kidsty Howes (keep to the left) the route drops swiftly to the shores of **Haweswater**, reaching the reservoir near the site of Riggindale Farm, a casualty of the flooding of the valley in the 1930s.

Go left at the foot of the ridge, across a bridge spanning Randale Beck, and then down the entire length of Haweswater on a clear path throughout, to Burnbanks.

Just after Measand Beck a last opportunity arises to take in the great sweep of mountains at the head of the valley.

Along the northwest shore, Birks Crag is the site of an ancient British fort, while the falls of Measand Beck, known as the Forces, offer a moment's pause. In its original state, before the waterworks activities, the hanging valley of Fordingdale, through which Measand Beck flows, ended in a massive fan of gravel and boulders spreading so far out it almost severed the lake. ◀

HAWESWATER

Haweswater, once of modest proportions, was enlarged in the 1930s to provide water for Manchester, and with it ended an era, for the building of the dam brought the demise of a number of valley farmsteads, and of Mardale itself, a tiny village with the legendary Dun Bull Inn, that now only those with long memories will recall. Passage of time has refashioned the harsh lines of man's intrusions, although drought conditions still lay bare the skeletal remains of the village.

Of Haweswater, Baddeley, claims, 'There is no aping of the grandeur of Windermere, the loveliness of Derwentwater, or the wildness of Wastwater, but – although it is a reservoir and somewhat artificial – not to have seen Haweswater would have been to fall short of a just appreciation of the beauties of English Lakeland.' Carlisle-born novelist Sarah Hall's novel, *Haweswater*, is a rural tragedy about the disintegration of a community of Cumbrian hill-farmers, because of the building of the reservoir here in Mardale.

Burnbanks village began construction in 1929 to house the men working on the reservoir, and their families. For many years, long after the work was completed, their houses looked derelict – only a few were inhabited – but during 2005 all the properties were completely renovated, some built on the original footprints of the 1930s houses.

Across Haweswater the wooded slopes of Naddle Forest rise sharply to a rounded lump known as **Hugh's Laithes Pike**. A minor summit crowned by a large stone, the top is said to mark the last resting place of Jimmie Lowther, who after a riotous life contrived to break his neck steeplechasing while drunk. Having died too suddenly for a death's-door repentance, Jimmie could find no rest in his grave, and in spite of all the parson's efforts to lay his ghost, continued to trouble the villagers. Finally, weary of Jimmie's hauntings, the villagers dug up his body and re-buried it on the highest point of Naddle Forest, where he would bother them no longer. For all we know, he's still up there, haunting the occasional passer-by, though I have been less than diligent in verifying this possibility!

Just over 1 mile of road walking leads from Burnbanks to the hamlets of Bampton (Mardale Inn, tearoom, shop, post office, accommodation – see Appendix B) and Bampton Grange (Crown and Mitre Inn, accommodation). Either is a convenient stop between Patterdale and Shap.

Haweswater Beck in reflective mood – it can be turbulent at times

On reaching **Burnbanks**, go through a narrow gate onto a path meandering through a small woodland glade (signposted 'Naddle Bridge'). This enchanted, moss-hung place echoes loudly in spring and summer to the song of wood, willow and garden warblers. It is a brief and cathartic gateway from the splendour of Lakeland into the next phase of your journey. Through the woodland, Haweswater Beck gurgles peacefully, its water lapping ivy-covered rocks and boulders until, in no time at all, **Naddle Bridge** appears. ◄

Cross the road to a stile giving onto a unique and fascinating configuration of bridges – Naddle Bridge itself is double-arched, while sheltering in its lee stands a long-disused, grass-covered packhorse bridge. Within a few strides you cross a small feeder stream, Naddle Beck, by a wooden bridge.

Now go half-left to amble beside Haweswater Beck on a green path to a stile crossing a drystone wall. Once across the stile, a few paces left brings Thornthwaite Force into view, a modestly proportioned cascade, after which the beck assumes a broad and easy course, its

banks enlivened in spring by the bright yellow of lesser celandine and marsh marigolds. Heading downstream, Park Bridge is soon encountered (but not crossed), and after a short wander away from the beck to follow a minor stream lined with trees, a wider track forms, rising slightly to cross a side stream to a gate and step-stile. Turn right along a fence line, climbing easily to pass to the right of High Park barn. ▶

Shortly after the barn, bear half-left across pasture to a prominent gate and stile, about 200m away. Now cross two more fields on indistinct green tracks to reach Rawhead Farm, where a stile gives on to the farm access, keeping right of the buildings to a minor metalled roadway.

Cross the road and traverse a short damp stretch, bearing left through gorse before dropping to a road again near **Rosgill Bridge**. ▶

Do not cross Rosgill Bridge, but turn right onto a broad farm track, with the River Lowther off to the left. A short way on, turn onto the track leading up to farm buildings, but immediately go left (do not climb the farm track) on a narrow path beside a wall to a stepped and gated stile in a wall corner. Moving on, roughly parallel to a continuing wall and then a fence across a pasture to pass an area of low crags known as Fairy Crags.

Keeping ahead, a few more minutes brings the route to a gate and a delectable corner where Parish Crag Bridge spans Swindale Beck, a tributary of the River Lowther.

Climb steps above the bridge, and then strike directly across the ensuing field to a group of ruined farm buildings on the skyline. Pass through the enclosure there, and after a gate bear right to meet a minor road at a bend.

Head up the road for about 200m, and turn left through a gate at a signpost. Cross boggy ground to a gate, and through this cross an ancient earthwork in the form of a water-filled ditch and mound. Now take to an indistinct green path towards a wall. As the wall bears right, follow it briefly, but then pull half-left, crossing the shoulder of a sloping pasture dotted with several small

Briefly, there is a fine retrospective view of the fells surrounding Mardale and the lower ground northwards of the Lowther valley.

Rosgill Bridge spans the River Lowther, which flows from Wet Sleddale to meet the Eamont near Penrith, and between here and Shap Abbey the way is never far from its company or influence.

granite erratic boulders. On the brow of the pasture, Shap Abbey appears to the right, not immediately obvious among its ring of trees. Drop to cross a stream and keep on to reach and pass through a wall gap high above the River Lowther.

Through the gap, bear right and soon strike across a sloping pasture, aiming for the abbey. On approaching the abbey, take to a narrow path (not easily located) that crosses a slight hollow above the river, and climb to a gate in a wall. Through the gate, the route bears left, away from the abbey, to cross Abbey Bridge into a small car park, and then goes forward along an access road to climb out of the river valley.

SHAP ABBEY

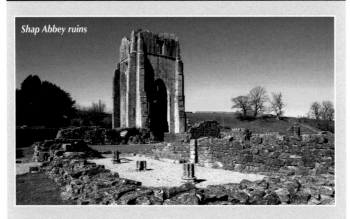

Shap Abbey ruins

The abbey at Shap was one of the many monastic houses established in England during the 12th century. It belonged to an order founded by the German Saint Norbert, and owes its foundation to a baron named Thomas son of Gospatric, who held lands in the Westmorland of William of Lancaster, the feudal lord of Kendale and Wyresdale.

Towards the end of his life, Thomas made arrangements for the establishment of an abbey on his own estates at Preston in Kendale, but before his death in 1201 he changed his mind, and instead granted the canons a site 20 miles further north on the banks of the Lowther. He gave them leave to quarry stone and to fell timber on his land. The place where the abbey was founded was then known as 'Hepp', meaning 'a heap', and referring to the megalithic stone circle today known as Shap Stones. Less than a hundred years later the name had changed from 'Hepp' to 'Hiap', and then to 'Shap'.

The new abbey was dedicated to St Mary Magdelene and sometimes referred to as 'St Mary Magdelene in the Valley'. Very little is known about the history of the abbey. The order was of Premonstratensian monks, and intended for those who wished to combine the life of prayer and discipline of a monk with parish work as priests serving local communities. Such men were known as 'White Canons', from the colour of the habits they wore. The history of such monastic orders in England closes during the reign of Henry VIII, with the end for Shap coming on 14 January 1540, when the last abbot surrendered the abbey's possessions to the representatives of the Crown. For his cooperation, perhaps, he was compensated with what was then the comfortable pension of £40 per year, his canons receiving smaller sums but enough to live off.

The abbey's lands were sold by the Tudor government to Sir Thomas Wharton, the governor of Carlisle, but in 1729, after the forfeiture of the Jacobite Duke of Wharton, they were purchased by Richard Lowther, of Mauld's Meaburn Hall. In 1948 the abbey ruins were placed in the guardianship of the Ministry of Works (now the Department of the Environment) for preservation as an ancient monument. Today it is in the care of English Heritage.

From the point where the car park access road and another road to the abbey meet, the right-of-way that the route follows turns abruptly upwards, climbing steeply up a pasture. The obvious access road is a much gentler gradient, but is not a right-of-way. At the top, a cattle-grid marks the start of road surfacing, as a narrow lane leads out to Brampton road at a bend.

From this point you can simply follow the road ahead as it winds round into the northern end of **Shap**, with the option of cutting off a corner of road by taking a bridleway which leaves to the left after about 300m, returning to the road about 300m later.

Off-road route via the Goggleby Stone

The shortest and most off-road route into Shap turns immediately right at the road bend onto a walled path to Keld Lane. This path is often wet and muddy for about 200m, improving thereafter as it heads for Keld Lane, another narrow, surfaced lane. Here, turn left for a short distance to the next corner, then go right at a footpath signpost along a walled track, but only for around 30m, when you can squeeze left through a gap-stile beside a gate giving into a field containing the **Goggleby Stone**, one of a line of stones thought to lead to the stone circle near Kemp Howe at the southern end of the village. (This can also be reached via a track which cuts down from the main road route at the turning south to **Keld**.)

Walk down the left-hand edge of the field, through a narrow section of walled path and into an elongated grassy pasture. Go up the pasture and ahead to a gate at the rear of houses. Pass through two gates to reach an estate road (West Close). Go left to a junction and right to walk out to meet the **A6** next to the fire station.

Along the final stretch into Shap, not-too-weary walkers may notice the change of bedrock from the granite of the Lakeland fells to the limestone that will now accompany the way. Not all the stones and boulders are limestone, however, for nearby, in the fields, are a number of huge boulders of granite. These are the **Shap Stones** (or Karl Lofts), thought by early historians to be relics of a monolithic monument. They are evidence of a double, mile-long avenue of single boulders (megaliths) extending northwest from a stone circle just west of Hardendale Quarry at the southern end of the village.

SHAP

Since 1970, when the M6 motorway opened, Shap has been spared the aggravation of the traffic that used to shake its very foundations. Not everyone applauded the stroke of highway-engineering genius that brought peace and quiet to this straggling village high on the moorland fringe of the Lake District, for as tranquillity set in, many jobs and livelihoods were lost. Once-prosperous shops, hotels, cafés, garages and other sundry services faced an immediate decline in trade, as everyone now bypassed the village, renowned for snow-blocked winter roads that often ensnared travellers.

Some shops, cafés, hotels and B&Bs still remain, however, to supply Coast to Coasters, but the economy of the village now largely rests on the prosperity of the nearby granite works and quarries, which add nothing to the otherwise wild beauty of the place.

Many of the houses, grey and not a little forbidding, date from the 18th century, while the market hall, with curious windows and round-headed arches, dates from a few years after the village was granted a market charter in 1687. Although quiet now by comparison, Shap remains an important staging post for walkers travelling east or west.

WEST TO EAST: SHAP TO PATTERDALE

Head north from the centre of the village as far as the side road for Bampton Grange, following this (largely without roadside verges) to a road bend where a narrow lane shoots off towards Shap Abbey.

Alternative off-route route: Leave Shap by turning left, on passing the fire station, into a small estate. Turn left again a moment later into West Close, and soon locate a signposted path (for 'Keld') on the right, passing between houses to a gate giving into a rising, elongated pasture. Go forward up and over the pasture, descending to a narrow gap-stile in a corner. A brief, narrow path then leads to another field in which stands the Goggleby Stone. Walk past the stone, following the right-hand wall to a gate and stile giving onto a narrow track. Turn right and walk out to meet a surfaced lane at a bend. At the lane, go left along Keld Lane for about 100m to a signposted path ('Bampton Road') on the right that follows a walled track. This is a lovely ancient route, and deserves more use. Sadly, it needs better drainage at the far end, though this is rarely a

> *real problem. When it does finally emerge on the Bampton Road, it is immediately at the end of the branching lane for Shap Abbey.*

Follow the lane as far as a cattle-grid, where the top of **Shap Abbey** comes into view. Cross the cattle-grid and soon leave the access road (which is not a right-of-way) to strike downfield to rejoin the access opposite the entrance to the car park for Shap Abbey.

Keep forward towards the car park and cross Abbey Bridge, which here spans the **River Lowther**. Go left through a gate, and then immediately climb steeply left to a ladder-stile. Over the stile, follow the rim of the drop to the river, and then head across the ensuing pasture on a green trod, bearing slightly left to reach a distant wall and another ladder-stile. Cross the stile to enter an undulating pasture across which there is no discernible path. Head down to cross a stream, bearing slightly away from the left-hand wall. Climb above the stream, heading for the highest of a line of power lines that guide you across to a wall corner, where you have a minor choice of route.

From the wall corner a permissive path runs left alongside the wall to a step-stile, immediately before which are the remains of an ancient earthwork in the form of a bank and ditch. Over the stile, a boggy path leads across rough ground to a narrow, surfaced lane. The right-of-way, however, runs from the wall corner across to a more northerly ladder-stile giving into an enclosed pasture. On the far side, a step-stile puts you on the narrow lane. Turn right and walk down the lane until it bends to the left, there leaving it by branching right to a ladder-stile giving into an enclosure containing a group of derelict farm buildings. Cross to another stile opposite, from which you strike half-left across the ensuing field to a wooded dell – aim for a gate. Pass the gate and drop beside a fence to gated Parish Crag Bridge, spanning **Swindale Beck**.

Over the bridge, go right alongside a fence (below Fairy Crag), which guides you to a stone stile below Goodcroft Farm. Beyond, the path curves round the end of a hill slope to another stile, and then follows a wall to a gate. Through the gate, go left on a broad track to **Rosgill Bridge**, once more (and for the final time) beside the Lowther.

On reaching a surfaced lane at Rosgill Bridge, immediately go left over a ladder-stile, and then bear slightly right up a grassy path that climbs through a spread of gorse to emerge (hopefully) opposite the entrance to Rawhead Farm.

Go up towards the farm, keeping ahead to a step-stile beside a gate, and then continue in the same direction across the ensuing pasture, rising gently and then descending to another step-stile beyond which you go half-left towards a gate and stile. A grassy path now leads to a group of barns – High Park – and here keep to the left of the barns, following a permissive path (though the right-of-way seems to pass to the right of the barns). Either way, a fence guides you down to a step-stile on the left – the first step-stile can be ignored. Continue further down to another, beside a gate, over which a clear track branches right to descend towards Haweswater Beck.

Cross a stile beside a gate, after which a broad grassy track bears away from the beck for a while to follow a small stream, re-joining Haweswater Beck at an old dam, beyond which lies Park Bridge. Turn towards the bridge, but don't cross it. Instead, go on alongside the beck to reach Thornthwaite Force. A ladder-stile above gives on to an indistinct grassy path that leads to **Naddle Bridge** (old and new). Cross the old bridge, and the ladder-stile on the other side. Then cross the road and a stile opposite to enter a lovely wooded glade, bright in spring with bluebells and stitchwort. Follow a clear path through the woodland, to emerge at a gate on the edge of **Burnbanks**.

Cross the village road onto a signposted path opposite – 'Fellside track via northwest shore of Haweswater to Upper Mardale'. Before long, the

Naddle Bridge – one of two bridges at this point

track climbs through trees and emerges above the intake, then follows a long and beautiful course above the reservoir as far as the foot of the ridge rising to Kidsty Pike, and reached just after in-flowing Randale Beck.

The ascent to **Kidsty Pike** is tiring, but the view from the top is inspiring, and its summit marks the highest point of the walk. *A short way beyond, it is worth diverting right (in clear conditions) to take a peep down into Ramps Gill (if you do this, then Rampsgill Head will actually be the highest point, being 12m higher than Kidsty Pike, from which it is easy enough to descend towards The Knott.* Stick to a clear track that keeps left of Rampsgill Head to meet the ancient Roman 'High Street' on the narrow neck of ground known as the Straits of Riggindale.

Turn right here and follow a path round to the minor summit called **The Knott**, avoiding its summit, and keeping to the path as it swings round beneath it. The path passes through a collapsed wall and shortly abandons the direct descent to Hayeswater and Hartsop village.

Bad-weather alternative: Once through the village of Hartsop, and just before reaching the valley road, turn right on a superb track that will lead all the way north to Rooking or Side Farm at Patterdale.

From below The Knott take the descending path heading right for **Satura Crag** and **Angle Tarn**. Beyond the tarn, the path skims past **Angletarn Pikes**, before threading an enjoyable way down to **Boredale Hause**, beneath the great mound of **Place Fell**.

Go left at the hause to overlook Patterdale, and then strike off to descend to an intake gate, there going left past **Rooking** and or right through another gate, arriving near the valley bottom at Side Farm. From here a broad track leads out to the village road at the George Starkey Memorial Hut.

INTO THE DALES

Wild Boar Fell from Severals Settlement (Stage 5)

As Shap is passed, you enter limestone country, quite a change after the ruggedness of the Lake District. Magnificent scenery awaits and walkers with a keen interest in prehistory will know that the ancient peoples of Britain found this corner of Westmorland (as it used to be) much to their liking. Many sites of archaeological and historical significance lie along this stretch. The region, too, is abundant in wildlife, and two large tracts of countryside are important breeding sites for birds.

The great swathe of land on Crosby Ravensworth Fell has been described as an 'Empty Quarter', and on a bleak day it can seem unwelcoming but it is an area of wild moorland and sheep farming, easy walking and botanic delights. Crosby Ravensworth Fell is a Site of Special Scientific Interest, and an important area for nature conservation, home to a range of moorland birds, some of which have declined significantly in recent years. Most notable among these are the golden plover, red grouse, redshank and curlew. These birds are characteristic of rugged, isolated uplands, and there is nothing more evocative than their call on the wind, especially the piping notes of the golden plover, the bird of wild places. But they are all sensitive to disturbance, especially in the breeding season, when they may desert their nests. In 2016, a large tract of

Limestone escarpments on the way up Nine Standards Rigg from Kirkby Stephen (Stage 6)

Crosby Ravensworth Fell, reaching almost to Shap, was included in the Yorkshire Dales National Park.

Between Kirkby Stephen and Keld the walk crosses the watershed of Britain, on Nine Standards Rigg. The original onward route from Nine Standards Rigg to Ravenseat was by Whitsun Dale, but this was often a quagmire, so the Yorkshire Dales National Park introduced seasonal variations to minimise erosional impact. Although any of the routes can be used at any time, the so-called 'blue route' through Whitsun Dale is recommended between August and November when, theoretically, the ground is firmer. This is the main route described in Stage 6. If all else fails, there is a fourth possibility, suitable for dire conditions only, and that is to follow the B6270 from Kirkby Stephen to Nateby, through Birk Dale and then into Keld – road walking all the way… but no bogs and no risk of getting lost.

Another decision lies ahead on Stage 7 – choice between the original high-level route between Keld and Reeth, or the gentler, low-level alternative through Swaledale. The former will appeal to those with an interest in industrial archaeology and the moorland tops; the latter is for those who enjoy a riverside ramble.

The final two stages of this section take you into the Vale of Mowbray – the northerly extension of the Vale of York, and an interlude that is almost wholly agricultural. This area is largely flat, and at Danby Wiske reaches the lowest point of the walk away from the coasts at little over 120ft (37m). But there is no need to march through impatient for higher altitudes. The low-lying land, barley fields, quiet farms and rural scenery of the vale add some valuable balance to the richness of the Coast to Coast feast.

STAGE 5

Shap to Kirkby Stephen

Start	Shap village centre car park (NY 563 150)
Finish	Kirkby Stephen centre (NY 774 087)
Distance	20¾ miles (32.9km)
Total ascent	2030ft (617m)
Total descent	2310ft (703m)
Walking time	10hr
Terrain	Once beyond the confines of Shap, open farmland pastures follow leading onto the vast openness of Crosby Ravensworth Fell. The descent to Orton once again crosses farmland fields and pastures. The onward route then crosses large upland areas of limestone; some road walking intervenes en route to Sunbiggin Tarn, followed by moorland across Crosby Garrett Fell and Smardale Fell before pastureland takes the walk into Kirkby Stephen.
Accommodation	Orton, Newbiggin-on-Lune (off route) and Ravenstonedale (off-route)

Once the motorway and granite works are left behind your first adventures in limestone country begin with a gentle climb up and over the Empty Quarter of Crosby Ravensworth Fell, rewarded by a visit to the charming village of Orton, and then another high moorland crossing over to Kirkby Stephen, with a bad weather option if navigation is likely to be too difficult. There is much of geological, historical and natural interest to observe along the way. It is difficult to imagine it today, but the great swathes of limestone moorland and pastures that are a prominent feature throughout today's trek, wild, windswept and lonely as they are, were once the scene of thriving communities; several settlements, mounds and sundry other prehistoric remains of uncertain purpose dot the landscape. Couple that with a proliferation in spring of limestone-loving wild flowers and a sky filled with bird song, and this gentle passage is one of the most memorable of the entire walk.

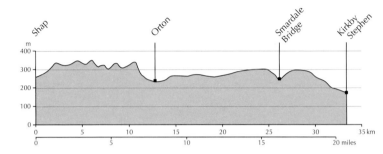

Walk southwards through Shap along the **A6**, finally leaving it by turning left onto a narrow housing-estate road (Moss Grove) directly opposite the Kings Arms Hotel at the southern end of the village (signed for Hardendale). In a short while, follow the road to the right (signposted), and go forward onto a broad track that soon bends left to cross the West Coast **railway line**. On the other side, the track continues parallel with the railway for a short distance before heading east along a walled track flanked by pastures.

Climb easily to a signpost at a path junction, and keep forward, still between walls, to a stile giving into a large pasture with a motorway footbridge prominent ahead. Cross the field to a stile near a gate in a field corner, and from it bear obliquely left to a through-stile in a wall, beyond which lies the motorway footbridge.

> While the view ahead, principally of the Shap granite works, is less than inspiring, the retrospective **view** is of a majestic skyline from distant Loadpot Hill, by way of High Raise, Kidsty Pike and High Street, to the long grassy ridge of Kentmere Pike. Soon these glimpses of Lakeland will be fewer and then no more, replaced by the fine, swelling domes of the Howgills to the south, as ahead the Pennine summits of Nine Standards Rigg, Mallerstang Edge and Wild Boar Fell start to capture our attention.

Cross the motorway bridge and continue right, parallel with the motorway for a short distance on a narrow path. From the corner of a walled pasture, near a collapsed drystone wall, the path slants upwards and left, across a slope dotted with granite boulders and hawthorn, to a gate in the corner of a wall that gives on to an open meadow near the **Nab**. Go forward on a green path to a narrow road.

Beyond and to the left rises **Hardendale Nab**, a minor limestone summit much less in stature now

map continues
on page 108

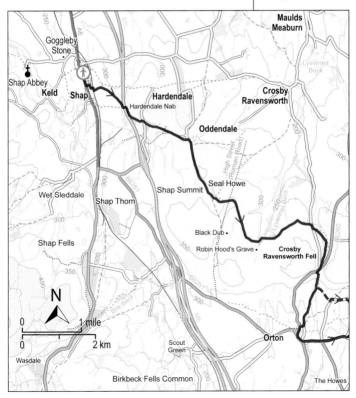

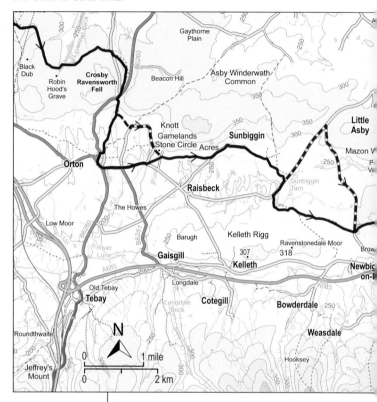

than of old, as huge chunks of it are removed from Hardendale Quarry, whose access road is plainly evident from here, looping southwards to cross the motorway.

Not far away to the north lies the hamlet of Hardendale itself, birthplace of John Mill, the Greek scholar (and great-grandfather of philosopher John Stuart Mill), who gave most of his life to transcribing the New Testament from manuscripts. He died in 1707, two weeks after finishing a work that had taken him 30 years to complete. Here, too, is a farm

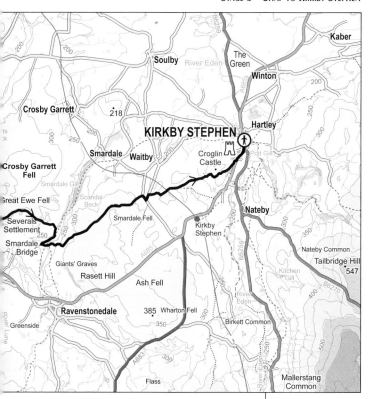

where Bonnie Prince Charlie and his officers stayed on the night of 17 December 1745, complaining about the high cost for food and the use of a room.

Cross the road and continue along a green path (signed for Oddendale), passing below a mainly grass-covered limestone lip, almost as far as a wall. Here, swing left to walk along the wall to a gate. Beyond the gate the path descends gently as it threads a limestone ledge to a stile just above the quarry access road. Steps lead down to the road and up the other side to a broad

Take care crossing the access road, both to avoid the huge lorries that use it, and to minimise the quantity of cloying limestone mud sticking to your boots.

limestone plateau, soon joining a broad, stony track, although not one frequented by the huge lorries that travel the quarry access. ◄

Across the access, bear left along the track, towards the hidden hamlet of **Oddendale**, but as it is approached, bear right, and shortly leave the road leading into Oddendale for a broad, gently rising track on the right – a Roman road – striking across the moorland expanse of **Crosby Ravensworth Fell**, and now within the extended Yorkshire Dales National Park.

> **Oddendale**, which sits on the carboniferous limestone of an escarpment that runs north-westwards from Kirkby Stephen towards Carlisle, is very much a shy and secluded place, a world apart from external haste and harassment. It lies at the heart of a vast area renowned for its wealth of prehistoric communities, no less than 11 early British settlements being found within a short compass. Oddendale stone circle (NY 592 129), a double ring of stones, lies only a short distance from the Roman road, and is worth a short diversion. An indistinct grassy path leads to it.
>
> The circle is part of the complex of cairns, stone circles and standing stones that includes the 'Shap Stone Avenue' of monuments, which is itself one of three important complexes of megalithic monuments in East Cumbria. The circle has seen a number of stages in its history that reaches back almost 5000 years, and is just a small part of a legacy around Shap and Crosby Ravensworth that is rich in Neolithic and Early Bronze Age field monuments.

The track continues rising easily, eventually levelling as it passes stands of woodland at Potrigg. Another plantation now appears on the left and soon a waymark is reached at a fork in the track (NY 598 119). Here, bear left, descending on a green path to the corner of the plantation off to the left. Beyond, a path climbs away from the plantation to cross a limestone edge and onward to descend via a couple of huge granite erratics to reach and cross the infant Lyvennet Beck.

Ahead, a cairn can be seen on the edge of a limestone rise, and beyond it a signpost and another cairn marks the site of an ancient tumulus. Before reaching the tumulus, the walk crosses the indistinct line of a **Roman road** linking forts at Low Borrow Bridge, in Lonsdale, and Brougham.

Much of this area is popular with breeding birds, and the way across it is intermittently waymarked – a good thing, too, for there is a grand feeling of **openness** here. Freed from the constraining summits and vales of Lakeland granite, the wind clears the mind, the sounds of moorland replace the subtly different music of the high fells, and the scenery rolls on forever to distant Cross Fell, the highest summit of the Pennines, and its acolytes, Little and Great Dun Fell, bringing an invigorating sense of freedom and self-satisfaction. Nearer to hand lies the serene loveliness of the Vale of Lyvennet, the onward route now substantially forming a ring around its headwaters.

Erratic on Crosby Ravensworth Fell

There are numerous 'alien' **granite boulders**, like those above Lyvennet Beck, dotted about the limestone country of the north. Brought to their final resting place at the whim of long-retreated glaciers, the larger ones, many with names, often serve walkers as useful guides, while more than a few have in the past been used to delineate parish boundaries.

Across Lyvennet Beck, keep forward along an ancient track. When this forks, bear left onto a green track through heather, bearing left towards a wall, which is finally met at a wall corner (NY 608 107).

Not far away stands a **monument** at Black Dub, claimed to mark the source of the Livennet (sic). Erected in 1843, it more significantly commemorates the passage of King Charles II who, in 1651, here 'regaled his army and drank of the water on his march from Scotland'. Worthy of note also, is the fact, no longer in any way apparent on the ground, that the walk has here crossed the line of the first road from London to Scotland, before the shelter, easier gradients and more hospitable terrain through the Shap fells found favour.

From the wall corner head east, descending beside a wall through low heather scrub to another wall corner. Here bear left towards a shallow gorge. Cross this and continue beside the on-going wall to another gully, better defined, and the course of a dried-up streambed.

The dried-up streambed twists southwards and conceals, only a short distance away, a large pile of stones with the fanciful name '**Robin Hood's Grave**'. Now, the great Forest of Sherwood did once extend much further north than its present-day residue, Robin's trusty lieutenant, Little John, is said to lie buried in a churchyard in Hathersage in the Peak. Maid Marion, I have heard tell, originally came from Wakefield. And history undoubtedly does record that Robin Hood travelled around quite a bit. But if the legendary hero's dying wish that he should be buried at the spot where his final arrow came to rest is to be believed, it would call for monumental quantities of credulity to believe he had the strength to flight it this far! His generally accepted resting place is at Kirklees, near Leeds.

Climbing easily, the route gradually moves away from the wall which has accompanied the way from Lyvennet Beck, and crosses a stretch of 'No-Man's Land' to head first for a large, walled enclosure and then down towards the minor road serving Crosby Ravensworth, reaching it by a step-stile opposite the Blasterfield Quarry.

Cross the road to the corner of a drystone wall. From this, strike towards the left-hand edge of a nearby plantation. Walk along the boundary, and when this ends, keep on in the same direction to rejoin the Crosby Ravensworth road almost at its junction with the **B6260** Appleby to Orton road.

Go right, towards Orton, to cross a cattle-grid, and immediately descend left on a green cart track to a gate in a wall corner (signposted 'Scar Side' or 'Orton Village').

After the refreshing moorland traverse from Shap, arrival at the edge of **Orton Scar** is a most satisfying moment. The domed heights of the Howgills serve as a backdrop to the broad patchwork expanse of the Lune valley and the rising Pennines, blue along the distant horizon. Even on a bleak day, the prospect of the onward journey to Kirkby Stephen is uplifting.

Beyond the gate follow the curving green path downwards (with a disused lime kiln on the left) towards a small plantation. Alongside the plantation, the descending track becomes enclosed between walls, and leads down to a gate. ▶

Walkers bypassing Orton, once through the gate, should go left as described below.

Walk downfield towards Broadfell Farm, there reaching a metal gate. Through this, keep to the right of the main farm buildings, passing through two more gates into a pasture. Descend to the bottom right-hand corner. Then, continue alongside a stream and wall to a gate in a wall corner beside a solitary beech tree. Beyond, the path continues and is soon re-joined by the stream, and passes down a field edge. Keep going forward to a gate giving on to a walled stony track on the northern edge of the village.

On reaching the first houses, go left to a road, and then right, walking down to a T-junction beside a bridge. Go right at the T-junction and walk out to the main village road (the church lies directly ahead). ◀ Turn left and walk down into **Orton** (a right turn is soon necessary if you want to visit the village tea room and the post office). Continue through the village to the turning for Raisbeck on the left at the southern edge of the village.

You can turn left instead here to take the easterly road through the village and visit the Wesleyan Chapel (1833).

Granted a market charter during the reign of Edward I (1272–1307), **Orton** lies in a beautiful spot at the foot of Orton Scar, and is overlooked by its 13th-century Church of All Saints, which stands on a knoll by the northerly approach to the village. It is one of the most charming of Westmorland villages. A farmers' market is still held here on the second Saturday in each month (see www.ortonfarmers. co.uk). In 1658, Oliver Cromwell granted a charter for a weekly market and an annual Whitsun fair. Other fairs were later permitted, and sheep and cattle traded.

Surrounded by trees and built around a village green between two streams, the village has a reputation for longevity, a considerable number of inhabitants having lived to a hundred so reluctant are they, perhaps, to leave such a beautiful setting. Many of Orton's cottages date from the 17th and 18th centuries. Petty Hall bears the date 1604 on a panel over the doorway and not far away stands Orton Hall, an extensive Jacobean mansion house in six acres of private grounds now serving as luxury self-catering accommodation. At the southern edge of the village stands a delightful double-arched bridge which separates the waters of Chapel Beck. Another attractive pedestrian bridge stands nearby, giving into the grounds of Orton Hall.

GEORGE WHITEHEAD

Probably the most famous of Orton's inhabitants was George Whitehead. Born here in 1636, he fell under the spell of the charismatic George Fox and became a Quaker while still a young man. This was a most perilous time for Quakers. They were universally hated by Anglicans, Presbyterians, and Baptists and it was commonplace to find people baiting them and beating them with sticks. Somehow, Whitehead survived this persecution and embarked on a personal crusade of a most remarkable order. Preaching widely, he argued at length with preachers and professors alike, and went to prison for his faith, as well as being placed in stocks and whipped.

At one point he managed to persuade King Charles II to free every captive Quaker, only to see them later thrown back into prison and robbed of their estates. From James II he secured immunity from persecution but it was not until after the Revolution that Parliament passed an Act recognising Quakers as citizens. If George Fox was the founder of the Society of Friends, George Whitehead, it has been said, 'was the law-giver, the Moses of his creed'. Unabashed, he stood before seven sovereigns, obtaining concessions that later found their way into the Quaker Magna Carta of 1696. He died in 1723, aged 86.

Bypassing Orton

This route will save ¾ mile (1.3km) if you are happy to give the Orton tea room a miss.

From the gate, go left across a low bridge spanning a stream gully, and then continue alongside a wall to the farm access for Broadfell.

Follow the access out to Street Lane, a minor road serving a handful of isolated farms. Go left up the lane to Scar Side Farm, then east to Friar Biggins Farm, and, shortly, Scarside Farm. A short way further on, a gate and stile on the left give access to a field. Strike across the field to another gate and stile, giving onto Knott Lane, a long-established bridleway leading north onto Orton Scar.

Cross Knott Lane to a stile (and gate) opposite.

Gamelands Stone Circle lies just south of this junction, over the east wall of the lane, and is of considerable size, with many of its original 40 or so stones collapsed but remaining.

From Orton, follow the Raisbeck road for 1 mile (1.5km), before leaving it by branching left to join a footpath which joins a bridleway about 300m further on when it meets Knott Lane (a wide, walled track that runs northwards towards the limestone fell, **Knott**). ◄

Continue half right ahead on the bridleway (signed for 'Acres' and 'Coast to Coast via Sunbiggin') by crossing a stile and going forward alongside a wall until another stile/gate takes the route onto the opposite side of the wall, where it now remains. The way takes a well-defined line across numerous wall-enclosed pastures, and finally arrives at a gate and stile beside a small group of trees beyond which, directly ahead across one last field, lies the farm at Acres.

When you reach the narrow lane at **Acres**, turn left and, taking care against approaching traffic (some of which may be four-legged and en masse), walk up to Sunbiggin Farm, and then head east for Stony Head Farm, where the lane surrenders to a broad green track enclosed between walls (signposted 'Bridleway to Sunbiggin Tarn'). The track ends at a gate on the boundary of Access Land, after which it crosses heather moorland. Keep going for about 200m to a track **junction**, and here branch right, heading south, towards the Howgills that form the undulating southern skyline. When, a short way on, the track forks, keep left, and at the next track junction, now with **Sunbiggin Tarn** in view, turn right through another spread of heather dotted with gnarled hawthorns. Follow a wide track out to meet a road.

Now there is a choice of two routes, which may well be influenced by weather conditions. The main route now makes use of a line not lawfully available at the time of the first edition of this book; the other simply takes the road to the left and then heads south through Mazon Wath. The latter, though longer, is the wiser option in poor visibility (and given below).

On meeting the road, go right – southwest and apparently heading away from Robin Hood's Bay – to cross Tarn Sike bridge (NY 672 074). Now continue along the road for a further 200m, then leave it for a clear track southward through heather. Just southwest of a boggy hollow created by Tarn Sike, the path meets a cross track. Here turn left, heading roughly east, with Sunbiggin Tarn easing into view once more.

Sunbiggin Tarn, though undoubtedly a welcome oasis in these great limestone uplands, is a particularly sensitive area. Often, the raucous clamour of breeding gulls will pinpoint the tarn's whereabouts sooner by sound than by sight. The area around the tarn is a Site of Special Scientific Interest (SSSI).

Not always clear underfoot, the on-going path is an ancient highway – now classified as a Byway Open to All Traffic (a BOAT). The path leads down to a gate in a wall, near a large, walled enclosure, on the boundary between Orton and Ravenstonedale parishes. Beyond the gate the ground can be boggy and churned up, but leads on to a lovely broad green track across **Ravenstonedale Moor**. **Although there is a discernible track across the moor, this may not be best place to be in poor visibility for uncertain navigators.**

Walkers bound for Newbiggin-on-Lune should turn right at the road and follow it down to the village, a little over half a mile (1km) distant.

The track eventually passes along the southern edge of a large walled enclosure, and then bears left, climbing gently to meet the road to **Newbiggin-on-Lune**, almost opposite a stony track along which the route continues. ◀

Bad weather route (through Mazon Wath)

If taking the road option – a tedious tarmac plod but easy to follow – turn left on reaching the road and cross a cattle-grid just north of **Sunbiggin Tarn**, of which there is a lovely view.

Continue towards the junction with the Newbiggin road, and here bear right, cutting the corner a little, and then follow an undulating road past the scattered dwellings at **Mazon Wath**, and then on as far as a conspicuous stony track on the left about 300m south of a cattle-grid.

Cross the Newbiggin road and follow a stony track heading past the domed and fenced mound of a reservoir, and then east along the north side of a wall towards Ewefell Mire, before bearing away to a gate. Beyond, continue below **Great Ewe Fell** and Bents Hill, still parallel with the wall. The easy crossing, above the **Crosby Garrett Fell** intake, is delightful strolling, with time aplenty to take in the view.

Away to the right the Howgills, which have kept company with the walk since Orton Scar was crossed, are starting now to recede, replaced by the great swell of **Wild Boar Fell**, the **Vale of Eden**, **Mallerstang Edge**, **Hugh Seat** and **Nine Standards Rigg**. From the vicinity of Bents Farm a keen eye can just pick out the cairns on Nine Standards Rigg. That's where the walk is taking you.

Continue following the intake wall, passing the turning to Bents Farm. Stay with the wall, and, near a cluster of sheepfolds at a wall corner, press on through a gate and keep along the ensuing wall.

Ahead lies Severals Settlement – an extremely sensitive area of prehistoric significance. When I wrote the first edition of this guidebook, I abandoned the **right-of-way** across the site – the line originally stomped across by Wainwright. Instead, I advised an alternative route which continued along the wall until, at a prominent waymark, you could cross it by a stile. I am glad to say that this route is now the recommended route for the Coast to Coast Walk.

The clearer footpath is on the south of the wall, but on the north of the wall there is also a perfectly serviceable path. Take this to keep the wall on your right and stay with it until just above a dilapidated building, where you will find a through-stile and can cross the wall.

The significance of **Severals Settlement** (see www.british-history.ac.uk) cannot be overestimated – it is a most remarkable place, although it may not look it. Alas, for walkers very little is visible at ground level – hang gliders would get a better idea. Covering an area of about three acres, it is a complex of prehistoric British villages comprising walls, huts, dykes and pathways. But all you'll see today are primitive earthworks, raised banks and the vague foundations of former walls.

The site is listed as one of key importance to our understanding of living conditions thousands of years ago. The remains we see today are sparse, and fully understood only by those knowledgeable in matters archaeological. Most of the settlement lies to the south of the wall, though there are traces of two other settlements north of the wall, overlooking the wooded vale of Scandal Beck.

So, mark your passage with a moment's pause to let your mind run free, back in time a few thousand years.

Near the old railway building follow a green path to the right, to reach a gated bridge crossing the line, and turn right (ignoring the low stile on the right), to continue alongside a fence, then following a curving path descending to **Smardale Bridge**.

Cross Smardale Bridge, beyond which the onward path awaits, climbing easily along a broad, enclosed track to a gate. Rising easily, never far from the wall, the path arrives at a gate and ladder-stile before setting off, this time in parallel with a long and unusually thin enclosure, to cross the northern flanks of Smardale Fell before descending to a signpost. Just a little further on the accompanying wall, which marks the boundary of Access Land, bears left. Here keep forward, and cross the northern slope of Smardale Edge, following a bridleway to a gate and stile at a **minor road** (NY 746 072), leading left to Waitby.

On the springy turfed descent to the minor road there are **fine views** ahead of the high moorland Pennines of tomorrow, sweeping round from the now prominent Nine Standards Rigg to the haven of the Vale of Eden, framed between Mallerstang Edge and Wild Boar Fell.

Closer by, the path crosses **Limekiln Hill**, deriving its name from the proximity of two kilns, just off the main line, but one at least worthy of a short detour.

SMARDALE BRIDGE

Smardale Bridge is an ideal spot for a short rest before the final lap to Kirkby Stephen. The stream here is Scandal Beck, and its banks in spring play host to a wide variety of wild flowers, among which are dog roses, forget-me-not, herb robert, and monkey flower, while the stream itself is often covered with great rafts of white-flowered river water-crowfoot.

Running north from Smardale Bridge, the valley of Smardale is very attractive, and little known outside the immediate locality. The former railway has left a few scars and disused buildings, but its great viaduct is a wonder to behold. The flanks of the old railway line are renowned for a wide variety of wild flowers, including many not widely seen, and if your interest lies here, a short detour, using the low stile just after the railway bridge mentioned earlier, will bring ample reward.

At a number of sites near Smardale Bridge, maps mention 'Pillow Mounds', best seen while descending towards the derelict railway building. Closer inspection reveals that these are not natural formations, and are known locally as 'Giants' Graves', though their true origin is uncertain. Various notions have been advanced about them, including one which suggests that they were rabbit warrens constructed by the monks who farmed this area; there are many such structures on Dartmoor, for example. Pillow mounds are a characteristic structure of cony-garths, a cony, or conie, being a rabbit.

Crossing Smardale Fell – a beautiful, heathery expanse in late summer

Turn right on reaching the road to a junction 150m away, and then left, slightly downhill, for another 150m, leaving the road by a through-stile on the right (signposted 'Coast to Coast: Public Footpath to Kirkby Stephen').

Diagonally, cross the meadow that follows on a green path, past a barn and on to a **railway underpass** ahead.

> The line is that of the **Settle–Carlisle railway**, a route much loved by railway enthusiasts, and a stark reminder of the Midland Railway's determination to construct its own route to Scotland.
>
> The railway was built at enormous cost, both in terms of finance and human life. During the 1980s, affected by the ravages of time and the sheer inhospitableness of the climate, the future of the railway was called into question, as the Beeching spectre of financial viability once more reared its ugly head. A vigorous campaign to keep the line open was finally triumphant in April 1989, when the government announced that the line was indeed to remain open. Its numerous viaducts and tunnels, notably further south, near Ribblehead, and the regular steam locomotive excursions organised by enthusiasts for enthusiasts, will long remain as a proud testament to Victorian endeavour and achievement.

Just after the underpass there is yet more evidence of early settlements, among a scattering of hawthorns, on the right.

Go through the underpass and across the next field to a stile (waymark), continuing on a grassy path through a slight depression. ◄

Follow the on-going path to a gate and narrow lane, leading between the obsolete abutments of a dismantled railway, to turn right into the farmyard at Greenriggs. A waymarked route shows the way out onto the farm access, leading to a back lane into Kirkby Stephen.

> Just after leaving Greenriggs Farm, the remains of **Croglin Castle**, no more than a rampart and a ditch, stand in the field on the right, accessible, if you have the energy and the inclination, by a stile. The

site is thought to have been one of many hill forts constructed by the Brigantes, a Celtic tribe dominant in this area of the North, before the coming of the Romans.

The back lane, improving marginally as Kirkby Stephen is approached, may be followed all the way into town, keeping very much away from the rather busier main street (**A685**), though the latter may be joined at any one of a number of points.

In the end, an alleyway leads right, to the Black Bull Inn, while a short way further, a counterpart favours the Pennine Hotel, directly opposite the market place, from where the onward route departs. ▶

Walkers bound for the youth hostel should either join the A685 by one of the earlier opportunities, or turn right on reaching the main street near the market place.

Many walkers will have traversed this section from Shap in one day, and will no doubt welcome the chance to put up their feet, and maybe down a few pints! Others may have wandered across in a rather more leisurely fashion, stopping perhaps at Orton. But few will have done either without acquiring a sense of a **passage through time**, extending over two, three, maybe four thousand years into the dawning of Man's time in northern Britain. Opportunities to experience so much in so relatively short a distance are rare. Only a soulless, blinkered person could pass by without so much as a thought for our prehistory, and, thankfully, very few of those have the spirit or imagination it takes to become long-distance walkers.

And if this ancient fantasy land has aroused something within you, make sure it is well secured in your memory before advancing into the busy streets of Kirkby Stephen. This, in spite of the town's undoubted charms, is the 21st century, and something of a culture shock.

KIRKBY STEPHEN

An old market town, with a charter since 1351, Kirkby Stephen gives the impression of a place that doesn't quite know what it wants to be. First impressions make it seem larger than it really is, but the River Eden, slipping quietly round the back of the town, rather sharply defines its eastern boundaries, while low hill pastures start to rise within a hundred metres of the town's main road, to the west.

Although lying on the once-important route up the Eden valley to Carlisle, the town, was once overshadowed by its neighbour, Brough, whose massive castle dominated the strategic junction of the Carlisle route with the road by Stainmore from Scotch Corner, once the main road from London to Scotland. But the coming of the railways signalled Brough's ultimate decline, wiping out the coaching trade, at the same time boosting the fortunes of Kirkby Stephen, which, until fairly recently, had two railway stations although now only the Settle–Carlisle line remains.

Even when the Beeching axe fell, Kirkby survived on the strength of the expanding motor trade, proving a well-sited staging post for convoys of coaches taking workers from the northeast on holiday and day trips to Blackpool. In those heady days of wealth, a café in Kirkby was a licence to print money, and the whole town stayed bright-eyed and bushy-tailed well into the early hours. Coaches still stop there and the Coast to Coast Walk has seen to it that a steady plod of hungry wayfarers finds its weary way into the town in search of hotels, bed and breakfast, camp sites, and the hostel.

Kirkby's church, of St Stephen, is worth a visit. Rather like a small cathedral, it still bears traces of Saxon and Norman handiwork. In the former county of Westmorland, St Stephen's was second in size only to the church at Kendal, and has a stately nave notable for its length and its magnificent 13th-century arcades. Dalesmen have worshipped on this site since Saxon times, and, until the early part of the 20th century, heard curfew rung from the 16th-century tower each evening.

The old town was built for defence against border raiders, with narrow, high-walled passages and spacious squares into which cattle would be driven in times of danger. Indeed, those narrow passages provide the lynch pin for at least one local legend. In relatively recent times, two salmon poachers, it is claimed, escaped from the long arm of the law by fleeing in their Mini down the narrow confines of Stoneshot. The pursuing police, coming from Penrith and lacking essential local knowledge, endeavoured to follow in their patrol car, only to find themselves wedged between the walls, unable to go forward or back, or open the doors.

EAST TO WEST: KIRKBY STEPHEN TO SHAP

Leave the market place in Kirkby Stephen by a small alleyway adjoining the Pennine Hotel, or by a similar passageway near the Black Bull Hotel. Both lead to a quieter back road. Turn left along it, and follow the back road past West Garth Avenue and into a narrow passage flanked by garages and a drystone wall. Gradually the road deteriorates, ceases to have a metalled surface and becomes a farm access leading to Greenriggs Farm and **Croglin Castle**.

Enter the farmyard and turn right around the end of the buildings, shortly going left between the abutments of a double railway underpass. Keep ahead and soon pass through a wall by a gate, then follow the left-hand field boundary alongside a drystone wall with a group of barns just to the right. Continue to a stile, and in the next field head directly away, climbing easily on a green path to cross a fence (stile), and then keep on to reach a wall.

Another green path leads across the next field to an underpass beneath the **Settle–Carlisle railway line**. Go through the underpass and press on, aiming for a wall ahead, to the right of which there is a barn. Just after the barn, turn right, and continue easily across pastureland to a gap-stile in a wall, beyond which you reach a surfaced lane. Go left along the lane to a junction, and then right, following the lane to a gate and stile on the left, and there leaving it.

Follow a broad track across the northern shoulder of **Smardale Fell** before descending to a signpost near a wall. Now go forward, roughly parallel with the wall, which flanks an elongated enclosure. Keep on through a gate, and then descend by a wall to another gate at the head of a wide, walled track leading down to Smardale Bridge.

Cross the bridge and immediately turn right onto a rising path above the dale, and then bear right alongside a fence flanking an old railway line. Cross a gated bridge and bear right towards a ruined railway cottage. At the cottage, turn left and climb beside a wall. Continue up beside the wall, keeping above **Severals Settlement**, to reach a gap-stile and waymark at the top of the large enclosure. Here, cross the stile.

Now follow the wall, left, to a gate near a wall corner, and continue through this to reach and pass the turning to Bents Farm. The track presses on to a gate and forward alongside a wall, shortly approaching a fence and the raised mound of a reservoir. When you reach a rough, stony track, go forward along this to an unenclosed road. Which route to take now depends on visibility and the weather. In good conditions, the walk across the moor is invigorating. So, on reaching the road go forward down a broad track heading west. The immediate objective is a large walled enclosure about

Sunbiggin Tarn – a lovely outpost, popular with black-headed gulls

300m away. Pass along the southern edge of this, and then ascend gently onto the grassy expanse of **Ravenstonedale Moor**.

The track across the moor leads onto a gate in a wall that marks the boundary between Orton and Ravenstonedale parishes, from which the track climbs left onto heather moorland. Once in among the heather, **Sunbiggin Tarn** comes into view on the right. As you cross the moor, the track goes around the southern edge of a boggy hollow to a meeting of tracks. Visible off to the right at this point is a narrow road and Tarn Sike bridge. There is a direct track to the road from the junction, passing round the boggy hollow. Turn right along the road to cross Tarn Sike bridge and press on for another 200m to a bridleway signpost on the left.

> *Bad weather alternative: In poor visibility the crossing of Ravenstonedale Moor ahead may be confusing, although there is a discernible path all the way. Anyone not entirely happy with this is advised to turn right on meeting the road, walk through the hamlet of Mazon Wath, and then go up to the junction with the Asby road. There turn left, and 1.1 miles (1.8km) farther on, shortly after a cattle-grid, and due north of Sunbiggin Tarn, leave the road on the right at a bridleway signpost.*

From the bridleway sign, go onto a wide grassy track through heather. After about 100m the track bends left. Work a way up to a cross-path and there go left, climbing steadily to cross a wide, low ridge over which the track descends to another junction. Here turn left, and after about 200m go forward through a gate and along a walled track to Stony Head farm.

At the farm the track becomes a surfaced lane. Continue along this, passing Sunbiggin Farm, and go on as far as the farm at **Acres**. *Take care along this stretch of road, which is often use by farm vehicles and animals on the move.*

At Acres, leave the road by branching right through a gate and onto a bridleway for Knott Lane. Initially, head across a large sloping pasture towards a group of tall trees. Near the trees cross a stile to begin a more-or-less straight traverse of numerous pastures. Keep to the right of the first field barn, and then target another ahead, following a well-defined route linked by gates and stiles. Continue beyond the second barn, maintaining direction, and eventually reach Knott Lane, where there is a choice of routes depending on whether an overnight stay in Orton is intended.

Cross Knott Lane, with **Gamelands stone circle** to your left, and walk out to meet the main road linking Orton and Raisbeck. Turn right and follow the road to the southern edge of Orton. Go forward to the main road and turn right, up through the village (fork right just after the pub if you want to visit the post office or tea room – you can rejoin the main road by turning left opposite the post office). Continue as far as a road on the right (directly opposite the turning to All Saints Church). Turn right along the road to a junction on the left (just before a bridge spanning a stream). Here, go left onto another minor road.

> *Bypassing Orton: Cross Knott Lane and a stile to the right of a gate. Strike across the ensuing field, half-right, to reach a lane near Scarside Farm. Go right, and follow the road past Friar Biggins Farm, and soon reach Scar Side Farm, where the road swings left. After about 100m, leave the road by branching right onto a wide access heading for Broadfell Farm. Just before reaching the farm, leave the access by bearing right alongside a wall, and heading for a gate near the edge of a plantation. Through the gate, continue climbing on a clear track, passing a lime kiln and swinging left to a gate. From it, bear right to reach a road. Turn right.*

Walk as far as a signposted path on the left (for Broadfell Farm), and here pass between houses to then bear right onto a walled track leading away from the village. From a gate, keep forward, following a stream and taking a clear route to Broadfell Farm. Head for a gate at the left-hand edge of the main farm buildings, and then go forward through two more gates to reach the foot of a sloping pasture. Walk up-field to a gate at the edge of a plantation, and then continue climbing on a clear track, passing a lime kiln and swinging left to a gate. From it, bear right to reach a road. Turn right and cross a cattle-grid to the nearby junction with the Crosby Ravensworth road.

Take the narrow green trod between the two roads, which strikes across grassy moorland, roughly targeting a plantation ahead. On reaching the plantation, keep right of it, walking along its boundary. At the far end, bear left to a wall corner, and there rejoin the Crosby Ravensworth road. A short way on, leave the road by branching left to a step-stile over a fence.

Over the stile, continue across a low, heathery shoulder onto **Crosby Ravensworth Fell**, across which the route is waymarked. Gradually it leads on to descend beside a wall and into a well-defined dip, within which lies the mound of stones known as **Robin Hood's Grave**. Keep going beside the wall to cross another dip with a stream in it. Beyond this, bear left on a grassy track through heather to a wall corner, and there bear right. Walk roughly parallel with the wall, and when it bends right again, go with it, on a green track across moorland.

The on-going track gradually moves away from the wall to join an old track, crossing **Lyvennet Beck**, from which you climb to a couple of large erratic boulders on the skyline. Climb past these and continue to a waymark pole just beyond which the track forks. Branch left and immediately right and shortly cross a stretch of limestone pavement. Continue to a large marker pole on the site of a tumulus.

Descend now on a green path through more heather, aiming for the left-hand corner of a plantation, and from it bear half-right, passing a derelict sheepfold ('bield') and climbing gently to meet the course of a **Roman road**. Here, bear right along a broad green track – the course of the Roman road – and soon reach the straggly woodland at Potrigg and the denser plantation beyond. The moorland track is a delight to follow and sweeps down to the edge of the hamlet of **Oddendale**. *On the way, it passes the Oddendale stone circle, though this is off to the left and not identifiable from a distance, although worth a visit.*

As the track meets the village road, bear left along it for a short distance, and then leave it altogether by going left along a stony track that leads to the access road into the Hardendale Quarry. Steps lead down to, and up the other side from, the access, which needs to be crossed with care, both to avoid vehicles and to minimise the glutinous effects of limestone mud. Across the access, bear right to a step-stile from which you thread through limestone outcrops to reach a gate.

From the gate, descend on a broad green track and round the end of a mainly grass-covered limestone lip. Then go forward to cross the narrow road to **Hardendale** and walk up to a gate in a wall corner near The Nab, an isolated farmhouse.

Bear half-right from the gate, following an indistinct and narrow path as it descends through an area of granite boulders and hawthorn above the **M6** motorway. From below a wall corner, walk roughly parallel with the motorway to reach a fence that then guides you to a footbridge. On the other side, turn immediately right to a through-stile in a wall, from which you strike across a wide pasture to another stile near a gate in a wall corner. Now keep ahead to reach and walk beside a wall to a gate/stile, beyond which a walled track leads you on and down to the West Coast **railway line**. As you descend the track, your distant view is of the eastern fells of Lakeland, with High Street and the shapely peak of Kidsty Pike prominent in view.

Cross the railway line by a bridge and swing right into the edge of a small housing estate. Go to the second turning on the left and follow this out to the **A6**, opposite the Kings Arms Hotel. Now turn right and walk through the village of **Shap**.

STAGE 6
Kirkby Stephen to Keld

Start	Kirkby Stephen town centre (NY 775 086)
Finish	Keld road junction (NY 891 010)
Distance	Blue route: 11 miles (17.5km); red route: 11 miles (17.9km); green route: 12 miles (19.2km)
Total ascent	Blue route: 2115ft (645m); red route: 2085ft (635m); green route: 2120ft (647m)
Total descent	Blue route: 1575ft (480m); red route: 1535ft (468m); green route: 1575ft (480m)
Walking time	5–6hr
Terrain	Farmland leads upwards to the potential quagmire that surrounds Nine Standards Rigg. This, once civilisation is left beyond, is upland farming land and then bleak moorland beyond, the crossing of which ideally requires a fair day.
Accommodation	None en route

The main object today is the crossing of the watershed of Britain on Nine Standards Rigg. Because of the bogginess of the terrain and the threat of excessive erosion, the National Park has plotted three routes across for different seasons. The original route – now marked as the 'blue route' – is taken to be the default route here, but the other options are also described for those passing through in spring or summer. They do not vary greatly in length or ascent. The state of the terrain is the main consideration. The 'red route', which heads more or less south from Nine Standards Rigg over Lady Dike Head and Cogill Knott is recommended for May to July, while the 'green route', which avoids Nine Standards Rigg takes a lower line around the head of Dukerdale.

The route south of Nine Standards Rigg has always been problematic, because of the state of the ground conditions which are fragile, extremely boggy and with little vegetation. At times it had been difficult at best to follow the route originally proposed: walkers have found themselves lost here and in 2016 a walker became so immersed in the peat that the Kirkby Stephen Mountain Rescue team had to be called out to free him.

To combat this, almost 400 metres of reclaimed stone flags have been laid along parts of the route. These flags float on top of the damaged peat and give a better surface underfoot as well as protecting the underlying peat.

Funding from the Yorkshire Dales National Park Authority has been used to spread heather brash (cut moorland vegetation) over the bare peat to help regeneration, and a new stone marker positioned to identify the boundary between Cumbria and Yorkshire. Two new signposts are also strategically positioned along the route. This section of the Coast to Coast is not a Public Right of Way but accessed under Open Access legislation. To ensure future maintenance of the route, Cumbria County Council has agreed to adopt the section as a Right of Way.

Leave the market place (opposite the Pennine Hotel) by a short lane past public conveniences, and descending Stoneshot to swing left and meet the River Eden at Frank's Bridge.

The source of the **River Eden** is high up on the slopes of Mallerstang, on Black Fell Moss, not far away, also the birthplace of the Ure, and of the Swale, the river that will shortly accompany the walk for a good part of the remainder of its journey.

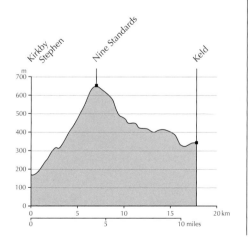

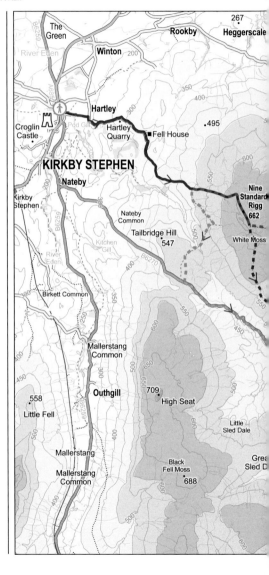

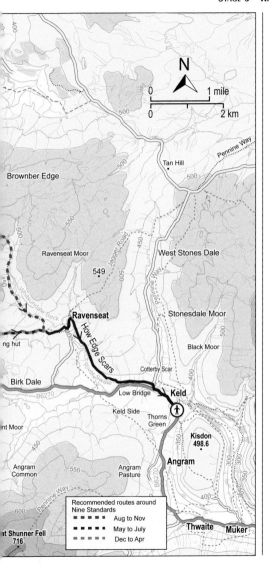

N

0 — 1 mile
0 — 2 km

Brownber Edge

Tan Hill

Pennine Way

Ravenseat Moor

West Stones Dale

549

Jagger Road

Pennine Way

Ravenseat

Stonesdale Moor

How Edge Scars

Whitsundale Beck

ng hut

River Swale

Black Moor

Birk Dale

Cotterby Scar

B6270

Low Bridge

Keld

nt Moor

Keld Side

Thorns
Green

Kisdon
498.6

Angram
Common

550

Angram
Pasture

Angram

Pennine Way

B6270

at Shunner Fell
716

600

Recommended routes around
Nine Standards
▪ ▪ ▪ ▪ Aug to Nov
▪ ▪ ▪ ▪ May to July
▪ ▪ ▪ ▪ Dec to Apr

Thwaite   Muker

The Eden, rising in a wild and magnificent setting, soon settles down to a sedate meander through its lush and fertile vale, finally condescending to meet the Solway Firth near Carlisle. To gaze on Eden's loveliness is to see the appropriateness of its name, as Wordsworth put it, 'fetched from Paradise and rightfully borne'. To travel its length is quite another story, and one evocatively told by Neil Hanson, sometime landlord of the Tan Hill pub, in his book *Walking through Eden*.

Cross Frank's Bridge, where an ever-present assembly of ducks sets up a cacophony of appeals for food, and turn right to follow the river for a short distance until it swings away, right, and then follow a path ahead, through gates, and by a quiet lane into the hamlet of **Hartley**.

> **Hartley** is a delightful place on the road to nowhere, 'A company of limes by a stream, silver birches, a little bridge, a few houses below the grandeur of the Pennines, this is Hartley, a quiet spot under a hill over 2000 feet high, with nine great stone cairns centuries old' (Neil Hanson, *Walking through Eden*).

Go right through Hartley for a while to a path on the left (signposted 'Nine Standards and Whitby'), descending to cross Hartley Beck by a footbridge, and then onto the road climbing to the vicinity of Hartley Quarry. Continue with the fell road, climbing steadily towards **Fell House** farm, a rather isolated outpost, where at last the gradient eases. The road runs on to its demise at a fork, where the way follows the left branch, a bridleway (signposted 'Nine Standards Rigg'), rising through a gate and onto **Hartley Fell**. ◄

There is a pleasing view southwards from here to Wild Boar Fell.

Continuing as a broad track the onward route is never in doubt, and soon joins company with a wall (on the right). Before long the wall bears southeast and then south near the point where Faraday Gill flows down from the slopes of Nine Standards Rigg.

Faraday Gill commemorates the local family whose offspring, Michael (1791–1867), was the physical scientist who discovered electromagnetic induction and other important electrical and magnetic phenomena.

Continue for a short distance until a track turns off (NY 810 067) heading down to the left. ▶

To follow the **blue route (August to November)** take the left-forking track to cross the gill at a ford and follow it on the other side for a short distance and then look for a narrow trod returning towards the gill, which is now followed along its true right bank. After a while the gill becomes more deeply incised, and offers a moment's diversion in a series of miniature cascades. Shortly, the route arrives at a walled enclosure, where the gill needs to be crossed, then continues ahead to a prominent cairn, not unlike those on the summit beyond.

As the cairn is achieved, so the **Nine Standards** come into view on the skyline ahead, for which you should now head, taking care to avoid a few wet (and deep) natural drainage courses.

The highest point of **Nine Standards Rigg** occurs at the trig pillar, a short way south of the Nine Standards.

This is where the three alternative routes – red, blue and green – begin.

The Nine Standards sit directly on the British watershed

NINE STANDARDS RIGG

Arrival at Nine Standards Rigg is a moment of some occasion. It lies on the watershed of Britain, that great north–south divide sending waters one way to the Irish Sea, and the other to the North Sea, although there are times on rainy days when you gain the distinct impression its sends them nowhere at all!

No one has yet come up with any historical fact about the origins of the Nine Standards. They stand on the former county boundary between Westmorland and the North Riding of Yorkshire, and, more than likely, therein lies their origin, although one fanciful notion suggests they were built to persuade marauding Scots that an English army was camped up there, which as Neil Hanson points out 'suggests a contempt for Scottish intelligence that even the English would find hard to maintain'.

Happily, after a prolonged period of neglect, the cairns have seen much restoration in recent years and are worthy of heritage protection. Recent research has shown that the nine cairns appear on old maps, and reference has been found in documents from the Brough Court indicating their existence as early as 1507. It is evident that they have adorned the Kirkby Stephen skyline for more than 500 years, and possibly much longer. Low-level oblique aerial photographs of the summit reveal the possible outline of a rectangular enclosure with the cairns running diagonally through it, and this may indicate some underlying archaeology.

On a clear and fine day there are few places that give a wider, more inspiring panorama of the massive, sprawling beauty of the wild moorlands of northern England than Nine Standards. It is the most far-reaching view seen on the crossing, extending from the mounds of Cross Fell, the Dun Fells and Mickle Fell in the north, to the lofty escarpment of Wild Boar Fell across the upper Vale of Eden. It is truly a place apart – somewhere certainly to take a break, to cast your eyes back the way you have come, to the now hazy-blue Lakeland heights. From here the route heads into the Dales, and Swaledale in particular, and although there is nothing to come that is higher than Nine Standards, it would be a mistake to think it is downhill all the way from here.

From the trig, both the Blue Route and the Red Route head south in the direction of **White Mossy Hill** to a signpost indicating the direction of these two seasonal routes.

Blue Route (August to November)
From the signpost take to a paved section that heads left across the moorland terrain, then descends eastwards,

keeping to the north of Craygill Sike, to that stream's eventual confluence with Whitsundale Beck.

> **Whitsun Dale** is a charming retreat, echoing to the call of curlew, buzzard and golden plover, where, on balmy days, the breeze sighs a soft accompaniment to a melody of light and shade, herons patrol the stream, and the miles that have gone and are to come seem like a distant world. Close by, the ever-growing beck fashions an indolent course, unhurried, reluctant yet to seek out its destiny of joining the Swale. Sheepfolds proliferate, their sometime occupants dotted about the fellsides, but there is otherwise little to betray the hand of man in this secluded spot.

Keeping on the west side of Whitsundale Beck, continue along its course to fenced enclosures at Fawcett Intake, where a stile facilitates onward progress to intercept the alternative route at NY 855 030, near a ruined barn just above Ney Gill.

Red route (May to July)
The red route also makes use of the path beside Faraday Gill, climbing east to the **Nine Standards** and then strikes south to the trig and undistinguished **White Mossy Hill** and to the signpost. From here the route continues in a roughly southerly direction across gloopy bog now partially flagged. ▶ The route bears gently to the right and then left towards a rocky outcrop (NY 828 043) and a pile of stones. Onward the objective is a tall but skinny cairn (NY 830 038). From this, continue roughly southward, basically targeting a track (not marked on the OS map) that leads east to rejoin the blue route.

Depending on the conditions, you may not precisely intercept this track, but an alternative objective that is more re-assuring is the Nateby to Keld road (**B6270**), and this will serve just as well, leaving it at Rowantree Gill (NY 831 028).

In 2016 and 2017, almost 400 metres of flagging were laid across the worst sections of Nine Standards Rigg. The flags start south of the trig point and weave through bare peat to reach the county boundary. The flags then split and cover part of both the blue and red route (approx 80 metres each way). This section was completed by the North pennines AONB. The Yorkshire Dales National Park has also carried out some flagging in Whitsundale.

Green route (December to April)

Apart from walking the road all the way, this is the easiest (but longest) way from Kirkby Stephen, but does not visit Nine Standards Rigg (although you could make an up-and-down diversion using Faraday Gill).

It is also feasible to stay alongside the wall, rather than climbing up and away, if conditions allow, following this around the head of Dukerdale.

Follow the main line as far as the turning into Faraday Gill, but then continue parallel with a wall, but gradually climbing from it to a sign at a junction that points, right, to a wind shelter. From here, drop back towards the wall, crossing Rollinson Gill (boggy) and then follow the wall as it gently descends across moorland to the Nateby to Keld road (**B6270**, NY 809 042). ◀ When the wall changes direction to head in a northwest direction, walk southwest and then south to reach the road.

Turn left along the road (B6270), and follow it for 1¾ miles (2.8km) to a steep-sided gully where Rowantree Gill meets the road (NY 831 028) – on a bad or tiring day there is merit in staying on the surfaced road all the way to Keld. Climb sharply out of the gill on an improving path that rises across moorland to intercept both the Red Route near Little Gill and, a little further, on a more pronounced track. Follow this past a shooting hut (NY 840 028) to be reunited with the main (Blue) line not far beyond a line of grouse butts that drop down the north side of Ney Gill.

Once the routes have combined, the onward way through the dale tends to keep above the stream, preferring the flanks of adjoining moorland to the twists and turns of the dale bottom. On approaching **Ravenseat** (possible refreshments at the farm), the route swings round beside a wall to cross Ney Gill on stepping stones, and then down to meet a minor road by which it enters this remote farming community.

Cross the bridge at Ravenseat and immediately go right, crossing a stream to a gate. Pass through the gate, and shortly turn right again through a gated stile setting the route off along the eastern bank of Whitsundale Beck.

The onward route is never in doubt. Pleasant walking now ensues, the beck never far distant and providing

Whitsundale Beck, near Ravenseat

attractive waterfalls to enhance an already appealing scene. Continue easily, negotiating a number of gates through walls, climbing half-left to a barn, and then by a slightly higher level to the quite surprising scenery of **How Edge Scars** and Oven Mouth, where, over countless years, the stream has done remarkable things to the landscape. ▶

Above Oven Mouth, and after a gate in a fence, the path forks. Go right here to pass a dilapidated enclosure, Eddy Fold, to the farmstead of Smithy Holme. A good path passes the farm and soon drops to meet the Kirkby Stephen to Keld road at **Low Bridge**, from where Keld is but a short distance away.

But you don't quit the high ground just yet. After a gate just before the final drop towards Low Bridge, look for a path going left above a collapsed wall. This leads above a limestone escarpment, **Cotterby Scar**, to meet the road climbing (left) to Tan Hill at a hairpin bend. The **River Swale** is now below, the first encounter with the river that is to be the walk's companion for some days to come.

If you wander off the route onto a conspicuous lower path, you are brought much closer to Oven Mouth, but can escape from by a steeply ascending path that climbs left alongside a wall.

At the Tan Hill **road**, turn right and descend to cross the Swale and reach the valley road for the final moments to **Keld** – roughly the halfway point of the Coast to Coast Walk. What lies ahead is every bit as good as what has been left behind (whichever direction you're travelling).

Until the Pennine Way found its way into this upper reach of the Swale, **Keld** was virtually unknown outside the dale. It is an ancient settlement of Scandinavian origin, its name, from the Norse, meaning 'a place by the river'.

The hamlet is attractively situated, the first village in Swaledale, surrounded by high moorlands, with the river bullying its way through the dale, crashing in a series of spectacular falls, or 'forces', out to the broader, greener pastures of Richmond and beyond. Catrake Force and Kisdon Force are the best of the cascades.

Once remote, it seems now that Keld has taken keenly to the benefits that the Pennine Way, and more latterly the Coast to Coast Walk, have brought in the form of travellers seeking a bed and nourishment. The youth hostel in a former shooting lodge along the 'main' road closed in 2008, but has since

NEDDY DICK

Not so long ago many of these 'isolated' communities largely managed their own affairs. In the heyday of lead mining in the area, Keld had a population of over 6000. Keld held its own sports day, Muker boasted a brass band, and all of them, not surprisingly, had their own 'characters'.

In Keld it was Dick Alderson, better known as Neddy Dick. Neddy's particular claim to fame, so it is said, was his ability to make music from stones. Apparently, while climbing near Kisdon Force one day, he dislodged a sliver of rock and heard a distinct musical ring as it fell against other rocks. Before long he had found enough rocks to compose a 'limestone scale', on which he would accompany his own singing.

His great ambition, alas unfulfilled, was to 'go on tour' with his geological one-man band piled on a donkey cart!

re-opened as Keld Lodge, a hotel with bar and restaurant. Bed and Breakfast signs adorn a few old
and attractive buildings, and one of the farms offers
a camp site, farmhouse accommodation and a
range of refreshments. But even so, the opportunities for an overnight stay, however delightful a prospect, are limited, and pre-booking essential.

EAST TO WEST: KELD TO KIRKBY STEPHEN

Leave Keld by climbing up to the **B6270** and then turning right to follow the
road as far as its junction with the road heading right for Tan Hill. Start up
this, but go only as far as the first bend, there leaving it for a path running
along **Cotterby Scar**, above Smithy Holme Farm, past the gorge of Oven
Mouth and on by pleasant pastures to Ravenseat.

On reaching **Ravenseat**, go left to cross a bridge on the access road to
this isolated community.

Head out along the road and, shortly after a cattle-grid, move right
to walk alongside a wall until it swings northwards to **Whitsundale Beck**.
Here the seasonal variations begin – blue, red and green routes. They are
waymarked and notices are posted to advise which route to take, although
the whole area is now Access Land. The **blue route** is the main route
described here but the others are outlined below.

Walk alongside the wall towards Whitsundale Beck, then go left,
following the course of the beck for a little over 1¼ miles (2km), until you
can leave the dale by turning left up beside Craygill Sike, climbing steadily
to join an older route near a peat grough and guidepost on the boundary
of the Yorkshire Dales National Park. Here, bear right to walk up to **Nine
Standards Rigg**, keeping ahead past the trig pillar to the **Nine Standards**
themselves. Descend from the centre of the line of 'standards' where a green
path departs left, at right angles, soon dropping to cross a drainage channel
beyond which the path continues to descend along the course of Faraday
Gill, aiming for and leading to a pile of stones and standing pillars at a site
known on old maps as Faraday House. Just before this, you need to cross
Faraday Gill and continue downwards to meet a rough, stony track running
to the right, parallel with a wall.

*Red route: From the wall corner continue in a westwards direction,
following the course of Ney Gill and later joining a shooters' track that*

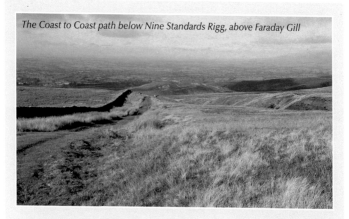

The Coast to Coast path below Nine Standards Rigg, above Faraday Gill

leads out to the B6270 near Rowantree Gill. The red route leaves the track before reaching the road by taking to such high ground as there is above Little Gill and heading roughly northwards towards a rock outcrop and slender, tall cairn, continuing then beyond to merge with the blue route beyond White Mossy Hill.Green route: This option makes use of the B6270 for about 2 miles (3km), as far as a bridleway leaving the road northwards from close by Jingling Cove. Although boggy underfoot in places, the bridleway is clear enough and leads north, north-east and north again to Rollinson Gill near which it encounters a more substantial track running north parallel with a wall.

The three routes meet at the foot of Faraday Gill (NY 810 067) to follow the track, which leads uneventfully down to a surfaced lane, at a bend, not far from **Fell House** farm.

Follow the road past the farm and on round **Hartley Quarry** to enter the village of **Hartley** itself, at a sharp bend. Shortly afterwards, a path goes left across a clapper bridge to a back lane. Follow this to the right for a short distance, to reach a quiet lane on the left leading to a gate giving access to a meadow across which a path leads on to the **River Eden**, soon crossed at Frank's Bridge.

Over the bridge, continue ahead and then right, up Stoneshot to enter **Kirkby Stephen** at the market place.

KELD TO RICHMOND

River Swale from Rampsholme Bridge, near Muker (Stage 7B)

Between Keld and Reeth, there is a choice of routes. One (described in Stage 7A) swings high onto the moorland, where it allows a thorough inspection of the remains of the lead-mining industry that once flourished in these parts, the other (the first half of Stage 7B) is a little longer but with much less height gain, and faithfully courts the River Swale. The former is described by Wainwright as 'a grim trek amidst the debris of a dead industry', while the latter will appeal to anyone who enjoys riverside rambles, a spectacular display of wild flowers, and the conviviality of rural pubs.

Walkers who have taken the high-level route from Keld to Reeth will find the next section, to Richmond, a complete and surprising contrast. The River Swale and its wooded valley is never far away, and the whole journey threaded with variety and interest – an old priory, two lovely, peaceful villages, and a landscape of limestone escarpments, copses, rich meadows and leafy becks serve as a perfect balance to the scars of industry recently left behind. Those who travelled the valley route, enjoying the lush richness of the English countryside at its best, will find their appetites even further indulged here.

STAGE 7A
Keld to Reeth (high-level route)

Start	Keld road junction (NY 891 010)
Finish	Reeth village centre (SE 038 993)
Distance	11 miles (17.8km)
Total ascent	2110ft (643m)
Total descent	2545ft (775m)
Walking time	5–6hr
Terrain	High-level trek across former industrial landscape and bleak moorland; fascinating but grim.
Accommodation	Reeth

The high-level route between Keld and Reeth can be confusing in poor visibility once above Gunnerside Gill. Miners' tracks and sledgates radiate in all directions, the litter of man's industry abounds, and however precisely the route description is worded, the potential for error is not insignificant. Keep your wits about you!

Leave Keld by a rough lane running southeast (signposted 'Kisdon Force' and 'Muker'), and soon branch left, and down, to cross the Swale by a footbridge.

Above East Gill Force the onward route is signposted, through a gate and climbing impressively above Kisdon Gorge, and soon, at a fork (NY 904 008), branching left to the ruins of **Crackpot Hall**.

> **Crackpot Hall**, commanding a superlative position above the Swale, would once have been a most attractive farmhouse. Alas, subsidence, caused by mining activities, hastened its demise, an end that came in the 1950s, and an event that must surely have saddened its occupants, in spite of the no doubt punishing existence that life among these isolated farming communities entailed. The farmhouse

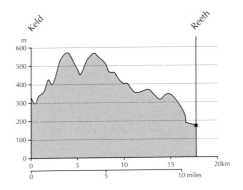

was built by Lord Wharton for his keeper, who managed the red deer that roamed the wooded hillsides of the 17th century and awoke every morning to an inspirational view. Tempting as it may seem so to think, the name of the farm is no comment on the mental state of its occupants, deriving instead from the 'pot' (pot hole or cave) 'of the crows'.

East Gill Force where the Coast to Coast and the Pennine Way meet

LEAD MINING

Throughout much of the remaining journey towards Reeth there is evidence in abundance of the **mining activities** that took place here – ruined smelt mills, chimneys, flues, old shafts, levels, hushes, spoil heaps, wheel pits, watercourses, reservoirs and dams. Although in the eyes of some they mar the landscape, they also form an essential ingredient of the experience of the Coast to Coast Walk to those who see it as a journey through history.

Lead mining probably began in the Dales before the arrival of the Romans, but the first clear evidence comes from 'pigs' of smelted lead bearing the names of Roman emperors, discovered at Hurst Mines just north of Reeth, and near Grassington in Wharfedale. It was also carried out by the Anglo-Saxons, by monks of the many monasteries and priories that dotted the pre-Henry VIII English landscape, and during Tudor times. But the activity reached its peak during the late 18th and early 19th centuries, and most of the physical remains that are encountered on the walk are relics of that time.

Just before reaching the ruins of Crackpot Hall, for example, the path crosses the line of Old Field Hush, a grooved scouring of the hillside caused by the artificial damming up of water above, which, when released, flushed surface debris and soil away to reveal much-prized minerals and ore, or at least the suggestion that a vein of ore might be present. The Old Field Hush was worked from 1738 to 1846, during a time of much squabbling between the Parkes brothers, owners of nearby Beldi Hill Mines, and Lord Pomfret, whose mines were in Swinner Gill.

Continue on the track rising behind Crackpot Hall, and past buildings of a former smithy. The view down the valley towards Muker is here exhilarating, as the path becomes narrow and rocky, turning under the crumbling sandstone outcrops of Buzzard Scar and into the awesome gorge of Swinner Gill.

At the head of the gill, at the junction with Grain Gill, is a fine stone bridge, while across the bridge are the ruins of **Swinnergill Mines**, with dressing floors and the decaying hulk of the smelt mill. The mineral veins worked by the lead miners are especially numerous on the north side of Swaledale. The veins run approximately W–E and NW–SE, so that

Lead mining ruins in Swinner Gill

the four tributaries of the Swale, of which Swinner Gill is the first, cut across a complex of veins allowing them to be discovered and worked. Swinner Gill well illustrates this, and further evidence will be found in Gunnerside Gill, Hard Level Gill and Arkle Beck.

In the gorge of Hind Hole Beck, to the left of Upper Swinner Gill lies the so-called Swinnergill Kirk, said to be a cave where, during times of religious persecution, those of the Catholic faith would meet and pray in secret. Quite why, having struggled so far into the wild heartland of these rolling hillsides, the necessity would still be felt to seek out the seclusion of a cave, is unclear, but it invests an otherwise bleak and inhospitable spot with a dash of much-needed colour. A more pragmatic view suggests that 'kirk' is Yorkshire dialect for a limestone gorge. The cave is very low, and doesn't look as though it could conceal many. Nor does it throw any light on how those who attended the kirk might have done so, there and back from their homes in the valley, unnoticed.

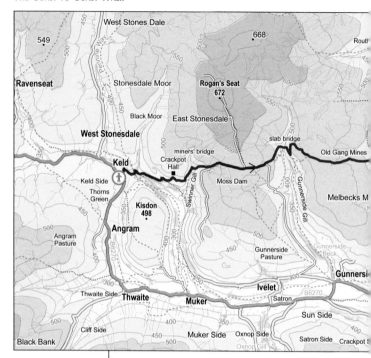

Botanists will also find a diversion into the gill
of interest. Its damp atmosphere and wet rocks and
ledges are home to a host of unusual flowers, ferns,
mosses and liverworts.

From the **miners' bridge** at the foot of Hind Hole
Beck and beyond the ruins of the smelt mill, the path
climbs stiffly for a while along the line of East Grain, the
gradient easing just before the broad scar of a shooters'
track. Now follow the track to the left, climbing easily
to the highest point on the moor, just after a fence, and
near a distinct branch to the left leading to the summit of lonely **Rogan's Seat**. At the high point of this
stretch, there is a glimpse, right, of **Moss Dam**, a relic of

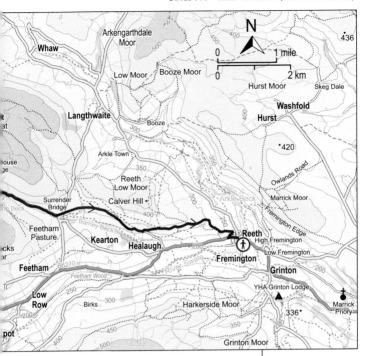

mining days, now almost concealed by the encroaching heather.

Continue ahead, descending gently as far as an old enclosure on the left. A short way ahead the main track bends right to head for Gunnerside. Before reaching this point look for two smallish cairns on the left (NY 931 013), leading to a larger one. Leave the main track here and follow a narrow path heading towards Gunnerside Gill. For a while the path skims along the rim of North Hush before moving away, northeast, to descend, steeply in places, to Blind Gill and the remains of the Blakethwaite Lead Mine.

Cross the stream by a **slab bridge** to reach the cloistered remains of a once fine building, thought to be a smelt mill.

Patterned fields near Gunnerside

Little more than a century ago the long ravine of **Gunnerside Gill** was a scene of intense mining activity. It is visited now only by walkers and those with an interest in industrial archaeology. For the latter, it must be a wonderland, for in spite of its present-day quiet, little imagination is needed to call forth the sounds of men labouring hard and long hours, often with bare hands and primitive tools. That this mangled landscape is a mess is obvious – it would take a generous eye to find beauty here – yet it is a compelling place to visit and, ironically, a perfect counterpoint to the surfeit of natural beauty that is Swaledale itself.

Behind the smelt mill, take a path zigzagging steeply up the hillside to intercept a green, terraced pathway. Turn right along this, with fine views down towards Gunnerside. Continue for about 200m and then look for a path angling back up the hill slope. The path is easily missed, but if it is just press on to the gash that is Friarfold Hush and Bunton Hush. A number of gullies lead to the moors above, but one, beneath a conspicuous fractured cliff, has rather more sense of purpose than the others, and rises easily to a low grassy ridge on the right, where a line of cairns is encountered, heading safely round and up to the highest ground.

Not surprisingly, the scenery is confusing, a mess of spoil, litter, gullies, hushes and collapsed walls. Here, by a large cairn, a broad gravel track is met – the main route – and followed ahead, through continuing devastation, with barely a blade of grass in evidence, to the **Old Gang Mines** at the head of Old Gang Beck.

> **Red grouse** breed on the tops, and twice I have almost unintentionally trodden on a nest of young birds that characteristically and with sudden alarm 'explode' from their nest, each bird going in a different direction to minimise the risk of capture by predators. It's a rare sight because you have to be almost on top of the well-camouflaged birds before they will move; but it's quite startling when they do.

In spite of the unremitting barrenness of the terrain, there is never any doubt about the onward route once the high moorland is reached, although there is precious little in the way of shelter for anyone caught out by a sudden change in the weather. The heather-clad moors are gone, replaced by an arid desolation that only man can create, sad but awesome in its bleakness. ▶

On a clear day a first glimpse may be had of the Cleveland Hills, still some way ahead.

Flincher Gill is crossed at **Level House Bridge**, a stone bridge, beyond which the track continues as roughly as ever, through a gate and onto the Old Gang Smelt Mill, built about 1770 and conspicuous by its tall chimney.

> The remains of **lead-mining activity** here are particularly extensive, and include furnace houses, arches of ore hearths and a system of flues – one flue leads up to a chimney on Healaugh Crag. The flues were constructed to create a draught for the furnaces. Much of the lead fume was condensed in the flues and could be recovered, which also prevented the poisoning of animals.

Easy walking now leads on to **Surrender Bridge**, where the beck is crossed by an unenclosed moorland road along which some of the television series 'All Creatures Great and Small' was filmed.

Stay on the north side of the beck and follow a signposted path above the Surrender Smelt Mill, then on through heather to the edge of steep-sided Cringley Bottom, a narrow ravine that can take you by surprise.

Cross the ravine, climb to a stile at the wall above, and go onto an improving path above enclosure walls. With no difficulty the path runs on through heather and grass to Thirns Farm, where it branches left, ignoring a descending lane to **Healaugh**. It climbs steeply to Moorcock Cottage (not named on maps), before once more skirting above enclosure walls, and below shapely if modest **Calver Hill**.

Above the farm of Riddings, keep ahead on a path across the moor to meet a wall corner, just beyond which a gate gives access to a hidden, and enclosed, green track, known as Skelgate. With unerring ease and superb onward views across **Arkle Beck** to the shattered wall of **Fremington Edge**, Skelgate will deliver you on to the **B6270** a short way west of the centre of Reeth. Go left along the road to enter **Reeth**.

REETH

Once the centre of great mining activity, Reeth (www.reeth.org) stands perched on a green plateau, from which its shops, inns and cottages gaze out across the luxurious vale it commands. The village was established in Saxon times as a forest-edge settlement, near the confluence of the River Swale and its most important tributary, Arkle Beck – indeed, the Old English meaning of the village's name is 'at the stream'. Holding such a strategic position, Reeth has, in recent times, acquired the title of 'capital' of Mid Swaledale. By the time of the Norman conquest this traditional market centre for the local farms had grown sufficiently to be noted briefly for its old lead mines by the compilers of the Domesday Book.

By the early 19th century, Reeth had developed into a thriving town, expanded by a long history of lead mining, in much the same way Cleator,

River bridge on the outskirts of Reeth

not far from the start of the walk, grew alongside the iron-ore industry on the Cumberland coastal fringe. But it was, perhaps surprisingly for a place commonly associated with harsh and rough forms of employment, almost as much the villagers' aptitude for producing hand-knitted gloves, stockings and sailor caps that helped the town to develop. People knitted whenever they could, to increase their family incomes, but the activity died out when machinery replaced the traditional needles, and men began to wear long trousers instead of breeches and stockings. This evocative aspect of life in Swaledale is explained in absorbing fashion in the Swaledale Fold Museum, hidden away near a corner of the village green. A renowned venue for numerous local fairs, agricultural shows and festivals, Reeth is a place to come back to.

EAST TO WEST: REETH TO KELD (HIGH LEVEL)

Leave Reeth on the **B6270** for about 250m to a signposted track, Skelgate Lane, on the right. Follow the track upwards and round to emerge at the intake wall. Go left, above the wall, keeping ahead as far as Moorcock Cottage, where the path descends to farm buildings at Thirns. Shortly after the farm, when the path forks, take the right branch, climbing gently.

A fine moorland path ensues, keeping ahead as far as the intervening steep-sided gully of Cringley Bottom. Cross the gully with care and continue through heather past Surrender Smelt Mill to **Surrender Bridge**.

Keeping on the north side of Old Gang Beck, a good track continues far into a region of industrial dereliction to a gate near in-flowing Flincher Gill. Turn left across a bridge spanning the gill and press on, rising steadily to the highest part of this broad and barren moorland crossing.

As Gunnerside Gill is approached, so the scenery becomes even more confusing. A large cairn marks the departure, left, of a good track down towards **Gunnerside Gill**, meeting a well-trodden terraced path still some distance above the valley bottom, and in an area of considerable spoil and debris. There are a number of ways down here, but the aim is to continue down to the remains of Blakethwaite Smelt Mill; the choice of route is yours.

Cross the stream by a bridge and start climbing by a zigzag path to reach the top of North Hush, before swinging away and gently upwards to arrive at a broad moorland shooters' track, near a group of modest cairns. Go right, along the track, ignoring its diversion towards the summit of **Rogan's Seat**, continuing ahead, still on a broad track, descending into **Swinner Gill**. Near more smelt mills, cross a fine arched stone bridge and pass beneath the cliffs of Buzzard Scar, before the path swings round to, first, an old smithy, and then the ruins of **Crackpot Hall**.

Just below Crackpot Hall the main line through Swaledale is re-joined. The path from Crackpot Hall continues above the river and Kisdon Gorge, gradually descending to meet the Pennine Way for a brief moment above East Gill Force. Here, by dropping to the river, the route crosses a bridge and climbs, right, to reach the village of **Keld**.

STAGE 7B
Keld to Reeth (low-level route)

Start	Keld road junction (NY 891 010)
Finish	Reeth village centre (SE 038 993)
Distance	12 miles (19.3km)
Total ascent	855ft (260m)
Total descent	1295ft (395m)
Walking time	6hr
Terrain	Riverside tracks and paths across farmland; some road walking.
Accommodation	Thwaite (off-route), Muker (off-route), Reeth

Rightly described as the Royal Road to Reeth, the low-level route between Keld and Reeth is riparian loveliness at its best, an extravagance of riverside wandering across meadows lush with wild flowers in spring and early summer. And the pastoral idyll continues after Richmond. The River Swale and its wooded valley is never far away, and the whole journey threaded with variety and interest – an old priory, two lovely, peaceful villages and a landscape of limestone escarpments, copses, rich meadows and leafy becks.

Leave Keld by a rough lane running southeast (signposted 'Kisdon Force' and 'Muker'), and soon branch left, and down, to cross the Swale by a footbridge. Above East Gill Force the onward route is signposted, through a gate and climbing impressively above Kisdon Gorge, and soon, at a fork (NY 904 008), branching left to the ruins of Crackpot Hall.

As **Crackpot Hall** is approached, ignore the path climbing left towards it, and instead descend, right, on a broad track continuing easily to join the River Swale below, near the foot of Swinner Gill. A clear, broad path now escorts the river out towards Muker.

Approaching Ramps Holme Bridge the path forks (SD 910 986), one branch ascending left, the other continuing ahead to the bridge. Take the path towards the bridge but, unless bound for **Muker**, keep on past it to another fork (both directions being signposted 'Gunnerside', though that to the left makes use of a minor roadway, and avoids the walk along the river). Take the right branch and continue to the first of many – very many – gated (and ungated) squeeze-stiles, to the right of a barn.

And on it goes – meadows, walls, barns, squeeze-stiles, buttercups and daisies in a seemingly endless succession until, at the end of one pasture, the path having re-joined the Swale, it leads on to a broad farm track, with a narrow riverside path dropping to the right. Take the riverside path, through the inevitable squeeze-stile, until the river and a wall on the left, close the meadow

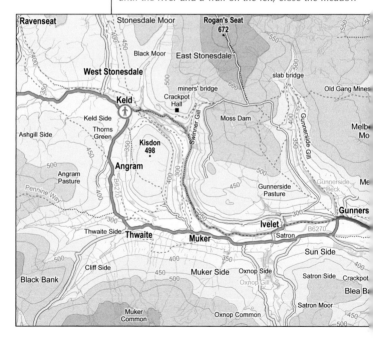

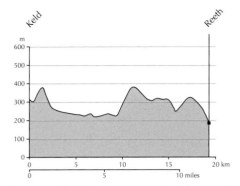

down at a stile, giving on to a narrow path into woodland above the river. At a gate the path descends once more to the riverside.

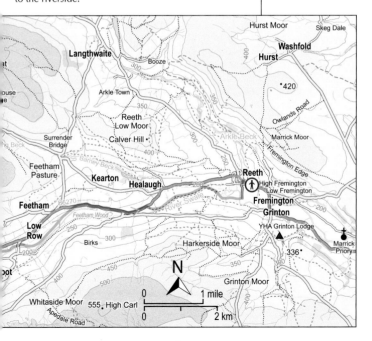

The shapely Ivelet Bridge spans the Swale

Near Ivelet Bridge the river flows languorously below walled fields rising to the distant summit of **Blea Barf**. Climb, by a gate, to Ivelet Bridge, a fine, single-arched bridge on the old corpse road from higher valley communities to Grinton, at one time the only church with hallowed ground to bury the dead.

An exhilarating view opens up ahead, of rich green pastureland, walled fields and sturdy barns, as the confines of the gill are left behind.

On the bridge, go left on the minor road leading to the village. At a telephone box turn right on a footpath to Gunnerside, where a minor road soon leads to a gravel path with a cottage on the left and a barn on the right. At a waymark, descend right on a narrow path through trees to a footbridge spanning Shore Gill. ◄

Once more the trail of meadows and squeeze-stiles takes over, until finally the path runs out onto a ledge between a fence and a steep drop to the river, soon to start descending. At a signposted track, bear half-left across a field for a final flourish of meadows and stiles before entering **Gunnerside** through an estate of modern, stone-built houses known as 'Flatlands'. ◄

Tea rooms and the pub are an excellent excuse to take a break here.

Cross the road at Gunnerside, and the bridge opposite, to reach the King's Head Hotel. Turn right in front of the pub (on a path leading to toilets). Immediately before the toilet block turn left through a gated stile into mead-owland for the now familiar arrangement of stiles and meadows, to reach the Swale once more just as it loops up towards the road.

A signpost on the riverbank directs walkers up a broad track to meet the road at a gate, immediately leaving it again by a step-stile into woodland. For a short distance follow a narrow path high above the river, to which it soon begins a steep and slippery descent, re-joining the riverbank at a stile. The path now continues along the top of flood banks flanked by a variety of trees – ash, holly, beech and sycamore – where projecting tree roots and the occasional remains of old fence posts make passage a little awkward in wet conditions.

Eventually the path is forced back to the road, which it is then obliged to follow until it can be left by a gate on the right (SD 968 975). Now follow a broad green track as it swings round to a squeeze-stile, passing outside a walled enclosure, and by means of a narrow green path following the edge of a field to cross a fence by a stile. For a while, stay with a field boundary and then head left across the middle of the meadow, towards a spot known as The Isles, where the path approaches the riverbank once more. ▶

A small flight of steps leads up to a stile giving on to Isles Bridge. Go a few paces left on the road to a footpath (signposted 'Reeth') which passes briefly along the top of a wall. Follow this round to join more flood banks, and later climb on top of a narrower wall with a drop to pastureland on one side and the river on the other – no place for anyone without a good sense of balance.

On finally quitting the wall the path re-joins the riverbank for a long and delightful trek to Reeth, finally escaping from the riverbank by a steep and slippery series of zigzags through scrubby **Feetham Wood**, following a signposted and waymarked footpath to join the road.

Go right along the road, dodging traffic for a about 1 mile (1.5km), until it can be left at a footpath sign ('Reeth: 1¾ miles') near a small parking area on the right. The path is seasonally overgrown for a short distance, following a fence on the left, the river on the right, then at a stile

This is a suitable spot for a brief halt to watch the antics of oystercatchers, dippers, grey wagtails and sand martins.

Along the trail to Reeth

it reaches the end of the meadow. Here it is necessary to ford in-flowing **Barney Beck**, something that can be awkward after rain, before continuing along the wooded banks of the river.

Finally, enter Reeth by a green path passing, but not using, a footbridge over the Swale, leading to an enclosed path. At the top of the enclosed path bear right, coming soon, at the first houses, onto a metalled back road. Follow this and, as it bends left (signposted), continue to the centre of **Reeth**, to meet the B6270.

EAST TO WEST: REETH TO KELD (LOW LEVEL)

Leave Reeth along the B6270, but soon go left down Langhorne Drive. At the bottom of the road, turn right along a quiet lane that soon deteriorates into a rough, enclosed path leading down to the River Swale. Ignore the conspicuous footbridge across the Swale a short distance ahead, but keep on the true left bank of the river, shortly to cross in-flowing **Barney Beck**. Keep on to meet the road again.

After about 1 mile (1.5km), the road is left by branching down a path descending into **Feetham Wood**. Before long the path re-joins the river, following its course all the way to Isles Bridge. Go left on the bridge for a few strides, then, without crossing it, drop right to follow a riverside path once more, until flushed up onto the road for a short distance, escaping back to the river at the first opportunity. A walk along flood banks follows, until the path briefly touches on the road before charging across a string of meadows to enter **Gunnerside** near the King's Head Hotel.

Turn left at the King's Head, and cross the bridge spanning Gunnerside Beck to be faced with two roads ahead. Take the one on the left – it soon leads to an estate of modern stone-built houses known as Flatlands, passed by a signposted route to reach a meadow leading out towards the Swale. On approaching the river, the path climbs high above, to begin a series of meadows and stiles leading to the village of **Ivelet**. Here, turn left and follow a surfaced road to Ivelet Bridge. Leave the road by a gate on the right before crossing the bridge, and follow the Swale on a green path through countless meadows as it swings round towards Ramps Holme Bridge. Continue ahead, ignoring the bridge, to start northwards with the Swale a little more distant now. Follow a broad, clear path to the foot of Swinner Gill, cross the gill and start climbing steeply to arrive directly beneath **Crackpot Hall**, where it joins the high-level route for the remaining section into **Keld**.

Crackpot Hall has clearly seen better days

STAGE 8
Reeth to Richmond

Start	Reeth village centre (SE 038 993)
Finish	Richmond Market Place (NZ 171 008)
Distance	10½ miles (16.8km)
Total ascent	1320ft (402m)
Total descent	1555ft (475m)
Walking time	5hr
Terrain	Farm- and estate-managed meadows and pastures; some woodland; some road walking.
Accommodation	Fremington, Marrick, Richmond

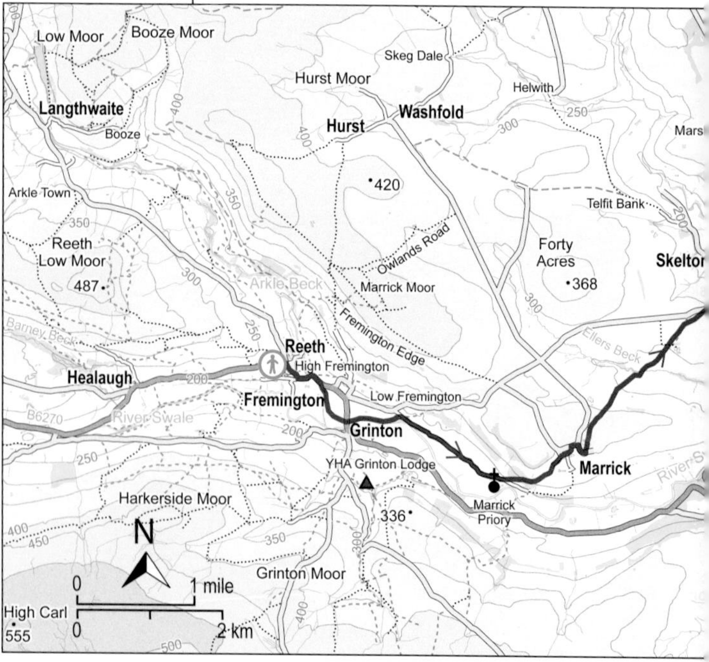

Leave Reeth at the southern end of the village square and follow the road to cross the bridge over the Swale. A short distance away, at a wicket gate on the right, a signpost indicates a path to Grinton. Take this to rejoin the river for a short while, then move slightly away from it on a green path across pastureland as far as Grinton Bridge. Approaching Grinton Bridge note the impressive form of **Grinton Lodge** high on the moors above. Once a shooting lodge, it is now a youth hostel.

Cross the road at the bridge, and rejoin the riverbank on the other side of it. Reluctantly, the path soon has to leave the river, rising to join the metalled access road to **Marrick Priory**. Take to a clear path across the grassland a little to the north of the priory access road, if you want something more gentle beneath your feet. Or, go right,

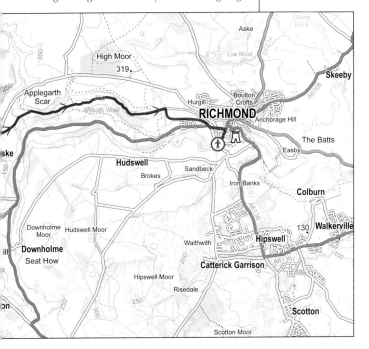

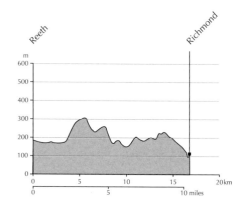

along the access road, a simple and meandering stroll with the priory ahead, beckoning from its verdant surrounds.

Marrick Priory was a 12th-century Benedictine priory, occupied by nuns from 1154 until Henry VIII had his way with it, after which it became a ruin, with only the tower remaining. Later it was to become the parish church and a separate farm. In the late 1960s the priory buildings were converted into an outdoor education and residential centre. It is not open to visitors but you are allowed to have a look around the grounds.

Near the priory entrance a track crosses a cattle-grid, reaching within a few paces a gate and stile on the left (signposted 'Marrick'). Follow this path to a bench at the entrance to Steps Wood.

Go through the gate and enter the woodland, climbing easily on a paved way, known as the 'Nuns Causeway' or 'Nunnery Steps', linking the priory and Marrick village. On leaving Steps Wood, follow the path along the edge of a few fields, through gates, to reach a converted Wesleyan chapel at the entrance to Marrick. Follow the lane ahead and at a junction (signposted) bear right, continuing to a T-junction near a phone box.

Turn right here to another junction (noting the interesting sundial on a nearby cottage). At the junction again go right, following the lane (a dead end) past the old school, shortly to turn left (signposted) up a rough green lane leading to a series of stiles across brief fields.

The path skirts dilapidated sheds and rusting farm equipment, gently climbing all the time, until, at its highest point, the fields broaden, a more satisfying vista opens up ahead, and the route begins a steady descent to a broad track serving Nun Cote Nook farm.

At the track go right, through a gate, and almost immediately left (signposted), continuing across broad meadowlands to the charmingly renovated cottage at Ellers. Pass around Ellers and cross **Ellers Beck** by a footbridge, then slanting up the next two fields to reach a gate near the access track to Hollins Farm. ▸

Follow the track right for a short distance, and then, without entering Hollins Farm, go left, skirting a small copse to a stile. Cross the next field to a wall, and follow the wall left and, just as it enters a confined pathway, use a gate on the right to cross the ensuing field diagonally to gain the once-important road linking Reeth and Richmond, there descending steeply, right, into **Marske** village.

Beyond Hollins Farm, Hutton's Monument, a towering obelisk in view for some while, commemorates Matthew Hutton, a member of the once-influential family that lived at Marske Hall.

Marske lies in an insignificant side valley of the Swale, a delightful retreat quietly going about its own business, where, it seems, only the tread of walkers disturbs the peace. The grounds of nearby Marske Hall add much to the village's natural loveliness, while the 12th-century church of St Edmund is worth a moment's pause.

The Huttons were the dominant family at Marske Hall for many years, producing two Archbishops of York, but, as W Riley mentions in *The Yorkshire Pennines of the North-West* (1934), 'The dale has bred men of another kidney besides bishops.' His grandfather used to tell of, 'the carryings-on there used to be in the big houses in his day, when the gentry wouldn't let their guests leave the table till they were too drunk to walk upstairs to bed; and the common folk were just as bad – mad on cock-fighting and coursing'.

Go down the road, amid splendid scenery, especially the view northwards of the upper valley of Marske Beck, and passing on the right the ornamental grounds of Marske Hall. Near the river, at a meeting of roads, go left, over Marske Bridge and uphill to a T-junction.

Turn right at the junction and continue along the road for about 600m, until by a stile on the right access can be gained to a series of fields crossed by a narrow path that later drops to cross wooded Clapgate Beck by a footbridge. A prominent path then slants upwards to a conspicuous cairn, which turns out to be on an access track leading to West Applegarth Farm, and passes beneath the limestone cliffs of **Applegarth Scar**.

Continue to, and around, West Applegarth Farm to a barn ahead and a little to the right. Drop down, right, slightly towards the barn, and go through a narrow gate near a wall corner. Keep on past the barn to another stile and then across a field to reach the access track to Low Applegarth Farm. Cross straight over this to the next stile, pass close by High Applegarth, and so gain the road leading to East Applegarth. Before long, however, leave the road at a stile on the left to cross a pasture well above the farm. At a stile just above East Applegarth the path meets a rough track climbing from the farm, and this is followed through an untidy landscape to enter **Whitcliffe Wood** (Whitecliffe on the OS map).

Popular as a local walk, **Whitcliffe Wood** and the nearby scar have a relaxing air about them, a winding-down opportunity as Richmond is approached. This whole stretch, through the seemingly endless 'Applegarth' farms, is a haven of quiet retreat, perched high above the Swale. It is here, as the route crosses Deep Dale, that the Yorkshire Dales National Park (wherein the route has been since Oddendale, near Shap) is finally left behind.

Just north of East Applegarth, a spot known as Willance's Leap is associated with Robert Willance, a worthy citizen of Richmond who in 1606 was hunting on horseback on the tops when mist descended. In his haste to get home he missed his way, and contrived to spur his horse over the cliff edge. In the fall to the valley 200 feet below the horse was killed, but its rider surprisingly survived, albeit with a broken leg. Willance, who lived to become an alderman of Richmond, celebrated his deliverance by presenting the town with a silver chalice as a thanksgiving.

As you leave Whitcliffe Wood, a broad track runs on the High Leases, soon to become a metalled road (Westfields) leading down directly into Richmond. Before long it is possible to go through one of a number of low stiles on the right at the top edge of West Field for a parallel, but easier underfoot, descent to the town, either returning to Westfields, or continuing to the bottom corner of the field just above where the Reeth road (**A6108**) joins Westfields on the edge of town.

Parish church, Richmond

This long descending approach to Richmond via Westfields meets the A6108 near a corner shop and post office. Follow the main road (Victoria Road) left and continue along it as far as the tourist information office. At a roundabout, go right into King Street, which leads to the cobbled market place, at the centre of which stands Holy Trinity Church.

RICHMOND

Richmond castle

Richmond (www.richmond.org) and the adjacent Vale of Mowbray are totally dominated by Richmond's castle, as they have almost certainly been since 1071. This was when the first earl, Alan of Richmond, Alan Rufus (or 'Alan the Red'), commander of the Norman rear-guard at the Battle of Hastings, received from William the Conqueror the not inconsiderable possessions of the Saxon Earl Edwin as a reward.

The name 'Richmond' comes from the French 'riche-mont', meaning 'strong hill', and many of its first inhabitants were French. With a vast inner courtyard, and built on a siege-worthy scale in a commanding position, the castle was a formidable fortress. Two kings of Scotland, William the Lion and David II, were imprisoned here, and there is a suggestion that at least one other was (and presumably still is) present. Legend recounts that a local man, a potter named Thompson, while seeking to escape the tongue of his nagging wife, stumbled on an entrance in the rocks beneath the castle. He claimed to have found a huge cavern where King Arthur and his knights were sleeping, biding their time until their return. Alas, Thompson, when called upon to do so, was unable to find the entrance to the cave again. Whether this was the same man who discovered the king and his knights in a cave below the Bwlch y Saethau, near Snowdon in North Wales, while escaping from a nagging wife, is not recorded!In similar vein is the story of how soldiers quartered in Richmond determined to test an old tale that a secret underground passage ran from the castle to Easby Abbey. Unwilling to make the journey themselves, through long dark tunnels with precarious roofing and foul air, they filled the head of a young drummer boy with visions of treasure and sent him into the tunnel. As the boy struggled on, he rattled away at his drum, while the soldiers above ground traced its muffled sound through the streets of the town. Fainter and fainter came the sound of the drum until, near the site occupied by the former grammar school, it ceased altogether. It is said that on a quiet night you can still hear the sound of drumming, very faint and distant, coming from underground.

On a more verifiable note, Richmond's market place is the largest horseshoe market place in England, and was once the outer bailey of the castle. It was re-cobbled in 1771, when Matthew and Mark Topham were paid sixpence a yard to find stones and set them in place. They may not have had to look far, for the present-day obelisk is on the site of a medieval cross that was pulled down in the same year. The Chapel of Holy Trinity, which stands in the centre of the market place, was founded in 1135. It has been altered and repaired many times, and has seen service as a court, prison and school.

Below the castle walls lies a labyrinthine network of narrow alleyways and back streets, 'wynds', formed by groups of quaint, haphazard buildings that would give modern planners apoplexy. Throw in the Culloden Tower, built in 1746 to mark the defeat of Bonnie Prince Charlie by the Duke of Cumberland, and the odd folly or two, and the whole town becomes an open-air museum of the grandest kind, and a tribute to those people of Richmond who have helped to preserve its unique character through the centuries.

EAST TO WEST: RICHMOND TO REETH

Cross the market place and go down King Street to a roundabout near the tourist information office. Turn left along Victoria Road until, near a corner shop, you can leave the town, and climb steadily along a back road (Westfields), which later runs on as a broad track, past High Leases and into **Whitcliffe Wood**.

On leaving Whitcliffe Wood, the path passes beneath Whitcliffe Scar and continues towards East Applegarth Farm. A waymarked path keeps above the farm and runs on to the vicinity of High Applegarth, Low Applegarth and soon the last of the farms, West Applegarth, close by the edge of **Applegarth Scar**.

Take the broad access away from West Applegarth as far as a large cairn, and here descend left to cross Clapgate Beck by a footbridge. Cross the ensuing fields to rise gradually to a surfaced road leading left to the village of **Marske**.

Descend through the village, cross a stream, and at a road junction follow the road ahead, past Marske Hall, and ignoring a side road to Skelton. A stiff pull ensues. Continue up the road to a stile on the left opposite a cottage. Through this, cross the next field diagonally right to reach a gate and stile, and then keep along the field-boundary wall to pass Hollins Farm (keep to the right of the farm), and so gain its access road. Turn right along the access for a short distance to a gate on the left, and from it head across two fields to the cottage at Ellers. More green paths cross fields and lead to an access serving Nun Cote Nook Farm, which is followed, right, for a few strides until a path climbs left across yet more fields to reach the village of **Marrick**.

The onward route is clear enough, and leads to an enclosed lane running down towards the old village school. The road here swings round the school and heads towards a row of cottages. Go left here to a junction, and then left again along a quiet road, keeping left at another junction to leave the village past a former Wesleyan chapel.

Always hugging the wall on your left, the path presses on to the top edge of Steps Wood, where a paved way, known as the 'Nuns' Causeway' or 'Nunnery Steps', leads to the bottom edge of the wood, and on by a descending path to Marrick Priory. Go right along the road leading away from the priory, eventually leaving it at a stile on the left to descend to the **River Swale** once more, following the course of the river as far as Grinton Bridge. Cross the road at the bridge and head diagonally right across fields, swinging round to meet the road close by Reeth Bridge. Follow the road, left, over the bridge and up into the centre of **Reeth.**

STAGE 9

Richmond to Danby Wiske

Start	Richmond market place (NZ 171 008)
Finish	Danby Wiske village centre (SE 336 986)
Distance	14 miles (22.8km)
Total ascent	575ft (175m)
Total descent	885ft (270m)
Walking time	7–8hr
Terrain	Low-level farmland and riparian meadows never far from the Swale; a little road walking.
Accommodation	Brompton-on-Swale, Catterick, Scorton

Your first walking in the Vale of Mowbray continues to track the course of the River Swale pretty closely, through settlements and farmland and past the ruins of Easby Abbey, until you bid the river farewell just before Bolton-on-Swale. Between here and Danby Wiske the route makes use of a succession of farmed fields to link these two charming villages. In a few places, notably close to farms, the going underfoot is less than ideal, but the route overall is a great joy to follow.

If you need to hurry, it is possible to hoof it along a quiet and obvious back road route from Ellerton Hill, via Streetlam, to Danby Wiske – but only if you need to!

Cross the market place and descend via New Road, Bargate and Bridge Street to Richmond Bridge. En route you will find an antiquated street lamp and, near the Green, another sundial on a wall. ▶

> **Richmond Bridge** dates from 1788–9, and was built by two different contractors, one operating for Richmond Corporation and the other for the county council. It spans the Swale, which from its exuberant, fast-flowing youth high above Keld has grown to full stature, slower and more mature as it sets out

The Green was once an industrial suburb of Richmond, the 'rough' quarter, as it has been described. Here there used to be a tannery, dye works, corn mill, fulling mill and brewery.

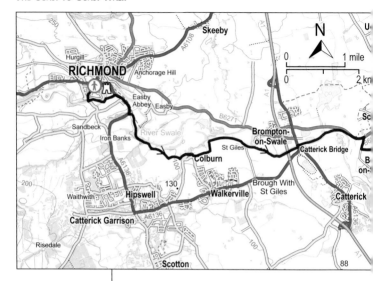

across the farmlands of the Vale of York to join the River Ure, and so become the Ouse.

Cross the bridge and shortly turn left into playing fields. Keep left and follow the edge of the field, with the ramparts of the **castle** towering high above, to enter woodland and climb to reach another field at a stile. Follow a green path going left, and as this starts to descend, locate a kissing-gate on the right by which the route gains a paved way in front of a row of houses (Priory Villas).

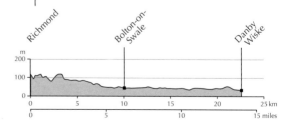

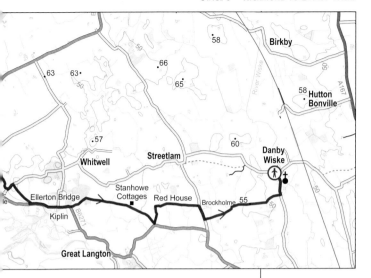

At the end of the houses, keep ahead and slightly left, to join the main road (**A6136**). Turn right and follow the road until, at a sharp bend, and just after crossing in-flowing Sand Beck, the route goes left (signposted) to take a service road leading to the sewage works, which contrast rather sharply with the ruins of **Easby Abbey** across the Swale, although the view of the ruins is somewhat obscured by undergrowth.

> **Easby Abbey** was founded in 1152 for a group of Premonstratensian Canons, last encountered at Shap Abbey. Its rather more substantial remains are also open to the public.

At the sewage works, skirt around the boundary on a clear path for a whiffy five minutes that leads to a stile entering woodland. A muddy path treks on through the woodland and crosses a footbridge, finally climbing to escape from the trees and undergrowth not far from the ruins of Hagg Farm.

Press on past the ruins along a narrow trod through undergrowth, and then by an improving path climb an easy brow before aiming across the next field to a stile in the far corner. Descend along a field boundary (left), and in the next field aim a quarter right on a narrow path to reach a concealed stile on the edge of more woodland. In company with a small stream, continue to a driveway leading into, and through, the hamlet of **Colburn**, crossing a bridge and passing a pub before coming to a lane end.

As the lane bends right, go forward on the village lane, and continue to a signpost (on the right) indicating a turning (left) at The Barn. Keep ahead to a field gate. Go along the edge of a pasture but leave it before a fence at the end of the second pasture by bearing left and shortly right towards St Giles Farm.

> Nearby is the site of **St Giles Hospital**, one of many run under monastic orders, although there is little to see on the ground from the route. The site was excavated as recently as 1990, and revealed a large number of skeletons that were all removed to York for further research.

Do not enter St Giles Farm, but go left on a path to meet its access track at a stile. Bear left, and only a short while later go left over a step-stile and forward along a field boundary, crossing the boundary fence at another step-stile tucked in a corner about halfway down the field edge. Now a path continues along the top of a bank above the Swale, later merging with a broad track that leads on to Thornbrough Farm.

On approaching the farm, pass through a gate and go forward past farm buildings onto a gravel track. As this swings to the right, leave it and descend very steeply, left, beside a fence to the banks of the Swale. Pass beneath the A1(M), and from a kissing-gate on the other side go forward towards a defunct railway bridge. Pass beneath this too, and on the other side circle right at the edge of the racecourse overflow parking area and use steps to climb up to the railway trackbed. Cross the bridge, and then descend steps to gain a surfaced track that leads forward to the A6055, joining it at Catterick Bridge.

Pass under the A1 and press on, keeping straight ahead, to pass beneath a defunct metal railway bridge, shortly beyond which the route bears to the right towards Catterick racecourse, crossing the end of an overflow car park to reach the **A6136** (the old A1), with Catterick Bridge on the left.

> **Catterick Bridge**, more or less as we now see it, was commissioned by seven local gentries in 1422, and built by three stonemasons, each of whom put their mason's mark on the stones of the old bridge. The bridge took three years to build, at a total cost of £173 6s 8d.
>
> Beside the bridge, the **Bridge House Hotel** (closed when visited in 2019), was also built in more spacious days, and had a style and charm often lacking in these days of mechanisation and standardisation – its atmosphere and tradition dated back to the old coaching days. In 1442, the hotel was known as the George and Dragon, and an important halt between London and Scotland. Until 1950 the present hotel was owned by the Lawsons of Brough Hall, Catterick.
>
> The area around the hotel has great historical interest, dating to the time when Catterick Bridge was a Brigantian city, then known as 'Cherdarich', meaning 'the camp by the water'. When the Romans arrived they extended the city into a great military centre, and Dere Street, the main Roman road to the north, forded the river at Catterick Bridge. The Romans renamed the area 'Cataractonium', though this is an ancient British word, borrowed by the Romans.

Cross the road with care to a gated squeeze stile giving access to a meadow. Follow the Swale until after passing through an elongated pasture the route is diverted

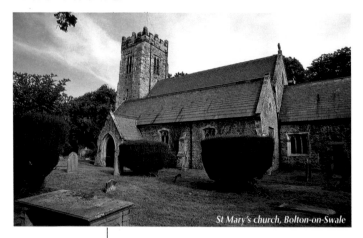

St Mary's church, Bolton-on-Swale

Here bid farewell to the Swale, which has been our companion since it was first met near Keld. It slips away to join the Ure, remaining in the distance for a while longer.

up to meet the B6271. ◀ Turn right beside it, walking for about 40m, and then entering a car park for the Scorton Walk. Immediately turn left through a gate onto a permissive path that parallels the B-road until it joins a right-of-way path at a pair of gates. Now keep forward to arrive at a surfaced track. Follow this southward and take the first turning on the left (Flat Lane), which leads you out to the B6271 at Bolton-on-Swale.

St Mary's Church is a delightful structure, its clock tower constructed of exquisitely hued sandstone blocks. Brothers of the Abbey of St Mary's in York originally built the church in the early 14th century. There were certainly earlier churches – Saxon and Norman – on this site, and what remained of those was incorporated into the present Gothic design.

But the principal feature of interest here is the monument in the churchyard, dedicated to one Henry Jenkins, whose claim to fame was that from his birth at nearby Ellerton in the year 1500, he lived to be 169, dying at Ellerton in 1670. Henry made his living from salmon fishing and thatching cottages, but he remembered being sent as a lad of 12 with a cartload of arrows to meet the Earl of Surrey's army on its march northwards to the Battle of Flodden (1513). The churchyard monument is a fitting tribute to the man, even if the mason did rather miscalculate his word spacing.

At St Mary's Church, go left along the lane to a stile on the right, just after a large building in private grounds. In the ensuing field, follow a path, left, which escorts lazy Bolton Beck round the field edge to a step-stile. In the next field, follow the edge, and do the same again in the next field to reach a dilapidated stone bridge on the left. Cross the bridge and a stile, and then walk downstream to meet the access track to Layland's Farm. Cross the farm track, and in the next field follow the beck to a stile near a bridge, giving onto a lane near Ellerton Hill.

Go left along the minor road to Ellerton Hill, and here leave it by going right onto a wide track to pass houses and reach a large field. Now follow a bridleway along the field boundary down to a hedge gap, and forward to a gate giving onto the B6271 at **Ellerton Bridge**.

Follow the road (left) for about ½ mile (1km) to a sharp bend (to the right) with trees on both sides of the road.

On the way, you pass the entrance to **Kiplin Hall**, built as a hunting lodge in 1620 for James I's Secretary of State, George Calvert. Its design in red brick was unique in Jacobean architecture, and it is today one of the finest buildings of its period in Britain.

As the road bends to the right, go left onto a broad track leading to Ladybank House and other properties. Continue past them to enter an enclosed path that ends as it enters the corner of a large arable field. Follow the right-hand field margin to a gate, just before which a ditch is crossed. Follow the ongoing field-edge path to the ruins of **Stanhowe Cottages**. ▶

Press on beyond the cottages until another stream is crossed, just after a gate. A short way on, at a hedge

The field paths here have long been maintained by the local farmer to encourage birdlife and the growth of wild flowers.

177

Stanhowe Cottages would once have been filled with the bustle of farming life

corner with farm buildings away to the left, keep forward across the field to a hedgerow corner and, further on, a solitary large tree, beyond which the field boundary leads out to meet the B6271 once more, at a bend. Here turn left, without touching on the main road, and head north towards Red House Farm, following a public bridleway. Just after passing Red House Farm, turn right to Moor House Farm, and pass the farmhouse to reach a gate on the right giving into a field. Turn left along the field boundary (often very 'farmy') to a step-stile. Over this, turn right through a gate and over another stile before heading slightly left across a pasture to step-stiles either side of a basic bridge spanning a stream.

Strike across the next field to another stile, and maintain the same direction in the ensuing field to locate another narrow footbridge over a field-edge ditch. Cross the next stile, and then follow the right-hand field edge to a gap and a clear path running out to meet the Streetlam road, not far from **Brockholme Farm/** Green Croft.

Turn right along the road for about 400m, and then leave it by branching left onto a broad access track leading

up High Brockholme. When the access bears right to the farm, keep ahead and soon reach the edge of a large pasture. Go down the right-hand edge of this. On the far side, go left to a stile beside a gate. Cross the stile and turn left, to be confronted by a wide gap in a hedgerow. Ignore this, and turn right up the field edge until it reaches a gate giving into an enclosed track, lightly wooded with willow scrub and often overgrown. ▶ Follow the field edge left, and shortly swing right along one last field margin to reach the road into **Danby Wiske**. Go left along the road to enter the village.

Field edge path, approaching Danby Wiske

In spite of the tangle, this is a lovely stretch, finally reaching daylight again at the head of an arable field.

> The **village church** is a delight, although its dedication is unknown, the records being destroyed when Scottish raiders came this way in the 12th century. Danby Wiske itself dated from Saxon times, so there was almost certainly a Saxon church on this site. The early Norman church that succeeded it has largely been incorporated into the later Norman/ Early English church we see today. It has a lovely Norman tympanum over the south door, along with a Norman font and Jacobean pews.

EAST TO WEST: DANBY WISKE TO RICHMOND

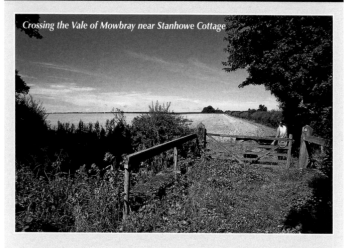

Crossing the Vale of Mowbray near Stanhowe Cottage

To leave Danby Wiske, go left at the White Swan, down Mounstrall Lane for about 600m, finally leaving the road at a gate on the right (signposted) to follow a field-edge path. On the way, the route passes Danby Wiske's beautiful Norman **church**, which is without dedication and well worth a brief diversion.

Walk up the field edge until you can bear left along a hedgerow towards woodland. Soon, you enter a long and quite delightful stretch of enclosed trackway, seasonally overgrown, but a lovely sheltered interlude. It ends at a gate giving into a gently sloping pasture. Walk down the right-hand edge of the pasture, and at the bottom continue into the next.

Lower down, the route goes left with the field boundary to a step-stile beside a gate. Cross this, and walk up the left-hand edge of a large field, eventually reaching the access track serving High Brockholme Farm. Walk out along the access to meet a surfaced lane.

Turn right, walking along the lane for about 400m, and leaving it opposite the entrance to another farm (Green Garth, but shown as **Brockholme** on the map). Now follow a field-edge path to a hedge gap, and through this walk around the end of a field to a stile giving onto a concrete slab bridge. Cross the next two fields, often cropped over, and eventually deal with a couple of stiles either side of a sleeper bridge just before Moor House Farm. Head for a stile just before a gate. Go through the gate and around the farm perimeter to reach another gate. Through this, go left to a track junction, and left again past **Red House Farm**, and walk out along a broad track to reach the **B6271**.

Without touching upon the B-road, turn immediately right onto a signposted path that follows a field edge, and maintains much the same direction across lovely countryside to walk up to the ruins of **Stanhowe Cottages**. Keep on past the cottages, always at the field edge (either right or left), eventually to reach a field corner where an old gate gap gives onto an enclosed path that leads up to cottages at Ladybank House. Go past the cottages, and keep on to reach the B6271 once more.

Now follow the B-road, right, for a little over half a mile (1km), on the way passing Kiplin Hall. Just before **Ellerton Bridge**, a signposted bridleway on the right takes you through a gate, a hedge gap, and up a field edge to reach houses and cottages at Ellerton Hill. Keep forward past these to reach a T-junction at a lane. Turn left.

Walk down the lane until, just before a brick bridge, you can leave it by crossing a stile on the right. Follow the course of Bolton Beck on the left (all the way, in fact, to Bolton-on-Swale), initially round a field edge to an access track serving Layland's Farm. Cross this, and keep forward alongside the beck to a dilapidated bridge. Cross the bridge and turn right, still following the beck and a field-edge path across fields and stiles, until eventually the path runs into a field corner at the edge of **Bolton-on-Swale**. Turn left towards the **church**.

Opposite St Mary's Church, take the side road leading up to the B6271, near the village pump, and head right along the road for a short distance to a broad track, Flat Lane, on the left. Follow this through its various twists and turns until it almost emerges onto the B-road once more. Just before reaching the road, turn left along a wide field-edge path, and shortly keep onward beside a fence through the site of former gravel works to a gate giving into the end of a long pasture. Go forward along the left-hand edge, almost immediately encountering the **River Swale**, the first close encounter with the river that is to be followed almost to its very source.

Now follow the course of the river all the way to Catterick Bridge, where a gated squeeze-stile gives onto the A6055. Cross the road with care, going through a gate and then ahead on a surfaced track to steps leading up onto a defunct railway trackbed and bridge. Cross the bridge, and descend steps on the other side, circling left at the edge of the overflow car park for the racecourse, to pass through a metal gate and beneath the A1(M).

From a gate beyond the A1(M), climb steeply left beside a fence to a gravel track leading, right, to Thornborough Farm. Pass the farm buildings to a gate.

Now keep forward beside fences on a broad track. When, later, the track dips to the right, leave it and go left onto a path along the top of a slope above the Swale. Keep on to a step-stile in a corner, and over this follow the right-hand field margin to another stile giving onto the access track to **St Giles Farm**. Head towards the farm, but soon leave it at a stile on the right. The path strikes across a field on the site of St Giles Hospital, to another stile, and then along the top edge of Colburn Beck Wood, shortly going left at a stile and along a field boundary to meet a farm access.

Turn right along the access and keep forward eventually to emerge on the edge of the village of Colburn at The Barn.

Turn right on the village lane, shortly going left to pass the Hildyard Arms, crossing a bridge, and then going ahead onto a quiet driveway leading into woodland and alongside a stream. Follow the accompanying path as it rises from the woodland to cross a field, and then another. At a stile, cross the next field to a slight brow, beyond which the path continues through a seasonally overgrown path to the ruins of Hagg Farm.

The path beyond Hagg Farm re-enters woodland, following a path that finally emerges into daylight at a stile, and not far from sewage works. Follow the boundary fence of the sewage works to meet its access road, and then press on to meet the main road (**A6136**) at a bend. Turn right along the road for about 700m, leaving it at a signposted road on the left, and continuing in front of a row of houses (Priory Villas) to pass between barns. In the field that follows, take a green path ascending slightly to the left until more woodland is entered, running out eventually on the edge of a playing field beneath the ramparts of **Richmond Castle**.

Follow the playing-field boundary ahead to reach the road into **Richmond**, and here turn right, cross Richmond Bridge, and then ascend ahead to the town centre via Bridge Street and New Street, finally to arrive at the market place.

STAGE 10

Danby Wiske to Osmotherley

Start	Danby Wiske village centre (SE 336 986)
Finish	Osmotherley (SE 456 972)
Distance	12 miles (20km)
Total ascent	862ft (263m)
Total descent	469ft (143m)
Walking time	5hr
Terrain	Farmland; a little road walking.
Accommodation	Ingleby Cross

More easy rural walking ensues, taking the route to the very edge of the Cleveland Hills. This is a perfect time to relax and plod on happily, in preparation for the effort that the hills and moors to come will demand. This is a gentle, soothing stretch, where everything is tidily in its place, birds call constantly from flower-decked hedgerows, cows peer at you inquisitively as they go about their daily munching, and all the villages are neatly trimmed and washed. Beginning with some unavoidable road walking, it is the brief passage that prepares the way for the grand finale.

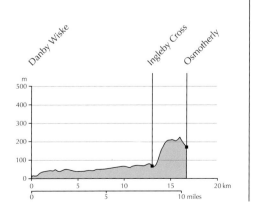

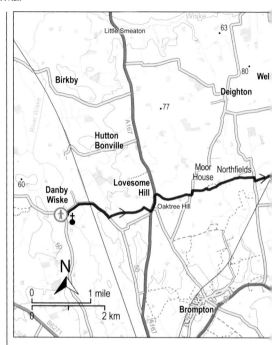

Follow the road ahead through Danby Wiske, passing the White Swan Inn, and soon to cross by a single-arched bridge the overgrown stream that is the **River Wiske**. Continue along the road, crossing the East Coast **railway line** and going past the turning down to Lazenby Hall, with grass verges from time to time to ease the plodding. After about 1¼ miles (2km) the road reaches a junction with Crowfoot Lane.

Go left here and follow the road to the busy **A167** at **Oaktree Hill**. Cross the road and go left until, just after Oaktree Farm (on the left), a rough track (gate and stile) leaves the road, right.

Head along the track, flanked by hedgerows, and later keep ahead with a hedgerow on the right to a stile. Once across the stile, the path, seasonally subdued by

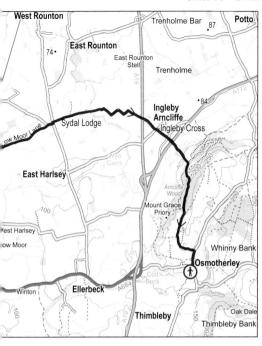

overgrowth, fights its way along a narrow tract of ground towards White House Farm, where it starts to improve. Without approaching the farm, continue ahead, as captivating glimpses of the Cleveland Hills appear between gaps in otherwise cloaking hedgerows. Finally, the track reaches a minor back road, Deighton Lane, at a bend. Go left for a short distance, but only as far as a farm access leading to Moor House.

Go forward, keeping the farm buildings to the right, and following a grassy strip and a small stream; then head towards the ruins of **Moor House Farm** (SE 379 994). Cross a stile/bridge combination near an open barn and follow a field margin away towards **Northfields Farm**. At the end of the field, cross another stream. In the large meadow that follows, head directly

Long Lane is a
less well-known
Roman road.

for Northfields Farm on a green path, aiming a little to the left of the buildings, and locate a stile across an intermediate fence, on the left. Ahead and at a step-stile (waymarked), the path reaches a farm access. Now go left to pass round the buildings at Northfield House Farm, and there swing right to pursue the access road to its junction with Long Lane. ◄

Here the route goes right along the metalled surface for 200m until, at a signposted farm access, it heads left and through a gate (cattle-grid) towards Wray House Farm. On reaching the farm buildings, go right down a short access track to a gate and step-stile, with a marked railway-crossing point directly ahead. Ignore this crossing, however, and instead go to the left along a hedge-row, and then head across the field to a concrete stile at a pedestrian crossing of the **railway**.

Once safely across the railway, traverse the field that follows to a bottom corner where there is a metal footbridge between stiles. Cross this, and in a few strides come to the edge of another field. Now head left along the field margin, trekking around two sides until it meets **Low Moor Lane**, a surfaced minor lane that takes the route on for a while, to the left, and passes close by Harsley Grove Farm. Here go right on a gravel track to pass Deepdale Farm.

Throughout the whole of the crossing from Danby Wiske, the scenery is entirely **pastoral**, the land given over to agriculture, and the walking of the easiest kind, with barely a gradient to be encountered anywhere. In every direction, cultivated farm fields, hedgerows and coppices stretch as far as the eye can see. The retrospective view is of the hills of Swaledale, now seeming far, far away, while ahead the Cleveland Hills are almost beneath our feet.

As the gravel extension of Low Moor Lane meets a road at a bend, go right for a short distance to another road, and there go left, but leaving it almost immediately by turning down an access track to **Sydal Lodge**.

On the approach to Sydal Lodge, continue ahead through a gate to a stile and gate near a large open barn. Keep the farm buildings on the right, and continue ahead on a narrow grassy path along the left-hand field edge, until diverted right to a mid-field signpost. Here, bear left and descend to a footbridge, once more meeting the River Wiske on its continuing and vain search for excitement. ▶

Cross the footbridge and immediately ascend an arable field to reach the overgrown ruins of Brecken Hill Farm, where, in season, a feast may be had of plums and elderberry. Pass to the right of the buildings, and then carry out a series of rights and lefts around field margins and along access lanes, passing Longlands and Crinkle Carr farms, finally to reach the **A19**. Cross this busy dual carriageway, linking Northallerton and Stockton-on-Tees. ▶ Follow the lane ahead to **Ingleby Arncliffe**.

Although modest and slow moving, the River Wiske has given its name, as a suffix, to a number of villages along its route. It finally meets the Swale not far from Thirsk.

This crossing is probably the most hazardous moment of the whole walk.

Water tower, Ingleby Arncliffe

The history of **Ingleby Arncliffe** can be traced to the Norman Conquest. From the Domesday Book it appears that there used to be two manors held by the king – Engelbi and Ernclive – and it is from these that the present names derive. 'Engelbi' is thought to mean 'the village of the English', an allusion to the survival of an English settlement amid what would have been a predominantly Scandinavian population. 'ernclive', or 'eagle's cliff', almost certainly owes its name to the steep, wooded cliff to the southeast.

At Ingleby Cross, the route enters the North York Moors National Park, and can be said to have engaged upon the final leg, the remaining 50 miles (80km).

On reaching Ingleby Arncliffe, a quick left and right then lead down to **Ingleby Cross**. ◄

Leave Ingleby Cross down the road at the side of the Blue Bell Inn to reach and cross the **A172**, so gaining a metalled road (over a cattle-grid) leading to Ingleby Arncliffe church, a simple, uncomplicated structure backed by the gables of Arncliffe Hall.

Ingleby Cross welcomes walkers to the final leg of the Coast to Coast

Arncliffe Hall is a fine Georgian house, dating from 1754, and probably built by John Carr of York. The adjacent All Saints' Church was built in 1821 to replace a much earlier building on the same site. It is regarded as one of the finest examples of a rural church of the Regency period – one that has remained largely unchanged.

Climb easily for a while to the brow of a hill and a gate on the left, and continue on a fenced track towards **Arncliffe Wood**, part of the Forestry Commission's Cleveland Forest. Go right on entering the wood, and follow an undulating course through the forest.

MOUNT GRACE PRIORY

Just west of your route through the woods lie the ruins of the Carthusian monastery of Mount Grace Priory. Founded in 1398 by Thomas Holland, Duke of Surrey and Earl of Kent, and a nephew of Richard II, it was not completed until after 1440. Its full title is 'The House of the Assumption of the Blessed Virgin Mary and St Nicholas of Mount Grace in Ingleby', and it remains today of considerable ecclesiastical interest.

Life in these monasteries was one we would countenance today only with abject horror. Mount Grace housed 15 or so hermit-monks, living as solitaries in two-storey cells, 22 feet square. The ground floor had a fireplace and a wooden staircase to the room above, with a small garden separated from the next by high walls, in which the monk worked alone. Meeting their fellows only for matins and vespers, and the occasional feast day when services were held in the church, the monks would spend ten hours each day in their cells, reading, praying, eating and meditating. So that no contact might be made with the server, food was brought to the monks and passed through a right-angled hatch. The monks remained at Mount Grace for 140 years, until the dissolution in 1539.

Now in the guardianship of English Heritage, the priory is generally open to the public, and contains a reconstructed and furnished cell. If you can find the time, it is definitely worth diverting through Arncliffe Wood to the priory, where the austerity and greyness of the lives of those who lived and died there is most noticeably impressed on a receptive mind (www.nationaltrust.org.uk/mount-grace-priory)

OSMOTHERLEY

Osmotherley is a small, thriving village at the point where the Cleveland Way, the Lyke Wake Walk and the Coast to Coast Walk meet. Originally the community developed as an agricultural market village, but during the 18th and 19th centuries it was also a thriving industrial centre. Many of the houses date from these days, built in the period 1800–1830 to provide accommodation for workers in the alum quarries and jet mines, and constructed of traditional Yorkshire sandstone.

The village's name has always been a source of interest. In the Domesday Book it is recorded as 'Asmundrelac', Asmund being an Old Norse name. Later, under Anglian influence, this would corrupt to 'Osmund's ley', a 'ley', like a 'thwaite', being a clearing, but, as ever, there is a more imaginative tale to be told.

A local princess dreamt her son, Os (or Oswy), would drown on a certain day, and so on that day ordered a nurse to take him to a safe place. Roseberry Topping, then known as Odinsberg, the prominent cone-shaped hill near Great Ayton that has been in view for a while as the Cleveland Hills are approached, seemed safe enough. Certainly, the nurse found it a safe and comforting haven, for she fell asleep, allowing the baby prince to wander away. When the nurse awoke it was to find the prince lying face down in a hillside spring, dead. He was buried at Osmotherley. Later, his mother died of grief and was buried at his side, so 'Os-by-his-mother-lay'. Chronologically, it doesn't tie up, of course – perhaps the village should be 'Mother-by-Os-ley'! It is all highly improbable, but why spoil a good yarn with the truth.

At this point the Cleveland Way is first encountered.

The path rises steadily to a T-junction. Here go right and continue to the edge of the forest at a gate (SE 454 986), beyond which a track leads down to Osmotherley. ◄

Leave the forest at this point, following the Cleveland Way across fields, through three kissing-gates, past **Chapel Wood Farm**, until reaching the road leading into **Osmotherley**, there turning right into the village.

EAST TO WEST: OSMOTHERLEY TO DANBY WISKE

From the centre of Osmotherley, follow the main street north for about ½ km, then taking a bridleway on the left (signed Cleveland Way) soon bending round to the north past **Chapel Wood Farm** and heading for the edge of **Arncliffe Wood**. After three kissing-gates go through the gate into the wood to a broad forest trail, leaving behind the Cleveland Way.

The forest trail continues pleasantly and uneventfully, soon branching left at a junction and later passing the entrance to Park House. The route undulates a little, and the woodland here seems well populated with pheasant at certain times of the year. Beyond Park House a distinct branch goes left, leaving the forest to follow a fenced track to a gate giving onto a quiet back road at the rear of Arncliffe Hall and the parish church.

Follow the road, right, curving past the hall and church, to run to meet the **A172**. Cross the road and continue ahead to reach **Ingleby Cross**.

Continue up the lane, away from Ingleby Cross, and at the top, at **Ingleby Arncliffe**, go left, and then immediately right opposite a water tower, to follow a lane out for a hazardous encounter with the **A19**. Cross this busy, high-speed dual carriageway with care, and head off down a rough lane opposite. At Crinkle Carr Farm, follow the track as it swings left to Longlands Farm, and then follows a series of right and left turns to arrive at the ruins of Brecken Hill farm, now very much overgrown, but providing a feast of plums and elderberries at the right time of year.

Keep to the left of Brecken Hill and walk around the ruins, then bear left across an arable field to find a footbridge spanning the **River Wiske**. Head up the ensuing field, aiming for a stile and gate to the right of a large open barn. From the stile go forward through a metal gate to follow the farm access out to a lane.

Turn left briefly, and then right onto a road for Welbury and Northallerton. After about 200m, leave the road at a bend by branching left onto a gravel track (Low Moor Lane) that leads past Deepdale Farm and on towards Harsley Grove Farm. As Harsley Grove is approached, **Low Moor Lane** becomes surfaced and bears left, away from the farm, with a large fenced pasture on the right. When the fencing ends after about 800m (signpost), leave it by turning right and walking along a field boundary round two sides, to locate a half-concealed dip on the right leading to a narrow footbridge between stiles. Over the footbridge, cross the ensuing field to a concrete stile giving pedestrian access to a crossing of a railway line.

Safely across the line, go obliquely left to a hedgerow and fence leading to a stile near Wray House Farm. Cross a brief enclosure, and another stile, and then bear left along an access track that leads out to Long Lane, a minor Roman road.

Head up Long Lane for about 200m, and then turn left towards Northfield House Farm. Keep the farm buildings on the right, passing round them on an access track, soon to reach a stile giving into a meadow. A green path heads across the meadow, passing **Northfields Farm** and crossing an intermediate fence and stile. Keep on across a second meadow, and then along a field margin to the remains of **Moor House Farm**. Cross a stile/bridge combination, then head half-left to a footbridge spanning a stream. Now roughly parallel a small stream on the right to pass to the north of Moor House. Leave the farm buildings behind by taking the farm access track out to a minor road, Deighton Lane.

Turn left onto Deighton Lane, but after only a short distance, leave it by branching right onto a green lane flanked by hedgerows and passing White House Farm. Gradually, the green lane narrows and becomes overgrown, but it leads eventually to a stile and an open meadow. A hedgerow on the left guides you to a gate beyond which a rough track leads out to meet the **A167** almost opposite Oaktree Farm.

Head left, down the A167, and continue past Oaktree Hill Garage to leave the main road for a minor road on the right (Crowfoot Lane). Follow this to a T-junction where it meets the road to Danby Wiske. Turn right, and now simply follow the lane to **Danby**.

THE NORTH YORK MOORS

Leg-swinging freedom beckons on Carlton Moor (Stage 11)

Stretching from the outskirts of Thirsk in the west to the coast in the east, and about half that distance in a north–south direction, the North York Moors present an open, unenclosed, virtually uninhabited expanse of high moorland that seems to have been devised solely with walkers in mind. In reality, the moors are not one, but a huge collection, almost 150, each with its own name, although quite where one ends and the next begins is a matter for the geographers and cartographers.

Along the southern boundary of the moors lies the Vale of Pickering, feeding into its companion, the Vale of Mowbray to the west, while the northern extremities peter out at Teesside. It is not by chance that the whole of this area, looking on a map not unlike the outline of Australia, has been embraced within the North York Moors National Park. It is a beautiful and true wilderness, traversed by few roads, and most of those seemingly aimless. Here, pheasant run madly about the woodlands and grouse clatter through the low heather where once dinosaurs and pterodactyls roamed, making way for primitive man as climatic conditions became favourable.

Not unlike the moorlands of the Northern Pennines in character, the North York Moors are, however, rather

Steep undulations along the scarp edge before the drop to Clay Bank Top (Stage 11) (photo: J Williams)

less bleak than their westerly counterparts. This area is a touch more colourful and easier to escape from in an emergency – although when the mist rolls in, and everything is lost save for a few strides ahead, you may be forgiven for doubting that observation. There is much here to please walkers and naturalists, as well as geologists and industrial archaeologists.

You're on the last leg now, so to speak, and if you can afford the time, it would be enjoyable to tackle these final few days at a relaxed pace. But between Osmotherley and Blakey Ridge there are few opportunities on the line of the walk to find accommodation. Fortunately,

many bed-and-breakfast proprietors, with accommodation in the numerous villages that shelter beneath the Cleveland Hills and the eastern moors, will pick up walkers from virtually anywhere. In some instances, this means being able to spend more than one night at a particular location, with transportation at the start and end of each day to resume the walking.

Purists, of course, would never think of such a thing, but there are many advantages to it. Some concern hygiene, dry clothes, comfort and warm beds and others the possibility of having a day or two with a light rucksack for a change.

STAGE 11

Osmotherley to Blakey Ridge

Start	Osmotherley (SE 456 972)
Finish	The Lion Inn, Blakey Ridge (SE 679 997)
Distance	20 miles (32km)
Total ascent	3236ft (986m)
Total descent	2700ft (822m)
Walking time	8hr
Terrain	Undulating moorland hill slopes; woodland.
Accommodation	Faceby, Kirkby, Lord Stones Country Park, Chop Gate (all off-route)

Today you travel in company with the Lyke Wake Walk and the Cleveland Way and tackle your last serious ascent, up onto Urra Moor, with an option to contour round some of the earlier summits in the day. From Urra Moor it's all pretty plain sailing. Few walls or fences encroach onto these gently rolling moors, contrasting sharply with the patterned fields viewed from the northern escarpment, here known as the Cleveland Hills. The loftiness of this vantage point arouses a great sensation of freedom and satisfaction.

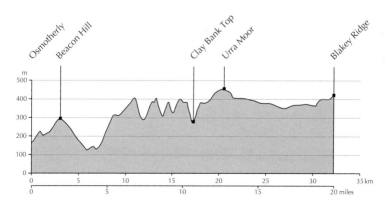

195

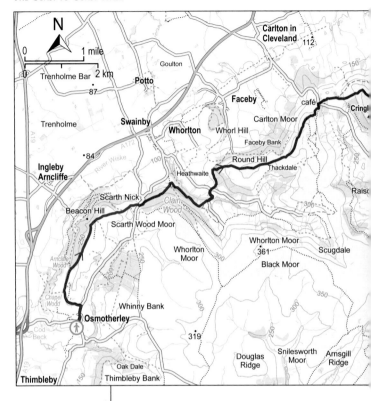

The Cleveland Way uses the National Trail white acorn on a black background.

From the centre of Osmotherley, follow the main street north for about ½ km, then taking a bridleway on the left (signed Cleveland Way) soon bending round to the north past **Chapel Wood Farm** and heading for the edge of **Arncliffe Wood**. After three kissing-gates go through the gate into the wood to a broad forest trail. Remain with the Cleveland Way, signposted as such for the next few miles. ◄

Climb away from the gate on a clear path through South Wood. At the top of the wood the path escorts a wall to a radio station, squeezing then between the

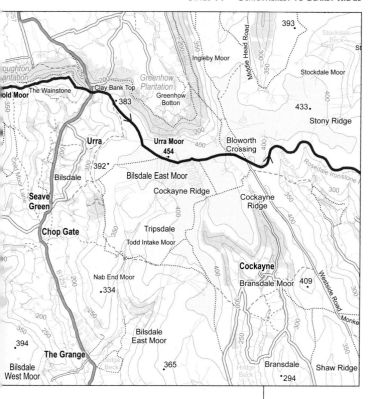

station and the wall to approach the summit of **Beacon Hill**, with the first wide-ranging views of the Cleveland Plain now coming into view, and a stunning view over heather moors of the onward route.

map continues on page 198

The trig point on the summit of Beacon Hill officially marks the start of the **Lyke Wake Walk** – a 40-mile trek across the moors that must be completed within 24 hours. These days the walk starts at the Lyke Wake Stone on a little mound opposite the first car park at the eastern end of Cod Beck Reservoir.

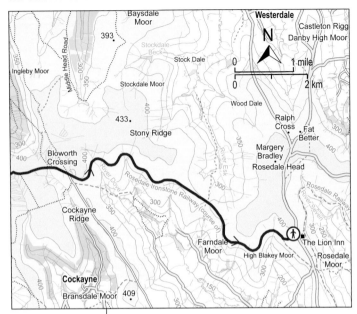

The Lyke Wake Walk began with an article in *Dalesman* magazine in August 1955, with the first challenge being taken up on 1 October 1955. Those first challengers, who included Bill Cowley, instigator of the walk, 'cheered each other on by reciting the Lyke Wake Dirge'. Normally sung at funerals in the 17th century 'by the vulgar people in Yorkshire', the dirge suggests that everyone, after death, must make a journey over a wide and difficult moor. Those who have done good deeds in their life – given away food and drink, silver and gold, written helpful guidebooks (?) – will receive aid and will cross the moor safely. But if not, the luckless soul will sink into hell flames – or Rosedale bog!

Continue away from the top of Beacon Hill to arrive at a gate. Another, just a few strides away, gives access to the heathery expanse of **Scarth Wood Moor**. Now an open track leads on across the moor, and is a particular delight in August when the heather is in bloom.

> **Scarth Wood Moor**, like most of the moors that make up the North York Moors, is of considerable prehistoric significance, and has a number of Bronze Age 'barrows', or grave mounds. Geologically, it is affected by three faults, the largest being along the line of Scarth Nick, soon to be encountered, and originally formed by an overflow of melt water from a huge glacier that once filled Scugdale.
>
> Ice sheets have advanced and retreated over the British landscape at least four times in the last two million years, a period of alternating warm and cold climatic conditions known as the Great Ice Age, which effectively refrigerated everything. The last period, known as the Devensian, did not end until about 11,000–10,000 years ago, when plants began to recolonise the moors, animals returned, and prehistoric people appeared on the scene.

When the path rejoins a wall (the handiwork of a community programme team working here in 1988), a low stone waymark for the Lyke Wake Walk (LWW) is soon reached. Here go left and descend to Scarth Nick, following the wall and ignoring more prominent tracks heading off to the right.

At **Scarth Nick**, reached by two flights of cobbled steps that do nothing for your knees, go left along the road to cross a cattle-grid, and then turn immediately right through a gate into forest.

> Scarth Nick is the crossing point of the **Hambleton Drove Road**, one of numerous routes taken by tough, weather-beaten Scottish cattlemen, hired to drive cattle from Scotland into England to sell at various market towns, even as far south as London.

When these drove roads were regularly in use it was a busy time for sheep and cattle farmers, the Industrial Revolution of the late 18th and early 19th centuries aggravating an already growing demand for beef that could not be met by English farmers. Ironically, it was the Industrial Revolution, and the invention of steam power, that sealed the fate of the cattle drovers, as steam power overcame leg power, and the new railway network made it possible to slaughter cattle locally and send carcasses to markets by rail. Already declining rapidly by 1850, by the turn of the century droving had ceased altogether.

The path through the wood soon joins a forest trail, where the walk continues ahead along level ground. At a break in the forest on the left (Cleveland Way sign and Lyke Wake Walk marker stone), leave the level forest trail by starting down a wide stony track. A few strides further on, a brief diversion leads onto a small balcony with a seat that offers a splendid view over the village of **Swainby** below.

Taking a breather on the seat above Swainby

Continue steeply down the track, and at the bottom, at a junction, go left and then almost immediately right (signposted) just before a gate. A fine path now follows the edge of **Clain Wood**, which contains spreads of bluebell and wood sorrel, both ancient-woodland indicator species.

After almost half a mile (1km) look for a stile on the left giving into a field. A grassy track leads down the field to a gate, beyond which lie the ford and footbridge at Piper Beck. Soon, join a narrow lane, turning left across Scugdale Beck, and shortly passing Hollin Hill Farm, walking up to a T-junction at Huthwaite Green.

Cross the road here to a gate, and take the enclosed path leading uphill towards Live Moor Plantation. At a gate you step outside the plantation boundary, to follow a fence round to another gate to re-enter the forest below a steep flight of cobbled steps clambering upwards to Live Moor. Keep ahead at an intermediate forest trail to a final gate giving access to the open moor. There is no respite just yet from the uphill toil, as the path tackles the shoulder of **Round Hill**. But then, at last, it finds easier ground, and lopes off energetically through acres of glorious heather (and a few sprouts of bell heather) in the direction of distant Carlton Moor.

From Live Moor the onward route is hardly in doubt, being paved the whole way, crossing Gold Hill and the edge of **Faceby Bank** to plod on up the broad, heathery expanse of Carlton Moor.

The presence on Carlton Moor of a broad strip of bare ground may puzzle for a while, especially if visibility is not good. It is the runway of a **glider station** in a barren, desert-like landscape, strewn with small rocks that seem to offer little prospect of a smooth landing. All this moorland is now Access Land, but the airstrip is excluded.

Sandwiched between this 'runway' and the escarpment edge, the path continues uneventfully to the summit

MINING ON CARLTON MOOR

Below the moor top, and shortly to be encountered, are some old jet mine workings. Jet in this region is synonymous with Whitby, although the history of jet mining and jet jewellery is much more ancient, beads of the light, fossilised wood having been discovered in Bronze Age burial mounds dating from 2500 to 3500 years ago. Jet was formed about 130 million years ago, when pieces of coniferous driftwood became buried by Jurassic sea mud.

In more recent times it was a retired naval captain who introduced two Whitby men to the art of turning on a lathe, leading to the production, from around 1800 onwards, of beads and crosses. By 1850, there were over 50 workshops in Whitby alone. Even so, jet would never have received the prominence it did had not Queen Victoria taken to wearing it as court mourning, following the death of Prince Albert. It was already generally recognised as an emblem of mourning, but with royal patronage a boom period followed, and those 50 workshops quadrupled in number, eventually giving employment to over 1400 men and boys. Jet is still carved in Whitby, and uncut pieces may be found by diligent searching on the beaches there.

Alum crystals, too, were a product of this remarkable region, with at least 25 quarries active between 1600 and 1871, and nature has not quite finished her work of disguising the massive shale heaps that litter Carlton Bank, and other places. The value of alum lay in its property as a fixative of dyes in cloth, a secret process mastered throughout Italy in the 16th century, and, towards the end of that century, by a member of the Chaloner family in Britain.

Requiring 50 to 100 tons of shale to produce one ton of alum crystals, its quarrying was a pick-and-shovel nightmare for the poorly paid labourers involved in the long, tedious process of extraction. Once won from the earth, the shale, piled in large mounds, had to be burned slowly, before soaking in water. Then the solution had to be boiled, crystallised and purified, a process that required scrub for the burning, water for soaking, coal for the boiling, and seaweed and human urine for the chemistry – an altogether messy and protracted way of going about business that came to a halt in 1871, with the closure of the Kettleness and Boulby works.

of **Carlton Moor**, marked by a trig pillar and a boundary stone.

The onward trail from the summit of Carlton Moor picks a cautious way down Carlton Bank, passing the edge of old alum quarries and large waste heaps of burnt shale.

On reaching a rough track, keep forward down a path to a narrow road. Cross the road and a stile to gain a green track going forward for **Cringle Moor**.

> You could take a slight detour here by turning right to **Lord Stones Café** (toilets and information centre here, and camping and camping pods in the country park), an unexpected and very welcome treat hidden beneath a raised embankment.
>
> Perhaps the café should go by the name 'Lords' Stone', since such a stone, known as the 'Three Lords' Stone', stands nearby on the former parish boundary. It commemorates the lords of the time – Duncombe of Helmsley (now Feversham), Marwood of Busby Hall, and Ailesbury, the latter at that time holding Scugdale.

From the café, the path goes left to pass a small copse, and then crosses to a broad green track heading for Cringle Moor.

> Before starting the ascent, the path forks, and there is a chance to take a **gentler route to Clay Bank Top** by branching left (signpost) along a gently rising, broad green footpath that traverses the northern slopes of the moors. This is an ancient pathway used by jet and alum miners. At one point the path is crossed by a bridleway used by all-terrain cyclists, so take care – at this point some of them will be completely out of control – it is easy to understand why when you see what they are descending.

Keep right (ahead) at a fork to a gate, and from there climb steadily to the nab of Cringle Moor at Cringle End, where a view indicator, a welcome stone seat and a boundary stone await. All the way to Clay Bank Top now, the on-going path is flagged, an undertaking begun in 1991. It's hard on the feet, but easy and speedy to follow.

*Descending to
Clay Bank Top*

The stone seat on Cringle End was erected in memory of **Alec Falconer** (alias 'Rambler'), a founder member of the Middlesbrough Rambling Club, who died in 1968. He promoted the notion of a long-distance walk along the hills and coastline of the North York Moors, but, sadly, died a year before the Cleveland Way was opened.

The highest point of Cringle Moor is **Drake Howe**, a Bronze Age burial mound, and the second highest point on this crossing of the Cleveland Hills. Its summit is set back from the path, and as a result is the only summit along this stretch that is not visited.

The onward path keeps to the escarpment edge above Kirby Bank, before descending steeply through a spill of boulders, stones and mining debris to the broad col before Cold Moor. From the col follow a wall (on the right) along a broad track to reach a streambed.

> Walkers who opted for the gentler route across the northern face of Cringle Moor will also reach this point. Here, a path descends and crosses the stream, then a stile, to continue along the boundary of **Broughton Plantation**, ultimately to arrive at Clay Bank Top by a sheltered and rather more level passage, though there is a little ascent involved.

Go right just before the stream, through a gate to follow a dilapidated wall ahead, and then left before continuing to the top of the moor.

The summit of **Cold Moor** is marked by a modest sandstone cairn, and is followed by a short and delightful walk along the escarpment edge, descending to a gate above Garfit Gap. Continue ahead along the line of a collapsed wall, passing through two gaps in lateral walls. A final short pull leads to the **Wainstones**, a tumble of

The Wainstones, a distinctive rock outcrop popular with climbers

boulders and rock outcrops that represent one of only a small number of rock-climbing opportunities in the North York Moors.

Various paths weave a way through the Wainstones, beyond which easy walking leads on across the plateau of Hasty Bank. Stay with the edge of Hasty Bank's escarpment (a pleasant prospect) before tackling the steep descent to the top of a plantation and wall corner (stile), from there descending a paved and stepped path beside the wall to meet the **B1257** Stokesley to Helmsley road at **Clay Bank Top**, more correctly known as 'Hagg's Gate'. ◄

A mobile snack bar sometimes turns up just left (north) of Clay Bank Top. Don't count on it, but it could provide extra sustenance.

Throughout the whole of this lengthy traverse, the highlight has been the **superb views** northwards and the dramatic escarpment dropping to forestry and farmland below, while the pinnacles of the Wainstones provide a stark contrast to the luxurious vegetation that has patterned the journey from Ingleby Cross. Clay Bank Top is an idyllic spot. The bluebell woods of Ingleby Bank stand on one side, with Bilsdale stretching far away on the other.

From Clay Bank Top the walk continues to the highest point on the North York Moors, Botton Head on Urra Moor. Very few signs of civilisation will be encountered along this stretch until the Lion Inn at Blakey Ridge.

Go through the road gate, following a paved path alongside a wall that marks the boundary of medieval Greenhow deer park, and follows an ancient packhorse trail once much used by smugglers. Initially the track climbs energetically, through a narrow cleft in a rocky barrier before reaching a gate, and there gaining access to the open moor of Carr Ridge.

From this point the walking is of the easiest kind, with **wide-ranging views** across a landscape of constantly changing colours, seen at its vibrant best in late summer and early autumn, when the heather is in full bloom and the sun and clouds combine to provide a limitless number of lighting variations to enhance the scene.

This is perhaps the finest stretch in the North York Moors, but potentially the most lethal in poor visibility. The great moor, badly damaged by fire in the 1930s and still recovering, has some deceiving contours. It might have been for this same reason that the justices sitting in Northallerton in 1711 decreed that **guideposts** should be erected throughout the North Riding of Yorkshire (as it then was). Opposite the trig point on the top of Urra Moor stands one such guidepost, the Hand Stone, with a rough carving on each side depicting a hand, and inscribed with the words 'This is the way to Stoxla' (Stokesley) and 'This is the way to Kirbie' (Kirkbymoorside). A short way further on, and probably much older, stands the Face Stone, depicting a crude face incised on the east face.

From the top of **Urra Moor** a broad track begins an easy descent to a spot known as **Bloworth Crossing**, where the onward route joins the embankments of the former **Rosedale Ironstone Railway**. At a line of grouse butts on the left, ignore a faint green path going left, but keep ahead instead to a slight boggy depression, climbing easily to the railway embankment. On reaching the trackbed, turn right, and follow this literally all the way to the Lion Inn – roughly 5 miles (8km) – at the head of Blakey Ridge, a long serpentine walk of the easiest kind.

The **Rosedale Ironstone Railway** was constructed in 1861 to carry iron from Rosedale over the watershed to the furnaces of Teesside. Iron Age man more than likely worked the Rosedale iron ore, but in 1328 Edward III granted land for that purpose to the nuns of Rosedale Abbey. Five centuries later the ore was dismissed as poor quality and worthless, only to be regarded later still as magnetic ore of the highest quality. Once the railway link was made across the moors, some five million tons were extracted in the first 20 years. By the later 1920s, however, the seams had worn thin, and a depression was looming, presaging the final end of the mining operations.

At a second gate shortly after Bloworth Crossing the route takes its leave of the Cleveland Way, but is not yet able to shake off the Lyke Wake Walk, which continues for some time yet. For a distance the railway bed contours neatly around the head of Farndale, a wild and beautiful valley renowned for its springtime display of daffodils, and once destined to be flooded to supply water to Hull, until a sense of natural justice prevailed.

After what seems like an eternity, the **Lion Inn** springs encouragingly into view on the skyline. As it is approached, the trackbed is left to pursue a path through heather leading up towards the inn (signposted 'LWW').

The old railway is in its own right, if you like, an ancient monument, a testament to **hard-working men** now long forgotten. We shall see it again soon, circling the head of Rosedale, but when at Blakey Ridge we step off it, its companionship and aid to a speedy passage are finally gone from beneath our feet. (A moment's pause and a silent word of gratitude for the men who, unwittingly, made part of our journey easy and comfortable to follow, would not go amiss.)

The path leading up to the inn comes first to a raised circular mound, Blakey Howe, an ancient burial mound used in more recent times for cockfighting.

EAST TO WEST: BLAKEY RIDGE TO OSMOTHERLEY

At Blakey Howe, head right, following a wall and descending slightly to meet the trackbed of the **Rosedale Ironstone Railway**. Once on the trackbed go right and follow this easy route for almost 5 miles (8km) around the head of Farndale until, at a gate, the Cleveland Way appears from the right, to lead onwards. Continue ahead, and a few hundred metres after a second gate, at a place known as **Bloworth Crossing**, leave the trackbed by descending left and then climbing from a boggy depression to begin the ascent of **Urra Moor**.

The summit of Urra Moor is Round Hill, the highest point of the North York Moors, and has an ancient guidepost, the Hand Stone nearby. Beyond the high point, the track eases onwards, gradually descending Carr Ridge, and then dropping suddenly through a narrow cleft into the rock lip before plunging down to **Clay Bank Top**.

Clay Bank Top is more correctly known as 'Hagg's Gate', and directly opposite the point at which the path from Carr Ridge meets the **B1257** Stokesley to Helmsley road, climb a flight of steps to gain a path rising beside a wall to a step-stile on the left, with a plantation on the right.

Low-level alternative: A speedy and less demanding alternative route keeps right at this point, along the edge of the plantation, bypassing Hasty Bank and the Wainstones. It later cuts across the northern slopes of Cringle Moor, following a route taken by the jet and alum miners who worked this area, to rejoin the main line of the walk just before reaching Lord Stones Café.

The main line crosses the step-stile to tackle the steep pull to Hasty Bank. The entire route from Clay Bank onwards was paved during the 1990s, and makes for speedy progress and, more to the point, safer progress in poor visibility. Only the passage through the Wainstones isn't paved, and this is obvious enough.

Once the ascent is complete, the path runs along the escarpment to reach the top of the **Wainstones**, a tumble of boulders and rock walls through which a number of paths thread a way. Below the Wainstones, take the paved path bearing left. This guides you down through lateral walls into Garfit Gap, and up to a gate. More ascent leads on to **Cold Moor**, followed by an easy descent to a gate. Follow the on-going wall round to another gate at a wall corner. *The alternative low-level route arrives here from the right, and the two routes rejoin briefly.* Through the gate, go left to a signpost. *Here, the low-level route branches right.* Go left and start climbing through mining spoil to reach a splendid escarpment path around the edge of **Cringle Moor**. The highest point of the moor, Drake Howe, lies off to the left, marked by a pile of stones.

Eventually, the path starts to descend slightly as it heads for a view indicator and stone seat at Cringle End. A paved path now descends to a gate, beyond which a broad green path (joined eventually by the low-level route) leads onward. When the fence on the left ends, either keep forward to continue along the route, or bear left to pass a small copse and so reach the **Lord Stones Café** (with toilets, refreshments and information).

Beyond the café lies a minor surfaced road, gained by a stile. Cross the road and continue forward on a narrow path through bracken that leads to a shale track leading to debris from former alum quarries. Cross the track, and pass through a gate to start ascending on a cobbled path, rising initially through quarry spoil, now almost completely covered by regeneration. The path soon reaches the summit of **Carlton Moor**, marked by a trig pillar and a boundary post.

An excellent, flagged path now leads on from the summit, a delightful airy traverse that soon passes a long, barren strip of ground used as a landing strip for gliders. The path is sandwiched between the airstrip and the northern edge of Carlton Moor, and then romps along in undulating fashion to Live Moor, before finally descending from the western edge of the Cleveland Hills to head for the next chapter in the walk, the Vale of Mowbray.

Once the top of Live Moor is crossed, the path continues gently downwards with stunning views ahead of Scarth Wood Moor, the waiting vale and the distant frieze of Swaledale fells. The on-going path leads past **Round Hill** and down to a gate giving directly into a plantation. A steep flight of cobbled steps follows, and this can be slippery when wet.

Marker for Lyke Wake Walk, Faceby Bank

At the bottom, pass through another gate, and follow the path left along the plantation boundary to another gate giving onto an enclosed path that emerges at Huthwaite Green, at the head of Scugdale.

On reaching Huthwaite Green, go ahead down the lane opposite the phone box, soon passing Hollin Hill Farm. Beyond, you cross Scugdale Beck, and soon afterwards a clear track (signposted) branches right for the lane to a footbridge (and ford) over Piper Beck.

From a gate, head slightly right, following a green track (rather than the waymarked bridleway) up-field to enter **Clain Wood** at a stile. Turn right to engage a lovely path through the wood, which is seasonally bright with bluebells and wood sorrel, both indicating that this is an ancient woodland. The path follows the lower perimeter of the woodland, and when it forks, branch right and keep going until you reach an access trail near a gate.

Turn left, and almost immediately branch right to begin a steady pull to the upper levels of Clain Wood. At the top of the ascent, a small 'balcony' on the right, with a seat, offers a moment's relaxation and a fine view over the village of Swainby below.

Back on track, turn right at a nearby junction (signpost and 'LWW' marker stone), and follow a level track until it forks. Here, at a signpost, branch right through the last of the woodland to emerge at the roadside just below **Scarth Nick**.

Turn left through a gate beside a cattle-grid, and up the road, and in a few paces take a signposted path on the right, climbing by a flight of cobbled steps to join a broad track at another low stone marker for the Lyke Wake Walk. Here, bear right onto a broad track that sweeps across the lovely heathery expanse of **Scarth Wood Moor**.

The track ends at a gate at the edge of woodland. Go through the gate, and the next one a few strides on, into the woodland. Now follow a path sandwiched between a wall on the left and a wooded escarpment on the right, soon reaching the summit of **Beacon Hill**, which marks the original starting point of the Lyke Wake Walk. Soon, the untidy ironmongery of Beacon Hill's radio station comes into view, with just enough room to let the path squeeze by before it starts descending through the delights of South Wood.

At the southern edge of the wood, the path emerges close by a gate. Leave the at this point, following the Cleveland Way across fields, through three kissing-gates, past **Chapel Wood Farm**, until reaching the road leading into **Osmotherley**, there turning right into the village.

STAGE 12
Blakey Ridge to Grosmont

Start	The Lion Inn, Blakey Ridge (SE 679 997)
Finish	Grosmont railway station (NZ 828 052)
Distance	13 miles (20.8km)
Total ascent	937ft (286m)
Total descent	2093ft (638m)
Walking time	5–6hr
Terrain	Undulating moorland hill slopes; some road walking.
Accommodation	Egton Bridge

After a few more miles of superlative moorland traverse today the route drops off the high moors over Glaisdale Rigg and down to the village of Glaisdale, saying farewell to the wilderness to follow the course of the River Esk east to Grosmont. If you can, allow a little time to pause in the charming village of Egton Bridge towards the end of the day.

Go left at the mound to reach the road between Hutton-le-Hole to the south and Castleton and Westerdale to the north.

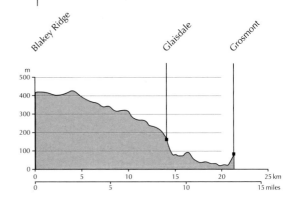

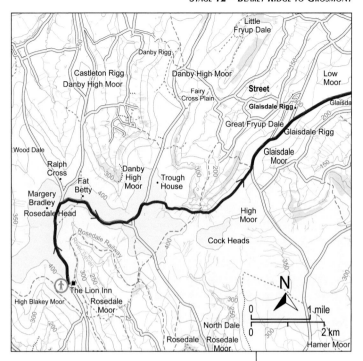

Head left along the road, which has ample grassy verges, high above Rosedale and its river, the **River Seven**. After about 1½ km you come to a large boundary stone on the left, known as **Margery Bradley**, and a path branching right across the head of Rosedale. This is the original line of the Coast to Coast Walk, and part of the Esk Valley Walk, but is often messy, saves little in time and misses out the iconic **Ralph Cross**. So, just follow the road, and don't forget to turn right.

map continues on page 214

Moorland crosses are a prominent and frequent occurrence on the North York Moors. There are more than 30 named crosses on the moors, probably a larger collection than anywhere else in

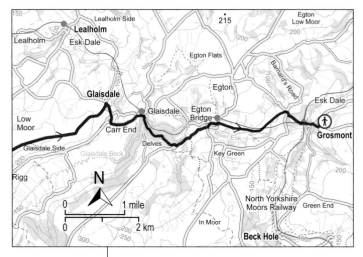

Britain. Reminders of the crucifixion of Christ, central symbol of the Christian faith, they first appeared on the moors during the 7th-century growth of Christianity in the region.

In 1974, the prevalence and significance of these moorland crosses was given a measure of official blessing when one of them, Ralph Cross at the head of Rosedale, and more or less central to the moors, was used as the emblem of the North York Moors National Park Authority.

Most of the crosses have lost their crossbars over time, and are now no more than bases or pillars. Used originally to guide travellers across the moors, they are found at (medievally) strategic points, and so indicate the line of ancient tracks and cross-moor routes. Anyone interested in studying these crosses will find Stanhope White's book *Standing Stones and Earthworks of the North York Moors* (1987) a good resource.

About half a kilometre after bending right an ungainly white-painted cross – known, for evident

reasons, as **Fat Betty** and formerly White Cross – is reached. Continue along the road for a short distance until a line of boundary stones going left marks the line of a possible shortcut, saving all of 100m. About another kilometre along the road after this first shortcut another narrow but clear path darts off to the left to reach a single-track road heading north across **Danby High Moor**. This bypasses a stretch of road down to a junction and doubling back, saving 300m.

However you reach the northbound road, follow it up a slight rise until a broad track branches right, towards an old shooting hut, **Trough House**. Take this track and a fine traverse of moorland now ensues, the path soon meeting Trough Gill Beck, and then circling the head of **Great Fryup Dale** across a landscape dominated by heather, bracken and bilberry, and passing an area where coal was once mined. This enjoyable interlude across **Glaisdale Moor** declines as the way meets another of the unenclosed roads crisscrossing this part of the moors, this one keeping to the high ground between Great Fryup Dale and Glaisdale.

The route turns north round a wide valley (photo: J Williams)

215

Turn left along the road, heading north, and after about 1.5km (1 mile) go right on a broad track just before the road reaches the conspicuous trig point of **Glasidale Rigg**. The track that follows, along Glaisdale Rigg, is an ancient highway, as many standing stones with directions on them testify, and leads easily and most pleasantly down to the village, with the abundant heather (not the last we will see) gradually giving way to grass as height is lost.

> **Glaisdale** is a sprawling village built on a series of hillsides that in the mid-19th century had a prosperous iron industry and helped to establish nearby Middlesbrough as a steel-producing town of considerable importance.

Finally reaching the village at the green, the onward route here turns right, staying with the meandering road through this strung-out village. With only short stretches of heather moorland to come, the time spent in the wilderness of the North York Moors can here be said to be at an end.

The route through Glaisdale could not be simpler – follow the road to the station. ◀

At Glaisdale **railway station** the road bends right to pass beneath the railway bridge. Immediately before the bridge, a path goes right (signposted) over a footbridge spanning **Glaisdale Beck** to enter East Arncliff Wood.

Before taking this route, however, a short diversion under the railway bridge is needed to visit Beggar's Bridge.

> **Beggar's Bridge**, it is claimed, is the handiwork of one Tom Ferris, a local man of modest means who fell in love with Agnes Richardson, the daughter of a wealthy farmer from Egton. The River Esk at this spot is always difficult to cross, the more so when in spate, but to see Agnes, Tom had to negotiate its watery ways. Agnes' father, however, seeing little in Tom's prospects, did his best to end the

A passageway just before the terrace where the post office is found leads to a quieter back road through the village, as does a narrow road opposite the Mitre Hotel.

THE HOB OF HART HALL FARM

Arthur Mee described the nearby valley as, 'a dale shut off from the world by the moors'. Not surprisingly, such an isolated community, one that even today is awkward to get to, is a source of folklore and legend. Prevalent in that folklore are many tales of hobs and goblins, and one such used to inhabit Hart Hall Farm on the edge of the village. Usually hobs are depicted as solitary, dwarf-like creatures, often shaggy-haired and ugly. They often work naked, and dislike clothes to the extent that a gift of clothing would be regarded as an insult, something that would annoy them intensely, causing them to become mischievous, vindictive or dangerous. Adept at hiding themselves from prying eyes, they work extremely hard and quickly, seeking no reward beyond an occasional word of thanks.

The hob at Hart Hall Farm was apparently a kindly fellow, and much loved by the inhabitants there. Once, when a hay-wagon wheel became jammed between two stones, with bad weather threatening, it became vital that the hay be brought in from the fields without delay. But all efforts to release the wheel failed, and the tired farm hands went to bed that night facing a harder than usual day's work in the morning. But during the night the hob got to work, using his great strength to release the wheel, and drawing the fully-laden wagon into the farmyard. When dawn came, the farm hands found the hay not only down from the fields and stacked, but the wagon prepared for the next day.

Tales like these are typical of these isolated communities. Always, it seems, the hobs were there when needed, helping with every chore around the farm, and always in secret. No one ever saw the hobs at work or heard them. Whatever our modern interpretation or opinions might be, they formed a real, and no doubt psychologically supportive, element in the lives of people destined to spend their lives in hard, rural toil.

relationship, inevitably forcing the couple to meet in secret. With so much opposition, it became clear that if he intended to have his bride, Tom had to make his fortune. Fortunately, he liked travelling, and left Glaisdale to join a ship at Whitby. Before long he found himself fighting the Spanish Armada, after which he (perhaps unavoidably) turned to looting Spanish galleons. Eventually he returned, and rose to become Mayor of Hull and Warden of its Trinity House. With his future assured, Tom built his famous bridge in 1619, and married Agnes.

Obviously serving a packhorse trade route across the moors, the bridge is a remarkable and pleasing structure, its sides leaning outwards to accommodate bulging side packs, or panniers. Soon the walk encounters a paved pannier-way as it enters East Arnecliffe Wood.

Retreat beneath the railway bridge to cross Glaisdale Beck, where the path climbs steeply for a while, leading on to an extended paved way, one of the centuries-old pannier-ways. Amid the quiet, green shelter of this natural woodland, the path seems longer than it is, concluding finally as it emerges onto a quiet road. Here turn left, down the hill to **Egton Bridge**.

Egton Bridge is one of Yorkshire's most beautiful villages, occupying a superb site on the River Esk, and flanked by great stands of trees and verdant loveliness. Its name comes from 'egetune', meaning 'town of oaks', and with its neighbour, Egton, on the hillside a short distance away, was given by William the Conqueror to his blacksmith in 1070.

As you arrive into Egton Bridge by the lane down to the Horseshoe Hotel, a path leads down to stepping-stones crossing the River Esk that makes for an interesting diversion, and an alternative way through the village (not advised if the river is in spate or the stones are wet). On the other side, walk out to the village road at The Old Mill (B&B), and turn right (shortly passing toilets) to rejoin the original route (left) near the church.

◄ On reaching Egton Bridge, at a T-junction near the Horseshoe Hotel, keep ahead to cross the road bridge over the **River Esk**. Soon, turn right to a junction between the church and the bridge, leaving the village by an enclosed way (signposted 'Egton Estates – private road'). Formerly this way was a toll road, and finally meets the valley road near a loop in the Esk, not far from Priory Farm. Turn right over a bridge and follow the road into **Grosmont**.

In their all-conquering manner, the Romans built a road through **Grosmont** (pronounced 'grow-mont'), and a fort to protect it, taking advantage of its strategic position at the confluence of two rivers, the Esk and the Murk Esk. There is scant evidence of Grosmont's ancient history, except that

THE MARTYR OF THE MOORS

Egton Bridge was once renowned for its Roman Catholicism, so strong that it was known as 'the village missed by the Reformation', and also for being the birthplace in 1596 of Nicholas Postgate.

Postgate, later called 'Blessed Nicholas Postgate, Martyr of the Moors', at the age of 25 went to be trained as a priest in France. After his ordination he was sent to England as a missionary, and spent the early part of his priesthood as chaplain to a number of wealthy families, his true role being concealed by his work as a gardener. Understandably, he always travelled in disguise and in secret to say mass, give communion and visit the sick. His love of gardening prompted him to plant flowers on his travels, and he is credited with bringing the wild daffodil to the moors, calling it the Lenten lily. He was finally betrayed at Whitby by an excise man called John Reeves, who set a trap and had him arrested while conducting a baptism at Red Barns Farm, near Ugglebarnby. Reeves received the princely sum of £20 for his work, and Postgate was charged with high treason, for which he was hung, drawn and quartered on 7 August 1679 at the age of 82.

Postgate's last resting place is unknown but relics of his work, and of the Postgate Society founded in his memory, can be seen at St Hedda's Catholic Church in Egton Bridge. During the first-ever visit to England by a reigning pope, in 1982, the late Pope John Paul II stood on Postgate's place of execution (now part of the racecourse at York) and prayed a litany of northern saints, including Nicholas Postgate among them.

As a footnote, the story goes that John Reeves, horrified by the outcome of his treachery, committed suicide by drowning himself in a deep pool at Littlebeck, ever since known as Devil's Dump.

Johanna Fossard, supported by the French priory of Grandimont, founded a priory here at the beginning of the 13th century. No trace remains today, but it is known to have occupied the site of present-day Priory Farm.

More recently, the building of one of the railway lines, in 1836, exposed a rich seam of ironstone, of the highest quality, which ultimately yielded over 100,000 tons of ore each year before the mining ended in 1871. The ore was transported by rail to

A 'proper' train at Grosmont station (photo: J Williams)

the coast at Whitby, for shipping to the Tyne, and the presence of railways still features largely in the everyday life of touristy Grosmont.

The Whitby–Pickering line opened in 1836 as a horse-drawn tramway to help the development of the inland timber, sandstone and limestone industries and ran until 1965. Shortly afterwards, in 1967, the North Yorkshire Moors Preservation Society was formed and managed to purchase the part of the line from Grosmont to Eller Beck. More bureaucratic wranglings ensued until, finally, on 1 May 1973, the North York Moors Railway was formally opened by the Duchess of Kent. Today with two lines, from Whitby to Pickering several times a day between the March and October half terms and, occasionally, from Whitby to Battersby along the Esk Valley, it is a highly popular tourist attraction.

EAST TO WEST: GROSMONT TO BLAKEY RIDGE

Keep ahead on the road through Grosmont and cross the railway line, soon bearing right under a railway line to leave the village by a pleasant lane to a bend in the nearby **River Esk**, not far from Priory Farm.

Just after the road crosses the first part of the river bend, go right towards Priory Farm, but before reaching the farm head left along a former toll road leading to **Egton Bridge**.

At Egton Bridge, go left to cross the river and follow the road to a junction with a minor road. Here, branch right (ahead) along the minor road for a little over half a mile (1km) until a path on the right gives access to East Arncliff Woods, through which passage is eased by the use of an ancient, paved pannier-way that eventually swings round and down to **Glaisdale Beck** on the edge of the village. Cross the beck by a footbridge, and then turn left to descend to the station. Just after crossing the footbridge, and beyond the railway viaduct on the right, stands Beggar's Bridge, which is well worth a diversion.

Follow the twisting road upwards through strung-out **Glaisdale** until, at the top of the village, at a green, a road goes left towards Glaisdale Hall Farm. The onward route now follows the line of an ancient highway, climbing at first by a grassy path and then into low heather across **Glaisdale Rigg**, high above the valley of Glaisdale to the south.

Gradually the trail broadens, and eventually meets a surfaced moorland road (from Lealholm to Rosedale Abbey) high on a narrow neck of land sandwiched between Glaisdale and **Great Fryup Dale**. Go left along the road for about a mile, leaving it by a rough track heading right (southwest), and swinging around the head of Great Fryup Dale to an old shooting hut, **Trough House**, shortly after which another unenclosed moorland road is encountered.

Between this point and the Lion Inn at the top of Blakey Ridge, the simplest way is to follow the road. The verges are good and (other than at weekends) there is little traffic. It is possible to shortcut a few obvious corners by delving into bog and heather to save a little distance, but hardly worth it. From the road just after Trough House, go left to a junction, and there turn right. Follow the road to another junction, passing a low moorland cross (Fat Betty, aka White Cross) on the right. Continue to a further junction near a car park, and not far from another moorland cross, **Ralph Cross**, which has been adopted as the symbol of the North York Moors National Park. At the junction turn left and walk on as far as the Lion Inn, passing a large and ungainly standing stone known as **Margery Bradley**.

As the **Lion Inn** is approached, a path rises right to an ancient raised mound, Blakey Howe. In more recent times it was used for cockfighting.

STAGE 13
Grosmont to Robin Hood's Bay

Start	Grosmont railway station (NZ 828 052)
Finish	Robin Hood's Bay (NZ 953 048)
Distance	15 miles (24km)
Total ascent	2275ft (695m)
Total descent	2350ft (720m)
Walking time	6–7 hours
Terrain	Moorland; farmland; woodland, and some road walking.
Accommodation	Sleights, Littlebeck, Hawsker

So this really is the final leg of the journey. It is one to be savoured and enjoyed, to be embarked upon both with a sense of happiness and of sadness – happiness at having achieved a personal goal and overcome such adversity as has been encountered, and sadness that such a good thing is coming to an end. There will have been bad days, almost certainly, when spirits were low, or feet and shoulders ached, or the pub or café closed two minutes before you arrived, but the greater part will be of good memories, unsurpassed scenery, historic moments (in more than one sense, no doubt), good companionship (perhaps), and walking of the highest order.

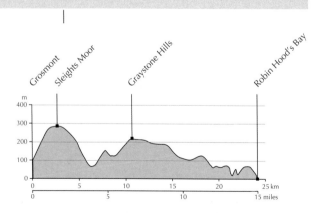

Leave Grosmont by climbing east (ignoring two roads going left to Sleights), and continuing up Fair Head Lane, a tiring pull at the best of times, but eased a little by fine retrospective views over the Esk valley. More significantly, Whitby Abbey can be seen in the distance on its clifftop site, as the final chapter of the walk draws to a close.

When the lane reaches the open moor (now Access Land), a line of standing stones known as the **Low Bride Stones** may be spotted to the south, and further on another set, the **High Bride Stones**, may be seen off to the right. The Low Bride Stones are something of a disappointment, lying haphazardly in a boggy depression, while the High Bride Stones make more of an effort to remain upright in the face of the elements.

Continue along the minor road for 700m beyond High Bride Stones, to a signpost (NZ 855 042) opposite a large parking area on the right. At the signpost, leave the road for a clear path through heather that shortly meets the **A169**. Turn left along the verge beside the A-road,

Coast to Coast signpost for Littlebeck on Sleights Moor

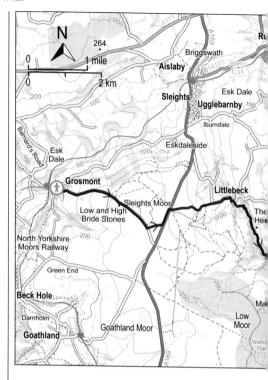

crossing it when you can safely do so. After 500m, come to a signpost on the right pointing to a gate that gives onto a bridleway heading left through heather to meet a stony track. Turn right along the track.

Press on down to the hamlet of **Littlebeck** and start ascending the road leading away from it. ◄ At a second bend go right, through a kissing-gate (signposted 'C-to-C' and 'Falling Foss'). Enter the woodland to begin a delightful but brief interlude in the company of Little Beck.

A good path leads on, negotiates a tributary stream, and leads to the unexpected sight of a spoil heap. Pass it to reach a muddy path leading to a huge boulder on the left, known as the **Hermitage**.

Littlebeck is a charming village, a secluded and sheltered community renowned locally for the extravagant beauty of its woodland.

The Hermitage is carved from one piece of rock, and could provide shelter for a sizeable group of visitors. It was constructed by George Chubb in 1790, and bears his initials. Quite why it was built appears to be unrecorded – it may simply have been to serve the purposes of a local eccentric, a form of 18th-century escapism that sees its modern counterpart in the blank-faced mobile phone-clutching brigades, who wander about our streets or sit immutably insular on trains and buses.

From the Hermitage continue along the higher of two paths that follow, and when this shortly forks, take the right branch to Falling Foss, a delightful waterfall in a wooded setting – at its best after prolonged rain. Nearby, Midge Hall is then reached by a footbridge. A stone block set in a gate pillar here bears the inscription 'Sneaton Lordship'.

Continue alongside the stream, with a larger, farm access bridge appearing on the left. Cross the access track and keep ahead to reach the stream at a ford. ◄

If the stream is in spate backtrack to the farm bridge and locate a path on the opposite bank that will bring you to the same spot.

The path continues ahead to meet a broader forest trail, at which go right, to cross a stream by a footbridge, continuing ahead on an improving path, passing a pond with bulrushes on the left, and keeping onwards to reach the vicinity of May Beck car park.

On reaching May Beck Bridge, go immediately left on the road, doubling back and following the rising road to, and beyond, a bend at New May Beck farm. As the road straightens, leave it, right, at a broad footpath that heads out onto Sneaton Low Moor. Ignore the prominent path bearing left onto the moor. Instead, from a signpost, head initially half-right through rushes onto a path that leads to a mid-moor signpost, and then on farther to a gate in a wall, close by a scattered stand of pine. Through the gate, turn left for Hawsker (note the interesting milestone nearby, right), and parallel the wall on a path at times board-walked.

At a field corner near the B1416, turn right to a gate giving onto the B-road. Cross the road to a stile opposite.

Now follow a narrow trod through low heather scrub across what is to be the final stretch of moorland. The path, marked by an occasional guidepost, is frequently wet, and passes through a couple of boggy depressions. This short stretch rejoices in the name of **Graystone Hills**, an appellation taking much descriptive licence. With a final boggy flourish, the path arrives at a gate, close by a raised tumulus on the right. Bear left to a stile.

Keep forward in the ensuing pasture before bearing left to arrive at a stile in a fence beyond which lies a broad track between hedges, leading to a surfaced lane and later bearing right into Low Hawsker. Bear right into Back Lane, and shortly cross the A171 to reach **High Hawsker**. Here roadside benches invite a moment's respite.

Hawsker has one of Yorkshire's many legendary links with **Robin Hood**, and since his bay is close by, it justifies retelling. The story is that both Robin and Little John, on a visit to Whitby, were accommodated at the abbey, where they were invited to demonstrate their archery skills. From the top of an abbey tower they each fired an arrow to the southeast, and each landed on Whitby Laithes, a stretch of ground, now a farm, near Hawsker. So impressed was the abbot with these shots that he ordered standing stones to be fixed where the arrows had landed, and to this day those places, Robin Hood Field and Little John Field, are still shown on maps (NZ 91 09). That the arrows would have had to carry a distance of just over 1¼ miles (2km) for this to be an accurate account is the sort of puerile currency that sceptics deal in to spoil a good yarn.

Leave the village up the road (signposted 'Robin Hood's Bay') to the right, noting a small well on the right bearing the initials 'TC' and the date 1790. Ascend the

Houses in High Hawkser

road to a right-hand bend, and here leave it, left, for a metalled road leading to, and past, a caravan site ('Sea View'). Another caravan site ('Northcliffe') is encountered a short way farther on. Just past the reception and shop, the road ends. Go ahead, then left, down through ranks of static caravans towards the North Sea.

A pause here to savour what you have achieved is most appropriate. Only a final scamper to Robin Hood's Bay remains, and we'll do that on all fours, if need be!

At the bottom end of the caravan park a track runs ahead to a small filtration plant protected by fencing. To the left of this a path continues down a field alongside Oakham Beck to rejoin the Cleveland Way and meet the coastal path directly above **Maw Wyke Hole**, a truly breathtaking moment. ◀

Now go right, following the coastal path, a popular, well-used and well-worn route that requires little description. Accompanying it most of the way is either a fence or a wall, sometimes both, usually on the seaward side, each field boundary crossed by stiles, as the route curves round North Cheek (Ness Point).

Shortly after passing a coastguard lookout station, the broad sweep of Robin Hood's Bay finally comes into view, a tremendous, uplifting moment as you gaze across the bay to South Cheek (Old Peak) and Ravenscar, where the Lyke Wake Walk, our sometime companion, meets its end.

Looking down on Robin Hood's Bay

Eventually, at a gate go left along a path enclosed by hawthorns to emerge on a grass track in front of a row of houses. This leads on to Mount Pleasant North, at the end of which turn left on the main road down into **Robin Hood's Bay**, ending in a final and steep descent, through the charming cottages and shops of the old part of the village, more correctly known as Baytown, to reach the seashore.

ROBIN HOOD'S BAY

Legend has it that Robin Hood found a quiet bay on the edge of the northern moors and decided on this as an ideal retreat from danger. Here, under the name of Simon Wise, he returned time and time again, keeping a small fleet of fishing boats, which he used to put to sea whenever danger threatened.

The village that bears his name was once a fishing community, with not a little emphasis on smuggling, although it has now caught the imagination of tourists, and is a popular holiday and weekend resort. Its houses and shops perch precariously at or above the water's edge, in imminent danger of collapse or flooding, many of its red-roofed houses so small and narrow that they have a 'coffin window' above the door designed to enable coffins to be removed.

At high tide the sea runs into the village street, and comes in alarmingly quickly. At low tide the Scars, a layer of harder rock underlying the soft boulder clay, run far out to sea, and are full of fascinating rock pools over which to gaze before returning to the prosaic ways of everyday life.

That's it – well done, you've finished. You can stop now… unless, of course, you dipped your boot in the sea at St Bees, or carried that pebble all the way across, in which case the necessary ceremonies must be observed.

Good organisation will see to it that champagne awaits the end of the journey. When I completed the first edition of this book, my celebration with friends, far out into the bay, caused a few wry smiles and looks of puzzlement – they had carried a bottle of champagne and fluted glasses for miles. When I completed the third edition, it was all I could do to keep up with my dog, who was heading for the sea to cool her feet.

But few of the visitors you will meet at Robin Hood's Bay will have much understanding of your achievement – success, in the final analysis, is a very personal thing. Few people will know of your triumph, and most of those will think you are mad. But no one can take from you the knowledge that you walked across England, Coast to Coast!

EAST TO WEST: ROBIN HOOD'S BAY TO GROSMONT

The North Sea at Robin Hood's Bay

Climb away from the seashore at Robin Hood's Bay, ascending steeply through the old part of the village (correctly known as Baytown) to reach the main road. Here, continue ahead and then turn right into Mount Pleasant North (signposted for the Cleveland Way, initially encountered only briefly but re-joined later and followed almost all the way to Ingleby Cross).

At another signpost, soon encountered, go forward through a gate to reach a path enclosed by hawthorns that finally ends at a kissing-gate giving onto clifftop pastures. Now simply follow the coastal path, the Cleveland Way, right, along the edge of numerous pastures, as far as **Maw Wyke Hole**, where the Coast to Coast Walk and the Cleveland Way part company. Here turn left for Hawsker, alongside Oakham Beck, to reach and pass directly up through a caravan site.

At the top end of the caravan site, go right past reception and a shop, and then follow the road out, through its various twists and turns, to reach a bend in the **B1447**, not far from the village of **Hawsker**. On descending into the village go left at the first junction, and then immediately right (for Sneatonthorpe) to cross the **A171** into Back Lane. Now simply follow this lane for just under a mile (2km) until it makes a sharp right-hand bend as it turns to Sneatonthorpe, just after Low Rigg Farm. Here, leave the lane by branching left onto an old lane that shortly runs on between hedges to a stile, where it enters Access Land, beyond which it bears right across a pasture to another stile giving onto the moorland expanse of **Graystone Hills**. Press on ahead, with the way through the heather and a few boggy patches waymarked from time to time. Eventually, the path reaches the **B1416** at a stile. Cross the road to a gate opposite and turn right parallel with the B-road, later following the field edge and a wall as far as a prominent signpost for Littlebeck. Here, turn through a gate and follow a narrow but clear path across Sneaton Low Moor, finally to reach a minor access road serving New May Beck Farm.

Turn left along the access and gradually descend to a bridge near May Beck car park. Just before the **bridge**, go right, along a forest trail, soon passing, on the right, a pond with bulrushes, and shortly reaching a footbridge. Cross the bridge and gain a broader trail, quickly leaving it, left, on a grassy path leading to a ford, and keep ahead to the ruins of Midge Hall.

At Midge Hall, cross a nearby footbridge and ascend a short distance for a delightful view of Falling Foss. Continue climbing easily to reach a higher path going left to a shelter carved from rock, **the Hermitage**.

From the Hermitage, press on, slightly left and down, to follow a woodland path and finally emerge onto a surfaced lane at the edge of **Littlebeck**. Take the road, left, out of Littlebeck, and when, after a steepish pull, it bends sharply to the right for Sleights, leave it by continuing forward along an enclosed stony track to reach open moorland, across which you climb easily to the A169 at the top of Blue Bank.

On reaching the **A169**, turn left and walk beside the A169 for 500m, crossing the road when you can safely do so. Leave the road at a step-stile on the right, giving onto a clear track across heather moorland. This reaches the minor road to Grosmont at a signpost opposite a large parking area. Turn right and follow the road into Fair Head Lane and down to **Grosmont**, on the way passing **High Bride Stones** and later **Low Bride Stones**.

APPENDIX A
Useful contacts

Youth hostels
Youth Hostels Association
Trevelyan House
Dimple Road
Matlock
Derbyshire DE4 3YH
Freephone 0800 0191 700
tel 01629 592700
www.yha.org.uk
customerservices@yha.org.uk

Independent Hostels UK
Speedwell House
Upperwood
Matlock Bath
Derbyshire DE4 3PE
tel 01629 580427
www.independenthostels.co.uk

National park authorities
Lake District Murley Moss
Oxenholme Road
Kendal
Cumbria LA9 7RL
tel 01539 724555
www.lakedistrict.gov.uk
hq@lakedistrict.gov.uk.

North York Moors
The Old Vicarage
Bondgate
Helmsley
York
North Yorkshire YO62 5BP
tel 01439 772700
www.northyorkmoors.org.uk
general@northyorkmoors.org.uk.

Yorkshire Dales
Yoredale
Bainbridge
Leyburn
North Yorkshire DL8 3EL
tel 0300 456 0030
www.yorkshiredales.org.uk
info@yorkshiredales.org.uk

Tourist information
Cumbria Tourism
Windermere Road
Staveley
Kendal
Cumbria LA8 9PL
tel 01539 822222
www.cumbriatourism.org
info@cumbriatourism.org

Yorkshire Tourism
Dry Sand Foundry
Foundry Square
Holbeck
Leeds LS11 5DL
www.yorkshire.com
info@yorkshire.com

St Bees
www.stbees.org.uk

Ennerdale
www.wildennerdale.co.uk

Reeth
www.reeth.org

Richmond
www.richmond.org

Robin Hood's Bay
www.robin-hoods-bay.co.uk

Public transport
Traveline
www.traveline.info

Rail
National rail timetables
tel 03457 48 49 50
www.nationalrail.co.uk

Northern Rail
www.northernrailway.co.uk

Esk Valley Railway
www.eskvalleyrailway.co.uk

North Yorkshire Moors Railway
www.nymr.co.uk

Bus
Arriva
www.arrivabus.co.uk

Stagecoach
www.stagecoachbus.com

Moorsbus
www.moorsbus.org
tel 0175 477216

Baggage carrying services
Brigantes Walking Holidays
and Baggage Couriers
Bob's Laithe
Halton Gill
nr Skipton
North Yorkshire BD23 5QN
tel 01756 770402
www.brigantesenglishwalks.com

The Coast to Coast Packhorse
Chestnut House
Crosby Garrett
Kirkby Stephen
Cumbria CA17 4PR
tel 017683 71777
www.c2cpackhorse.co.uk

Sherpa Van
Office 8, Mowbray House
Olympic Way
Richmond
North Yorkshire DL10 4FB
tel 01748 826917
www.sherpavan.com

Trail Magic Baggage
www.trailmagicbaggage.com/
coast2coast.html

Weather information
Met Office
tel 0370 900 0100
www.metoffice.gov.uk

Facebook
There is a Facebook group that posts
information and recommendations
about the Coast to Coast Walk:
www.facebook.com/groups/
CoastToCoastWalkUK/

APPENDIX B

Accommodation along the route

Every effort has been made to ensure the accuracy and currency of this list, but inevitably there will be inclusions that are no longer valid, and omissions not yet listed. If you find accommodation not listed below, please let us know, for inclusion on our lists: contact the author through the Cicerone Press website.

If you are an accommodation provider, wanting to be included in our lists, please also contact the author via Cicerone Press. Accommodation that lies a distance from the route of the walk often offer a pick-up and drop-off service; don't be afraid to ask.

There are a number of accommodation-booking companies that offer discounts, but it is invariably better to contact the accommodation direct, to obtain the best rate. If calling these numbers from outside the UK, drop the initial '0', and replace with '00 44'.

St Bees

Albert Hotel
1 Finkle Street
St Bees
Cumbria CA27 0BN
tel 01946 822 345

Ellerbeck Manor (B&B)
5 Ellerbeck Barns
Egremont Road
St Bees
Cumbria CA22 2UA
tel 07511 924 307
www.ellerbeckmanor.co.uk

Fairladies Barn (B&B)
Main Street
St Bees
Cumbria CA27 0AD
tel 01946 822 718

The Manor
11–12 Main Street
St Bees
Cumbria CA27 0DE
tel 01946 820 587 or 01946 822 250
https://themanor-inn.business.site

LuLu's (B&B)
The Old Station House
134 Main Street
St Bees
Cumbria CA27 0DG
tel 01946 822 600
www.lulusbistro.co.uk

Moorclose B&B
Outrigg
St Bees
Cumbria CA22 2TZ.
tel 01946 824 561
www.moorclosestbees.co.uk

Queens Hotel
Main Street
St Bees
Cumbria CA27 0DE
tel 01946 822 287

Seacote Park (camping)
The Beach
St Bees
Cumbria CA27 0ET
tel 01946 822 777
https://seacote.com/seacote-park/
tourers-tents

Seacote Hotel
The Beach
St Bees
Cumbria CA27 0ES
tel 01946 822 300
https://seacote.com/seacote-hotel

Stonehouse Farm (B&B)
Main Street
St Bees
Cumbria CA27 0DE
tel 01946 822 224
www.stonehousefarm.net

Tomlin Guest House (B&B)
Beach Road
St Bees
Cumbria CA27 0EN
tel 01946 822 284

Whistling Jack's Guest House (B&B)
Rottington
Cumbria CA28 9UR
tel 01946 821 550
www.whistlingjacks.co.uk

Sandwith

Grovewood House
Sandwith
Cumbria CA28 9UG
tel 01946 63482/07740 465 305
www.grovewoodhouse.com

Cleator

Ennerdale Country House Hotel
Main Street
Cleator
Cumbria CA23 3DT
tel 01946 813 907
www.bespokehotels.com/
ennerdalehotel

Grove Court Hotel
Cleator Gate
Cleator
Cumbria CA23 3DT
tel 01946 810 503

Jasmine House (B&B)
Low Farm
Moor Row
Cumbria CA24 3JA
tel 01946 815 795
www.jasminehousebandb.com

Cleator Moor

Parkside Hotel
Cleator Moor
Cumbria CA25 5HF
tel 01946 811 011
www.theparksidehotel.co.uk

Ennerdale Bridge

Fox and Hounds (Country pub,
camping)
Ennerdale Bridge
Cumbria CA23 3AR
tel 01946 861 373
www.foxandhoundsinn.org

Ghyll Farm (B&B)
Kirkland Road
Ennerdale
Cumbria CA26 3YA
tel 01946 861 330/07941 585 266
https://ghyllfarm.co.uk

Longmoor Head (B&B)
Ennerdale Bridge
Cleator
Cumbria CA23 3AG
tel 01946 861 497
www.longmoorhead.co.uk

Low Cock How (Farm B&B)
Kinniside
Cumbria CA23 3AQ
tel 01946 861 354
www.walk-rest-ride.co.uk

Shepherds Arms Hotel
Ennerdale Bridge
Cumbria CA23 3AR
tel 01946 861 249
www.shepherdsarms.com

The Cloggers (B&B)
Kirkland Road
Ennerdale Bridge
Cleator
Cumbria CA32 3AP
tel 01946 862 487

Thorntrees (B&B)
Ennerdale
Cumbria CA23 3AR
tel 01946 862 549/07810 495 001
www.thorntreesennerdale.co.uk

Ennerdale valley

Low Gillerthwaite Field Centre
(NY139141, hostel and camping)
Ennerdale
Cleator
Cumbria CA23 3AX
tel 01946 861229
www.lgfc.org.uk

Wild Wool Bunkhouse & Camping
Routen Farm
Ennerdale
Cumbria CA23 3AU
tel 01946 861 270
www.wildwoolbarn.co.uk

YHA Ennerdale (Youth hostel)
Cat Crag
Ennerdale
Cumbria CA23 3AX

tel 0345 371 9116
www.yha.org.uk

YHA Black Sail Hut (Youth hostel)
Ennerdale
Cumbria CA23 3AX
tel 0345 371 9680
www.yha.org.uk

Honister

YHA Honister Hause (Youth hostel)
Seatoller
Cumbria CA12 5XN
tel 0345 371 9522
www.yha.org.uk

Seatoller

NOTE: The postal addresses for properties at the southern end of Borrowdale can be misleading; check all addresses for Seatoller, Rosthwaite and Stonethwaite.

Glaramara House (Hotel)
Seatoller
Cumbria CA12 5XQ
tel 017687 77222
www.glaramarahouse.co.uk

Seatoller Farm (B&B and campsite)
Seatoller
Cumbria CA12 5XN
tel 017687 77232
www.seatollerfarm.co.uk

Seatoller House (Guest house)
Seatoller
Cumbria CA12 5XN
tel 017687 77218
www.seatollerhouse.co.uk

YHA Borrowdale (Youth hostel)
Longthwaite
Cumbria CA12 5XE
tel 0345 371 9624
www.yha.org.uk

Rosthwaite

Hazel Bank Country House (Hotel)
Rosthwaite
Cumbria CA12 5XB
tel 017687 77248
www.hazelbankhotel.co.uk

Royal Oak Hotel
Rosthwaite
Cumbria CA12 5XB
tel 017687 77214
www.royaloakhotel.co.uk

Scafell Hotel
Rosthwaite
Cumbria CA12 5XB
tel 017687 77208
www.scafell.co.uk

Yew Craggs (B&B)
Rosthwaite
Cumbria CA12 5XB
tel 017687 77348
www.yewcraggsborrowdale.co.uk

Yew Tree Farm (B&B)
Rosthwaite
Cumbria CA12 5XB
tel 017687 77675
www.borrowdaleyewtreefarm.co.uk

Stonethwaite (Borrowdale)

Chapel House Farm Camp Site
Stonethwaite
Borrowdale, Keswick
Cumbria CA12 5XG
tel 01768 777 256
https://chapelhousefarmcampsite.co.uk

Knotts View Guest House
Stonethwaite
Cumbria CA12 5XG
tel 017687 77604
www.lakedistrictletsgo.co.uk

Langstrath Country Inn
Stonethwaite
Cumbria CA12 5XG
tel 017687 77239
www.thelangstrath.co.uk

Grasmere

Bridge House Hotel
Church Bridge
Grasmere
Cumbria LA22 9SN
tel 015394 35425
www.theinnatgrasmere.co.uk

Chestnut Villa (Guest house)
Keswick Road
Grasmere
Cumbria LA22 9RE
tel 015394 35218
https://chestnutvilla.wordpress.com

Grasmere Hotel
Broadgate
Grasmere
Cumbria LA22 9TA
tel 015394 35277
www.grasmerehotel.co.uk

Heidi's Grasmere Lodge
Red Lion Square
Grasmere
Cumbria LA22 9SP
tel 07568 333 950
http://heidisgrasmerelodge.co.uk

Lake View House (Country House B&B)
Lake View Drive
Grasmere
Cumbria LA22 9TD
tel 015394 35384
www.lakeview-grasmere.com

The Lancrigg
Easedale
Grasmere
Cumbria LA22 9QN
tel 015394 35317
www.lancrigg.co.uk

The Little Inn at Grasmere
Red Lion Square
Grasmere
Cumbria LA22 9SS
tel 015394 35456
www.theinnatgrasmere.co.uk

Moss Grove Organic
Grasmere (on B5287)
Cumbria LA22 9SW
tel 015394 35251
www.mossgrove.com

Raise View House (Guest house)
White Bridge
Grasmere
Cumbria LA22 9RQ
tel 015394 35215
www.raiseview.uk

Thorney How (Hostel and Bunkhouse)
Thorney How (via Easedale Road and
Helm Close)
Grasmere
Cumbria LA22 9QW
tel 015394 35597
www.thorneyhow.co.uk

Traveller's Rest Inn
Grasmere (on A591)
Cumbria LA22 9RR
tel 015394 35604
www.lakedistrictinns.co.uk/travellers-rest

Tweedies Bar and Lodge
Grasmere
Cumbria LA22 9SW
tel 015394 35300
www.tweediesgrasmere.com

YHA Grasmere Butharlyp Howe
(Youth hostel and camping)
Easedale Road
Grasmere
Cumbria LA22 9QG
tel 0345 371 9319
www.yha.org.uk

Patterdale and Glenridding

NOTE: Walkers opting to stay in
Glenridding will add 1km+ to their day.

Chery Holme Guest House
Glenridding
Cumbria CA11 0PF
tel 017684 82302
www.cherryholme.com

Crookabeck Farm (B&B)
Patterdale
Cumbria CA11 0NP
tel 07979 345630
www.crookabeck.com

Crookey Cottage (B&B)
1 Crookabeck
Patterdale
Penrith
Cumbria CA11 0NP
tel 017684 82278/07833 184 488
www.crookeycottage.com

Fairlight Guest House
Glenridding
Cumbria CA11 0PD
tel 017684 82397
www.fairlightguesthouse.co.uk

Glenridding House Hotel
Glenridding
Cumbria CA11 0PH
tel 017684 82874
www.glenriddinghouse.com

Greenbank Farm (B&B)
Patterdale
Cumbria CA11 0NR
tel 017684 82292
http://greenbankfarmpatterdale.co.uk

Noran Bank Farm
Patterdale
Penrith
Cumbria CA11 0NR
tel 017684 82327

Old Water View Hotel
Patterdale
Cumbria CA11 0NW
tel 017684 82175
www.oldwaterview.co.uk

Patterdale Hotel
Patterdale
Cumbria CA11 0NN
tel 017684 82231
www.patterdalehotel.co.uk

Side Farm (Camping)
Patterdale
Cumbria CA11 0NL
tel 017684 82337

White Lion Inn
Patterdale
Cumbria CA11 0NW
tel 017684 82214
www.whitelionpatterdale.com

YHA Patterdale (Youth hostel)
Patterdale
Penrith
Cumbria CA11 0NW
tel 0345 371 9337
www.yha.org.uk

Bampton

Mardale Inn
Bampton
Cumbria CA10 2RQ
tel 01931 713 244
www.mardaleinn.co.uk

Norbrock House B&B
Bampton
Cumbria CA10 2RQ
tel 01931 713 351
www.bamptonteashop.co.uk

Bampton Grange

Crown and Mitre Inn
Bampton Grange
Cumbria CA10 2QR
tel 01931 713 225
www.crownandmitre.com

Shap

Brookfield House (B&B)
Shap
Cumbria CA10 3PZ
tel 01931 716 397
www.brookfieldshap.co.uk

Crown Inn (Pods and camping)
Main Street
Shap
Cumbria CA10 3NL
tel 01931 716 562

Greyhound Hotel (B&B)
Main Street
Shap
Cumbria CA10 3PW
tel 01931 599 995
www.greyhoundshap.co.uk

Kings Arms Hotel
Main Street
Shap
Cumbria CA10 3NW
tel 01931 716 277
www.kingsarmsshap.co.uk

New Ing Lodge (B&B, hostel, camping)
Main Street
Shap
Cumbria CA10 3LX
tel 01931 716 719
www.newinglodge.co.uk

Orton

George Hotel
Front Street
Orton
Cumbria CA10 3RJ
tel 01539 624 071
www.thegeorgehotelorton.co.uk

Raisbeck

Rookery Barn (B&B)
Raisbeck
Cumbria CA10 3SG
tel 01539 624 971

Nateby

(off-route, unless taking the B6270
off-season)

The Black Bull Inn
Nateby
Cumbria CA17 4JP
tel 017683 71588
www.nateby-inn.co.uk

Kirkby Stephen

Bollam Cottage (B&B)
Nateby Road
Kirkby Stephen
Cumbria CA17 4JN

tel 017683 72038/07580 165 045
www.bollamcottage.co.uk

Brockram Cottage (B&B)
121 High Street
Kirkby Stephen
Cumbria CA17 4SH
tel 017683 71214

Chapel Cottage (B&B)
14 High Street
Kirkby Stephen
Cumbria CA17 4SG
tel 017683 71249

Eden House (B&B)
65 High Street
Kirkby Stephen
Cumbria CA17 4SH
tel 017683 71891
www.edenhousebandb.co.uk

Fletcher House (Guest house)
Market Street
Kirkby Stephen
Cumbria CA17 4QQ
tel 01768 371013
www.fletcherhouse.co.uk

The Jolly Farmers (Guest house)
63 High Street
Kirkby Stephen
Cumbria CA17 4SH
tel 017683 71063
www.thejollyfarmers.wordpress.com

Kirkby Stephen Independent Hostel
Market Street
Kirkby Stephen
Cumbria CA17 4QQ
tel 07812 558 525
www.kirkbystephenhostel.co.uk

King's Arms Hotel
Market Street
Kirkby Stephen
Cumbria CA17 4QN
tel 017683 72425

Black Bull Hotel
38 Market Street
Kirkby Stephen
Cumbria CA17 4QW
tel 017683 71237
www.blackbullkirkbystephen.co.uk

Lockholme (B&B)
48 South Road
Kirkby Stephen
Cumbria CA17 4SN
tel 017683 71321
https://lockholme.co.uk

Old Croft House (Guest house)
Market Street
Kirkby Stephen
Cumbria CA17 4QW
tel 017683 71638
http://theoldcrofthouse.co.uk

Pennine Hotel
Market Square
Kirkby Stephen
Cumbria CA17 4QT
tel 017683 74997/07946 620 212
www.penninehotel.co.uk

Pennine View Park
Station Road
Kirkby Stephen
Cumbria CA17 4SZ
tel 017683 71717
www.pennineviewpark.co.uk

White Gill House (B&B)
Mellbecks
Kirkby Stephen
Cumbria CA17 4AB
tel 017683 72238

Pennine View Park (Camping)
Station Road
Kirkby Stephen
Cumbria CA17 4SZ
tel 017683 71717
www.pennineviewpark.co.uk

Keld

Butt House (B&B)
Keld
North Yorkshire DL11 6LJ
tel 01748 886 374
www.butthousekeld.co.uk

Frith Lodge (B&B)
Keld
North Yorkshire DL11 6EB
tel 01748 886 489
www.frithlodgekeld.co.uk

Greenlands (B&B)
Angram Lane
Keld
North Yorkshire DL11 6DY
tel 01748 886 532
www.greenlandskeld.co.uk

Hoggarths Campsite
Keld
North Yorkshire DL11 6LT
tel 01748 886 335
www.swaledalecamping.co.uk

Keld Bunkhouse Campsite and Yurts
Keld
North Yorkshire DL11 6DZ
tel 01748 886 549
www.keldbunkbarn.com

Keld Lodge (Hotel)
Keld
North Yorkshire DL11 6LL
tel 01748 886 259
www.keldlodge.com

Pry House Farm (B&B; Shepherd's Hut)
Keld
North Yorkshire DL11 6LT
Ttel 01748 886 845
www.upperswaledaleholidays.co.uk

Rukin's Park Lodge (Campsite, tea shop)
Keld
North Yorkshire DL11 6LJ
tel 01748 886 274
www.rukins-keld.co.uk

Swaledale Yurts (Park House)
Keld
North Yorkshire DL11 6DZ
tel 01748 886 159
www.swaledaleyurts.com/campsite

Tan Hill Inn (Pub and bunk rooms)
Reeth
Richmond
North Yorkshire DL11 6ED
tel 01833 533 007
www.tanhillinn.com
Pick-up and drop-off service from Keld

Thwaite

Kearton Country Hotel
Thwaite
North Yorkshire DL11 6DR
tel 01748 886 277
www.keartoncountryhotel.co.uk

Muker

Bridge House (B&B)
Muker
North Yorkshire DL11 6QG
tel 01748 886 461
www.bridgehousemuker.co.uk

Farmers Arms (Country pub)
Muker
North Yorkshire DL11 6QG
tel 01748 886 297
www.farmersarmsmuker.co.uk

242

Muker Village Store (B&B, tea shop)
Muker
North Yorkshire DL11 6QG
tel 01748 886 409

Stoneleigh (B&B)
Muker
North Yorkshire DL11 6QQ
tel 01748 886 375
www.stoneleighcottage.co.uk

Usha Gap Campsite
Long Close House
Muker
North Yorkshire DL11 6DW
tel 01748 886 110
www.ushagap.co.uk

Gunnerside/Low Row

Oxnop Hall (B&B)
Gunnerside
North Yorkshire DL11 6JJ
tel 01748 886 253
www.oxnophall.co.uk

Punch Bowl Inn (Country pub)
Low Row North Yorkshire
tel 0333 7000 779 (Freephone)
www.pbinn.co.uk

Scabba Wath (Bunkbarns and camping)
Low Whita Farm
Low Row, Reeth
North Yorkshire DL11 6NT
tel 01748 884 601
www.lowrowbunkhouses.co.uk/
scabba-wath-campsite

Reeth

Arkleside (B&B)
Reeth
North Yorkshire DL11 6SG
tel 01748 884 200
www.arklesidereeth.co.uk

Black Bull (Country pub)
Reeth
North Yorkshire
tel 01748 884 213
www.theblackbullreeth.co.uk

Burgoyne Hotel
On The Green
Reeth
North Yorkshire DL11 6SN
tel 01748 884 292
www.theburgoyne.co.uk

Cambridge House (B&B)
Arkengarthdale Road
Reeth
North Yorkshire DL11 6QX
tel 01748 884 633
www.cambridgehousereeth.co.uk

Hackney House (B&B)
Bridge Terrace
Reeth
North Yorkshire DL11 6TW
tel 01748 884 302
www.hackneyhousereeth.co.uk

The Manse (B&B)
Reeth
North Yorkshire DL11 6SN
tel 01748 884 136
www.themanseinreeth.co.uk

Orchard Caravan and Camping park
(and camping pods)
Back Lane
Reeth
North Yorkshire DL11 6TT
tel 07397 302 277
www.orchardcaravanpark.com

Springfield House (B&B)
Quaker Close
Reeth
North Yorkshire DL11 6UY

tel 01748 884 634
www.springfield-house.co.uk

Grinton

YHA Grinton Lodge (youth hostel,
camping and camping pods)
Grinton
North Yorkshire DL11 6HS
tel 0345 371 9636
www.yha.org.uk

Marrick

Nun Cote Nook Farm (Camp site)
Marrick
Richmond
North Yorkshire DL11 7LG
tel 01748 884 266
www.nuncotenookcampsite.co.uk

Richmond

Black Lion Hotel
12 Finkle Street
Richmond
North Yorkshire DL10 4QB
tel 01748 826 217
www.blacklionhotelrichmond.co.uk

Buck Inn
Newbiggin
Richmond
North Yorkshire DL10 4DX
tel 01748 517 300
www.thebuckrichmond.co.uk

Castle House (B&B)
9 Castle Hill
Richmond
North Yorkshire DL10 4QP
tel 01748 823 954
www.castlehouserichmond.co.uk

Cordilleras House
11 Hurgill Road
Richmond
North Yorkshire DL10 4AR
tel 01748 824628/07587 150 510
www.cordillerashouse.co.uk

Golden Lion (Pub)
43 Market Place
Richmond
North Yorkshire DL10 4QL
tel 01748 518 648

Frenchgate Guest House (B&B)
66 Frenchgate
Richmond
North Yorkshire DL10 7AG
tel 07889 768 696
www.66frenchgate.co.uk

The Frenchgate Hotel
59–61 Frenchgate
Richmond
North Yorkshire DL10 7AE
tel 01748 822 087
www.thefrenchgate.co.uk

King's Head
Market Place
Richmond
North Yorkshire DL10 4HS
tel 01748 850 220
www.kingsheadrichmond.co.uk

The Old Brewery Guest House
29 The Green
Richmond
North Yorkshire DL10 4RG
tel 01748 822 460
www.oldbreweryguesthouse.com

Pottergate Guest House
4 Pottergate
Richmond
North Yorkshire DL10 4AB

tel 01748 823 826
www.pottergateguesthouse.co.uk

River View (B&B)
Park Wynd
Millgate
Richmond
North Yorkshire DL10 4JS
tel 01748 824 474
www.richmond.org/stayat/riverview

Rosedale Guest House (B&B)
2 Pottergate
Richmond
North Yorkshire DL10 4AB
tel 01748 824 056/07894 726 132
www.richmondbedandbreakfast.co.uk

Stable Cottage (B&B)
6 Nuns Close
Richmond
North Yorkshire DL10 4AF
tel 07794 680 252

Strawberry House (B&B)
49 Maison Dieu
Richmond
North Yorkshire DL10 7AU
tel 01748 850 449
www.strawberryhouserichmond.co.uk

Turf Hotel
Victoria Road
Richmond
North Yorkshire DL10 4DW
tel 01748 829 011
www.turfhotelrichmond.co.uk

Victoria House (B&B)
3 Linden Close
Richmond
North Yorkshire DL10 7AL
tel 01748 824 830

West End Guest House (B&B)
45 Reeth Road
Richmond
North Yorkshire DL10 4EX
tel 01748 824 783
www.stayatwestend.co.uk

Willance House (B&B)
24 Frenchgate
Richmond
North Yorkshire DL10 7AG
tel 01748 824 467
www.willancehouse.com

Colburn, near Richmond

Hilyard Arms
Colburn
Catterick Garrison
North Yorkshire DL9 4PD
tel 01748 832353
https://thehildyardarms.wordpress.com

Brompton-on-Swale

Brompton-on-Swale Bunkbarn,
Richmond Road
Brompton-on-Swale
North Yorkshire
tel 01748 818 326
https://independenthostels.co.uk/
members/bromptononswalebunkbarn

Brompton on Swale Caravan and
Camping Park
Brompton-on-Swale
Richmond
North Yorkshire DL10 7EZ
tel 01748 824 629
www.bromptoncaravanpark.co.uk

Farmers Arms (Country pub)
Gatherley Road
Brompton-on-Swale
Richmond

North Yorkshire DL10 7HZ
tel 01748 818 062

Catterick/Catterick Bridge

Premier Inn Catterick Garrison,
(3km/2miles S of Richmond bridge)
Prince Gate
Richmond Road
Catterick
North Yorkshire DL9 3BA
tel 0871 527 9568 (national rate
applies)
www.premierinn.com

St Giles Farm (B&B)
Catterick Bridge
North Yorkshire DL10 7PH
tel 01748 811 372
www.coast2coast.co.uk/stgilesfarm

Scorton

The Farmers Arms
The Village Green Northside
Scorton
North Yorkshire DL10 6DW
tel 01748 812 533

Scorton Lodge (B&B)
Hospital Road
Scorton
North Yorkshire DL10 6DX
tel 01748 811 607

Danby Wiske

Ashfield House (B&B)
Danby Wiske
North Yorkshire DL7 0NH
tel 01609 771 628

Church Holme Camping
Mounstrall Lane
Danby Wiske
North Yorkshire DL7 0LY
tel 01609 600 618 or 07789 630 716
https://danbywiskecamping.co.uk

Inglenook (B&B)
Danby Wiske
North Yorkshire DL7 0NQ
tel 07957 836 215
www.inglenookbnb.co.uk

The Old School (B&B)
Danby Wiske
North Yorkshire DL7 0NQ
tel 01609 774 227
www.coast2coast.co.uk/theoldschool

Rawcar Farm (B&B)
Streetlam
Danby Wiske
North Yorkshire DL7 0AL
tel 01325 378 297
www.rawcar.co.uk

White Swan (Country pub)
Danby Wiske
North Yorkshire DL7 0NQ
tel 01609 775 131
www.thewhiteswandanbywiske.co.uk

Lovesome Hill

Lovesome Hill Farm (B&B)
Lovesome Hill
Northallerton
North Yorkshire DL6 2PB
tel 01609 772 311
www.lovesomehillfarm.co.uk

Northallerton

Allerton Court Hotel
Northallerton
North Yorkshire DL6 2XF

tel 01609 780 525
www.allertoncourthotel.co.uk

Ingleby Cross

Blue Bell Inn
Ingleby Cross
North Yorkshire DL6 3NF
tel 01609 882 272
www.thebluebellinninglebycross.co.uk

Elstavale (B&B)
Ingleby Arncliffe
North Yorkshire DL6 3LZ
tel 01609 882302
www.elstavale.co.uk

Ingleby House Farm (B&B)
Ingleby Arncliffe
North Yorkshire DL6 3LN
tel 01609 882 500 07745 238 406
www.inglebyhousefarm.co.uk

Park House (Guest house)
Ingleby Cross
North Yorkshire DL6 3PE
tel 01609 882 899
www.parkhousecountryguesthouse.com

Somerset House Farm (B&B)
Ingleby Cross
Ingleby Arncliffe
North Yorkshire DL6 3JP
tel 01609 882 555

Swan House (B&B)
Trenholme Bar
North Yorkshire DL6 3JY
tel 01642 700 555 07930 855 205
www.swanhousebedandbreakfast.com

Osmotherley

Cote Ghyll Caravan & Camping Park
Osmotherley
Northallerton
North Yorkshire DL6 3AH

tel 01609 883 425
www.coteghyll.com

Golden Lion (Inn)
6 West End
Osmotherley
North Yorkshire DL6 3AA
tel 01609 883 526
www.goldenlionosmotherley.co.uk

Mount Bank Farm (B&B)
Ellerbeck (2km W of Osmotherly)
Northallerton
North Yorkshire DL6 2TE
tel 07801 940 922
www.mountbankfarm.co.uk

Queen Catherine Hotel
7 West End
Osmotherley
North Yorkshire DL6 3AG
tel 01609 883 209
www.queencatherinehotel.co.uk

Three Tuns (Hotel and restaurant)
9 South End
Osmotherley
Northallerton
North Yorkshire DL6 3BN
tel 01609 883 301
www.threetunsrestaurant.co.uk

Vane House (B&B)
11a North End
Osmotherley
Northallerton DL6 3BA
tel 01609 883 406/07891 789 766
www.vanehouse.co.uk

YHA Osmotherly (Hostel and camping)
Cote Ghyll Mill
Osmotherly
North Yorkshire DL6 3AH
tel 0345 260 2870
www.yha.org.uk

Swainby

Blacksmiths Arms (Country pub)
2 Black Horse Lane
Swainby
Northallerton
North Yorkshire DL6 3EW
tel 01642 700 303
www.blacksmithsarms.com

Faceby

Four Wynds (B&B)
Whorl Hill
Faceby
Middlesbrough
Cleveland TS9 7BZ
tel 01642 701 315
www.fourwynds.co.uk

Clay Bank Top and Chop Gate

Beak Hills Farm (B&B and camping)
Chop Gate
Middlesbrough TS9 7JJ
tel 01642 778 371
www.beakhillsfarm.co.uk

Buck Inn
Chop Gate
North Yorkshire TS9 7JL
tel 01642 778 334
www.the-buck-inn.co.uk

Forge House (B&B)
Chop Gate
Cleveland TS9 7JL
tel 01642 778 166
www.coast2coast.co.uk/forgehouse

Maltkiln House (B&B)
Urra
Bilsdale
North Yorkshire TS9 7HZ
tel 01642 778 216
www.maltkilnhouse.co.uk

Newlands House (B&B)
Great Broughton
North Yorkshire TS9 7ER
tel 01642 712 619
www.newlandshouse.co.uk

Lordstones Country Park (campsite with
camping pods)
Carlton Bank
Chop Gate
North Yorkshire TS9 7JH
tel 01642 778 482
www.lordstones.com

Blakey

Lion Inn
Blakey Ridge
Kirkbymoorside
North Yorkshire YO62 7LQ
tel 01751 417 320
www.lionblakey.co.uk

Pickering

Heygate Farm (Farm B&B)
Haygate Bank
Rosedale Abbey
Pickering
North Yorkshire YO18 8RB
tel 01751 417355

Sevenford House (B&B)
Rosedale Abbey
Pickering
North Yorkshire YO18 8SE
tel 01751 417 283
www.sevenford.com

Glaisdale

Arncliffe Arms (Pub)
No 1 Arncliffe Terrace
Glaisdale
Whitby
North Yorkshire YO21 2QL

tel 01947 897 555
www.arncliffearms.com

Red House Farm (B&B)
Glaisdale
North Yorkshire YO21 2PZ
tel 01947 897242
www.redhousefarm.com

Station House (B&B)
Glaisdale
North Yorkshire YO21 2QL
tel 01947 897 409/07790 590 274
www.beggarsbridge.co.uk

Egton Bridge

Broom House (B&B)
Broom House Lane
Egton Bridge
North Yorkshire YO21 1XD
tel 07423 636 783
www.broom-house.co.uk

Horseshoe Hotel
Egton Bridge
North Yorkshire YO21 1XE
tel 01947 895 245
www.thehorseshoehotel.co.uk

The Old Mill (B&B)
Broom House Lane
Egton Bridge
North Yorkshire YO21 1UZ
tel 01947 895 351
www.theoldmillegtonbridge.com

Grosmont

The Geall Gallery (B&B)
Front Street
Grosmont
North Yorkshire YO22 5QE
tel 07768 743 633
www.chrisgeall.com

Grosmont House (B&B)
Office Row
Grosmont
North Yorkshire YO22 5PE
tel 01947 895 699
http://grosmonthouse.co.uk

Priory Farm (campsite)
Egton Bank
Grosmont
North Yorkshire YO22 5QG
tel 01947 895 324
https://prioryfarmwhitby.wordpress.com

Station Tavern (B&B)
Grosmont
North Yorkshire YO22 5PA
tel 01947 895 060
www.stationtavern-grosmont.co.uk

Littlebeck

Intake Farm (B&B)
Littlebeck
North Yorkshire YO22 5HA
tel 01947 810 273
www.intakefarm.com

Hawsker

Long Leas Farm (B&B)
Hawsker
North Yorkshire YO22 4LA
tel 01947 603 790/07966 109 069
www.swallowcottages.co.uk

York House (camping and camping pods)
Hawsker
North Yorkshire YO22 4LW
tel 01947 880 354
https://yorkhousecaravanpark.co.uk

Robin Hood's Bay and Fylingthorpe

Aldersyde (B&B)
Mount Pleasant South
Robin Hoods Bay
North Yorkshire YO22 4RQ
tel 01947 880 689
www.aldersyde-robinhoodsbay.co.uk

Bay Hotel
The Dock
Robin Hood's Bay
North Yorkshire YO22 4SJ
tel 01947 880 278
www.bayhotel.info

Birtley House (B&B)
Station Road
Robin Hood's Bay
North Yorkshire YO22 4RL
tel 01947 880566
www.birtleyhousebedandbreakfast.com

Bottom House Farm (B&B)
Robin Hood's Bay
North Yorkshire YO22 4PH
tel 01947 880 754
www.bottomhouse.co.uk

Clarence Dene (B&B)
Station Road
Robin Hood's Bay
North Yorkshire YO22 4RL
tel 01947 880 478
https://clarencedene.com

Fernleigh (B&B)
Mount Pleasant South
Robin Hood's Bay
North Yorkshire YO22 4RQ
tel 01947 880 523
www.fernleigh-robin-hoods-bay.co.uk

Grosvenor Hotel
Station Road
Robin Hood's Bay
North Yorkshire YO22 4RA
tel 01947 880 320
www.thegrosvenor.info

Hooks House Farm (camping)
Robin Hood's Bay
North Yorkshire YO22 4PE
tel 01947 880 283
www.hookshousefarm.co.uk

Lee-Side (B&B)
Mount Pleasant South
Robin Hood's Bay
North Yorkshire YO22 4RQ
tel 01947 881 143
https://lee-side.co.uk

Lynnfield House (B&B)
Station Road
Robin Hood's Bay
North Yorkshire YO22 4RL
tel 07919 412 075
https://lynnfieldhouse.co.uk

Manning Tree (B&B)
Mount Pleasant North
Robin Hood's Bay
North Yorkshire YO22 4RE
tel 01947 881042
www.manningtreebnb.co.uk

Raven House (B&B)
Victoria Terrace
Robin Hood's Bay
North Yorkshire YO22 4RJ
tel 01947 880 444
www.ravenhouse.rhbay.co.uk

Saxon Villa (B&B)
Thorpe Lane
Robin Hood's Bay
North Yorkshire YO22 4TH

tel 01947 880 812
https://saxonvilla.co.uk

Skerry Hall Farm (B&B)
Sledgates
Robin Hood's Bay
North Yorkshire YO22 4PP
tel 01947 881 156
www.skerryhallfarm.co.uk

Smugglers (B&B and bistro)
The Dock
Robin Hood's Bay
North Yorkshire YO22 4SJ
tel 01947 880 099
https://boathouserhb.co.uk

Thorpe Green House
3 Sledgates
Fylingthorpe
North Yorkshire YO22 4TZ
tel 01947 880 339/07530 694 370
www.thorpegreen.co.uk

Thorpe Hall
Middlewood Lane
Flylingthorpe
North Yorkshire YO22 4TT
tel 01947 880 667
http://www.thorpe-hall.co.uk

Victoria Hotel
Station Road
Robin Hood's Bay
North Yorkshire YO22 4RL
tel 01947 880 205
www.victoriarhb.com

The Villa (B&B)
Station Road
Robin Hood's Bay
North Yorkshire YO22 4RA
tel 01947 881 043/07898 388 579
www.thevillarhb.co.uk

APPENDIX C
Further reading

Thousands of books have been written about the Lake District, the Yorkshire Dales and the North York Moors, covering numerous topics. Knowing something about an area before you go, or being able to follow up on discoveries made during the trip, will help you get the most out of experience. Here is a selection to choose from.

Books

Baddeley, MJB. *Thorough Guide to the English Lake District* (Dulau & Co, 1880–1913)

Barrowclough, David. *Prehistoric Cumbria* (The History Press, 2010)

Black's Picturesque Guide to the English Lakes (Adam and Charles Black, 1841–1888)

Brumhead, Derek. *Geology Explained in the Yorkshire Dales and on the Yorkshire Coast* (David and Charles, 1979)

Fraser, Maxwell. *Companion into Lakeland* (Methuen, 3rd edn 1943)

Hanson, Neil. *Walking through Eden* (Pavilion Books Limited, 1990)

Harding, DW. *The Iron Age in Northern Britain* (Routledge, 2004)

Ingleby, Joan and Hartley, Marie. *The Old Hand-knitters of the Dales* (Dalesman Publishing, 1991)

Lefebure, Molly. *Cumbrian Discovery* (Victor Gollancz, 1977) *The English Lake District* (BT Batsford, 1964)

Marshall, JD. *Portrait of Cumbria* (Robert Hale, 1981)

Mee, Arthur. *The Lake Counties: Cumberland and Westmorland* (Hodder and Stoughton, 1937)

Monbiot, George. *Feral* (Allen Lane, 2013)

Prosser, Robert. *Geology Explained in the Lake District* (David and Charles, 1977)

Raistrick, Arthur and Jennings, Bernard. *A History of Lead Mining in the Pennines* (Longmans, Green & Co, 1965)

Rhea, Nicholas. *The North York Moors* (Robert Hale, 1985)

Raistrick, Arthur (ed) *North York Moors National Park*, National Park Guide No 4 (HMSO, 1966)

Riley, W. *The Yorkshire Pennines of the North-West* (Herbert Jenkins,1934)

Scott, Harry J. *Portrait of Yorkshire* (Robert Hale, 1965)

Singleton, Frank. *The English Lakes* (BT Batsford, 1954)

Symonds, HH. *Walking in the Lake District* (W&R Chambers, 1947)

Turnbull, P and Walsh, D. 'A prehistoric ritual sequence at Oddendale, near Shap'. *Transactions of the Cumberland and Westmorland Antiquarian and Archaeological Society* (1997: 11–44)

Wainwright, A. *A Coast to Coast Walk* (Westmorland Gazette, 1973, Frances Lincoln, 2003)

Walton, John K, and Wood, Jason (eds). *The Making of a Cultural Landscape* (Ashgate, 2013)

Waugh, Edwin. *Rambles in Lake Country* (John Heywood, c1898)

Wordsworth, Dorothy. *Illustrated Lakeland Journals* (Collins, 1987)

Websites
Transactions of the Cumberland and Westmorland Antiquarian and Archaeological Society www.cumbriapast.com

SIMILAR CHALLENGES
YOU MIGHT ALSO BE INTERESTED IN...

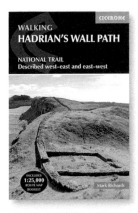

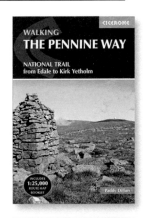

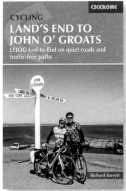

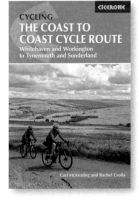

visit **www.cicerone.co.uk** for more detail
and our full range of guidebooks

LISTING OF CICERONE UK GUIDES

For full information on all our
guides, books and eBooks,
visit our website:
www.cicerone.co.uk

CICERONE

Trust Cicerone to guide your next adventure,
wherever it may be around the world...

Discover guides for hiking, mountain walking, backpacking,
trekking, trail running, cycling and mountain biking, ski touring,
climbing and scrambling in Britain, Europe and worldwide.

Connect with Cicerone online and find inspiration.

- buy books and ebooks
- articles, advice and trip reports
- podcasts and live events
- GPX files and updates
- regular newsletter

cicerone.co.uk

Aerial view of Ennerdale and its lake from the summit of Angler's Crag (Stage 2)

THE COAST TO COAST WALK

The Coast to Coast Walk is an iconic 188 mile (302km) long-distance walk which crosses England from St Bees in Cumbria to Robin Hood's Bay in Yorkshire, traversing three National Parks as it goes. Usually tackled in a two-week stretch, occasionally over rugged and remote terrain, it is still within the reach of well-prepared novice backpackers.

Contents and using this guide

This booklet of Ordnance Survey 1:25,000 Explorer maps has been designed for convenient use on the trail and includes:

- a key to map pages (page 2–3) showing where to find the maps for each stage.
- the full line of the walk with some variant sections
- an extract from the OS Explorer map legend (pages 99–101).

The companion guidebook, *The Coast to Coast Walk*, describes the full route from west to east (with summary route description east to west), alongside all that you need to plan a successful trip and lots of information about local history, geography and wildlife, and places to stay.

© Cicerone Press 2017
ISBN-13: 978 1 85284 926 9
Reprinted 2020, 2023 (with updates), 2021
Photos © Terry Marsh 2017

© Crown copyright 2017
OS PU100012932

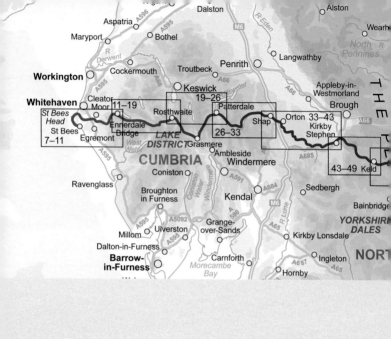

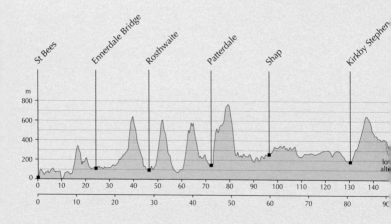

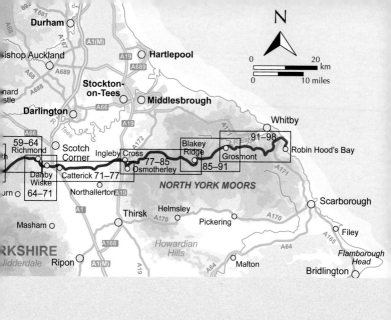

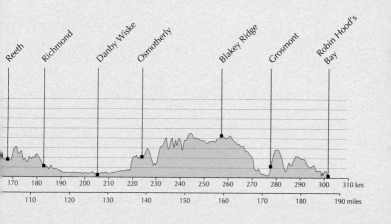

Reeth · Richmond · Danby Wiske · Osmotherly · Blakey Ridge · Grosmont · Robin Hood's Bay

59–64 Richmond
64–71 Danby Wiske
71–77 Catterick
77–85 Osmotherley
85–91
91–98

River Swale

THE COAST TO COAST WALK

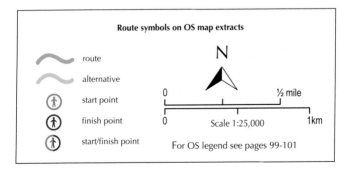

Route symbols on OS map extracts

route

alternative

start point

finish point

start/finish point

N

0   ½ mile

0   Scale 1:25,000   1km

For OS legend see pages 99-101

St Bees Head

St Bees Head

Fairladies Farm

Out Rigg

Quarries (dis)

B 5345

Deep

Pow Beck

Abbey Wood

ST BEES CP

High House

Peartham House

Quarry (dis)

B 5345

Wood Lane

Sch

Sch

Rottington Hall

Rottington

Rottington Cottages

FBs

Christy Meadow

Seabarrow

Abbey Farm

Priory (rems of)

12

St Bees

Sch

Eaglesfield

Peckmill

CH

Hotel

Gutter Foot

Wks

PO

FB

IRB Sta

Peckmill

FBs

Mean High Water

Mean Low Water

P

PC

P

PC

-38

St Bees to Ennerdale Bridge

Start   St Bees
Finish   Ennerdale Bridge
Distance 15 miles (23.9km)
Time   8hr

Pattering Holes

Sheepfold

Tomlin

South Head

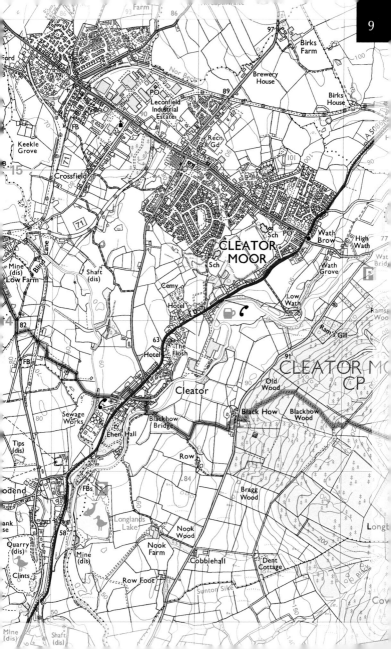

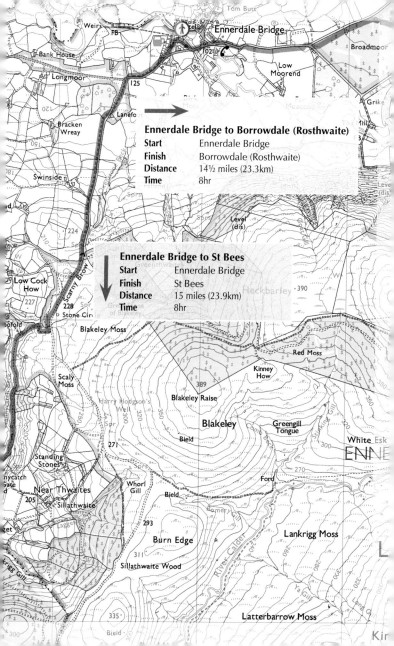

Ennerdale Bridge to Borrowdale (Rosthwaite)

Start	Ennerdale Bridge
Finish	Borrowdale (Rosthwaite)
Distance	14½ miles (23.3km)
Time	8hr

Ennerdale Bridge to St Bees

Start	Ennerdale Bridge
Finish	St Bees
Distance	15 miles (23.9km)
Time	8hr

Croftfoot

Howside

Whins

Woodfoot

How Hall
Farm

Ford

Alternative route

FB

Broadmoor

Rothery Sike

Spr

Grike

P

The Mill

Weir

Weir

FB

Bleach
Green
Cottages

Spr

Robin Hood
Chair

Level
(dis)

Crag Farm
House

Anglers Crag

Revelin Crag

Waterfall

Levels
(dis)

Crag Fell

523

522

Bield

Cairn 488

451

Level
(dis)

Grike

Min
(dis)

Bield

Sheepfold

Black
Pots

Shaking Gill

Buck Hole

White Esk

ENNERDALE AND KINNISIDE CP

Whoap

Sheepfold Bield

Gill Beck
Sheepfolds

Steel Brow
Floutern Crag
Level (dis)

Waterfall

Herdus

Cairn

Cairn

Great Borne

616

Shelter Cairn

Shelter Cairn

Cairn

Scaw Well

n Farm

Sheepfold

Rake Beck

Scaw

rd

16

Brown How

Sheepfold

Sheepfold

Bowness

Bowness Knot

333

Bowness Plantation

Sheepfold

Smithy Beck

Settlement

dale Water

273

Latterbar

Nine Becks

Char Dub

Level (dis)

Boat How

363

The Side

Stair Knott

Boathow Crag

Mart Knott

FBs

Sail Hills

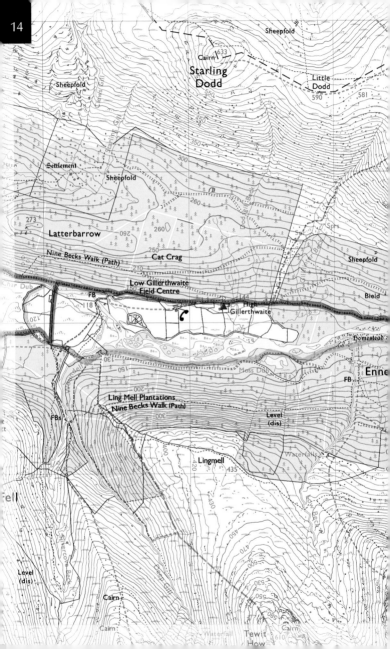

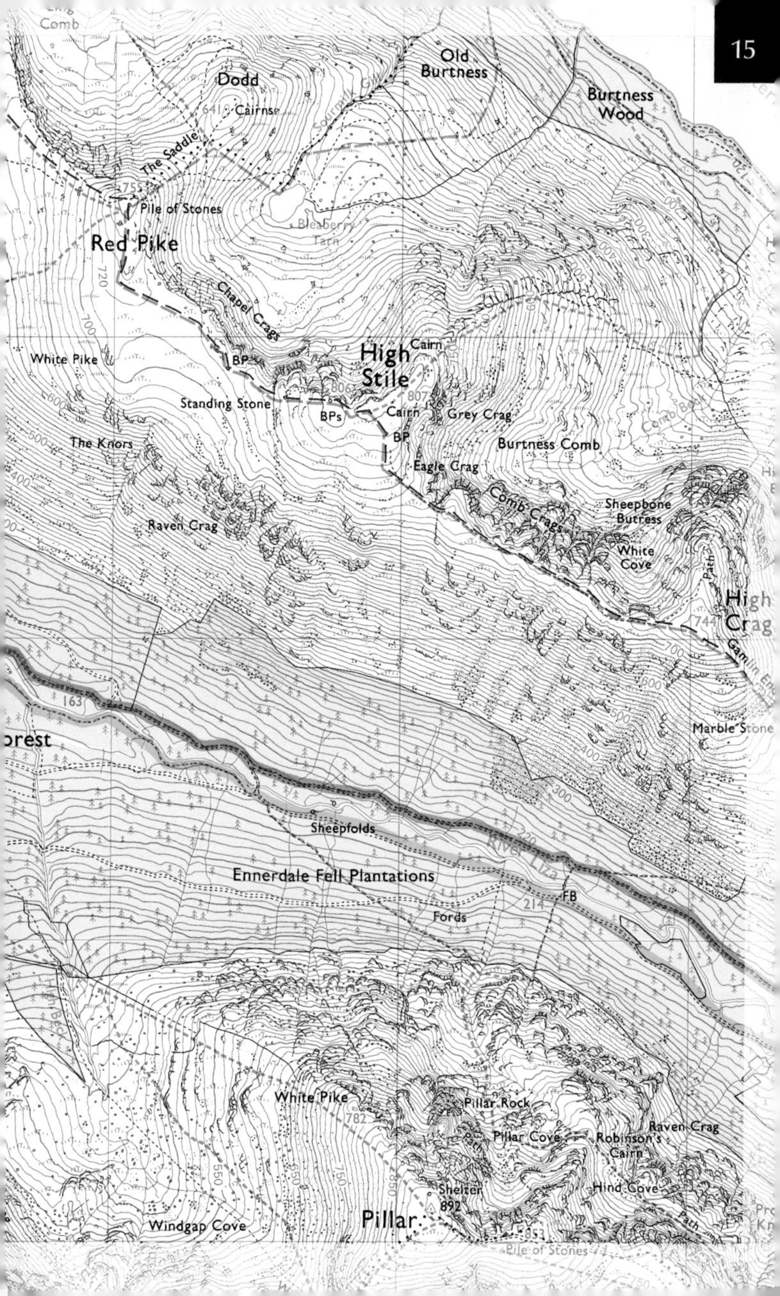

Comb

Dodd

Old Burtness

Burtness Wood

Cairns

The Saddle

755

Pile of Stones

Blesberry Tarn

Red Pike

720

Chapel Crag

High Stile

Cairn

White Pike

BP

807

Cairn

Grey Crag

Standing Stone

BPs

Cairn

Burtness Comb

The Knots

BP

Eagle Crag

Sheepbone Butfress

Raven Crag

Comb Crag

White Cove

High Crag

744

Path

163

Gamlin End

Marble Stone

orest

RIVER LIZA

Sheepfolds

Ennerdale Fell Plantations

Fords

214

FB

White Pike

782

Pillar Rock

Pillar Cove

Robinson's Cairn

Raven Crag

Shelter

892

Hind Cove

Path

Windgap Cove

Pillar

Pile of Stones

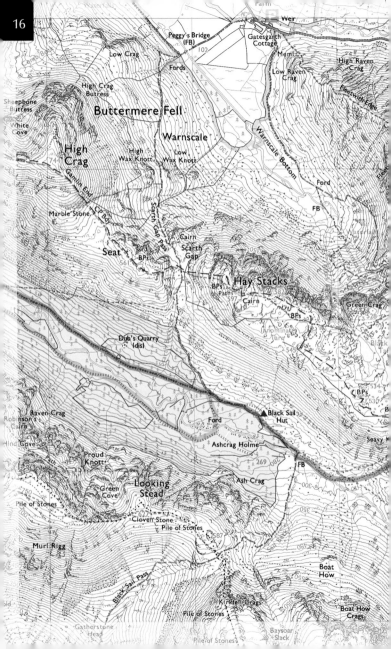

Weir

Peggy's Bridge
(FB)
Gatesgarth
Cottage

Low Crag

Meml

High Raven
Crag

Fords

102

Low Raven
Crag

Fleetwith Edge

High Crag
Butress

Sheepbone
Butress

Buttermere Fell

White
Cove

Warnscale

Warnscale Bottom

**High
Crag**

High
Wax Knott

Low
Wax Knott

Ford

FB

Gamlin End

CP Boy

Marble Stone

Scarth Gap Pass

Cairn

Seat

Scarth
Gap

561

BPs

BPs
Path

Hay Stacks

Green Crag

528

Cairn

BPs

Dub's Quarry
(dis)

Innominate
Tarn

544

BPs
530

Raven Crag

Robinson's
Cairn

Ford

Black Sail
Hut

Seavy K

Hind Cove

Proud
Knott

Ashcrag Holme

269

FB

Green
Cove

**Looking
Stead**

Ash Crag

Pile of Stones

587

Clovett Stone
Pile of Stones

Murl Rigg

Boat
How

Black Sail Pass

Pile of Stones

Kirk Fell Crags
Pile of Stones

Boat How
Crags

Gatherstone
Head

Baysoar
Slack

Pile of Stones

Gatesgarthdale Beck

156

Moss Crag

Buckstone Hows

Low Crag

Maiden Stone

Honister Crag

Yewcrag Quarries (dis)

Black Star

Wet Knotts

Levels (dis)

550

with Pike

Honister Quarries (dis)

Quarry (dis)

Stang How

Honister Pass

Fox Fold

Hopper Quarry (Slate)

Bell Crags

331

Dismantled Tramway (Path)

Slate Mine

Wks

Honister Hause

Seatoller Fell

Level (dis)

Dubs Quarry (disused)

Drum House

Fleetwith

Little Round How

Sheepfold

Dubs Bottom

Great Round How

Waterfall

Mines (dis)

BPs

Grey Knotts

Raven Crag

398

Level (dis)

Seathwaite Slabs

Southmilk Gill

BPs

Piles of Stones

Gillercomb

Hanging Stone

Cairn

715

BPs

Brandreth

Brin Crag

Moses' Trod

Gillercomb Head

BPs

Base Brown

Cairn

646

Strawberry Gill

Fawn Crag

Tongue

BPs

Blackmoor Pols

610

BP

Greenhow

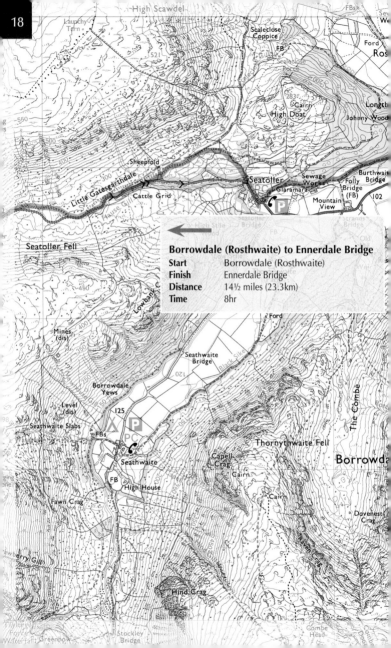

Borrowdale (Rosthwaite) to Ennerdale Bridge

Start	Borrowdale (Rosthwaite)
Finish	Ennerdale Bridge
Distance	14½ miles (23.3km)
Time	8hr

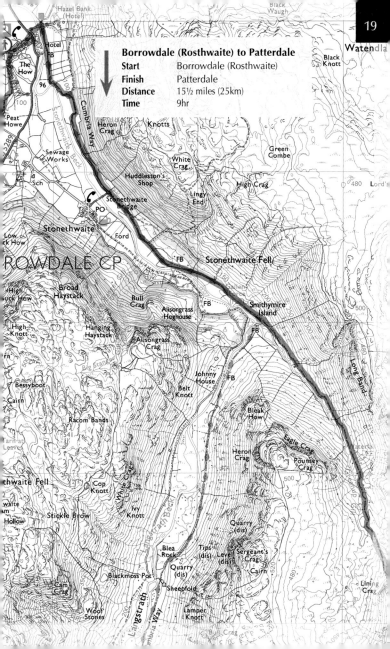

Borrowdale (Rosthwaite) to Patterdale

Start	Borrowdale (Rosthwaite)
Finish	Patterdale
Distance	15½ miles (25km)
Time	9hr

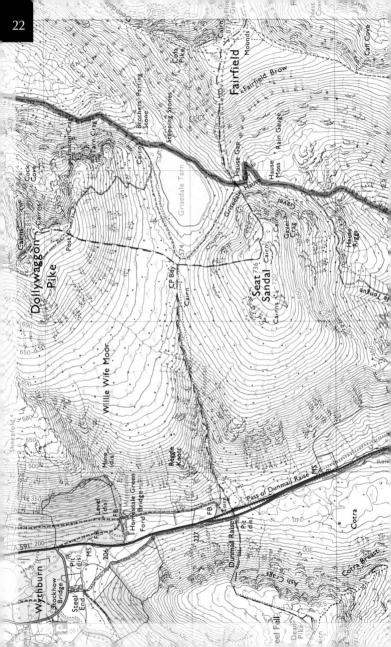

Grasmere
Heron Pike
Helm Crag
Easedale
Stone Arthur
Riggs Crags
Stone Cove
Blind Cove
Butter Crag
Brackenwife Knotts
Rowan's Ground
Cairn
(Cairn)
Level (dis)
Ford
Fords
FB
FBs
High Broadrayne
Mill Bridge
Low Mill Bridge
Winterseeds
Knott Houses Farm
Travellers Rest
Pit (dis)
River Rothay
Cemy
Butharlyp Howe
Goody Bridge
Easedale Road
Thorny How
Underhelm
Lancrigg
Easedale Beck
New Bridge
James's Quarry (disused)
Brimmer Head Farm
Quarries (disused)
Jackdaw Crag
White Crag
High Raven Crag
Low Raven Crag
Ghyll Foot
Helmside
Town Head
MS
Dam
Bracken Hause
Gibson Knott
Bield
Meml
Hotel
A591
B5287
PC
Great Tongue
Tongue Gill
700
650
620
600
550
460
400
360
320
270
190
150
135
151
200
280
90
89
106
621
614
612
570
500
450
380
405
350
300

24

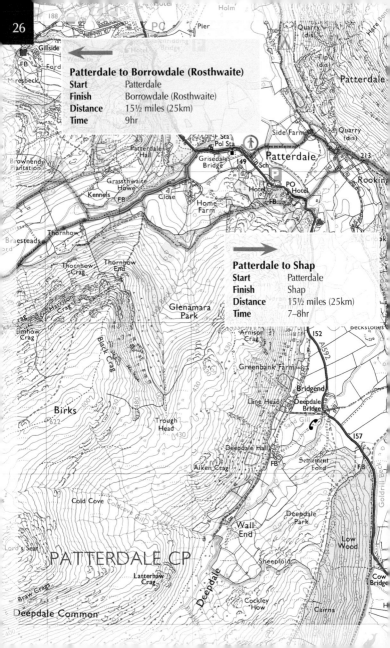

Patterdale to Borrowdale (Rosthwaite)

Start	Patterdale
Finish	Borrowdale (Rosthwaite)
Distance	15½ miles (25km)
Time	9hr

Patterdale to Shap

Start	Patterdale
Finish	Shap
Distance	15½ miles (25km)
Time	7–8hr

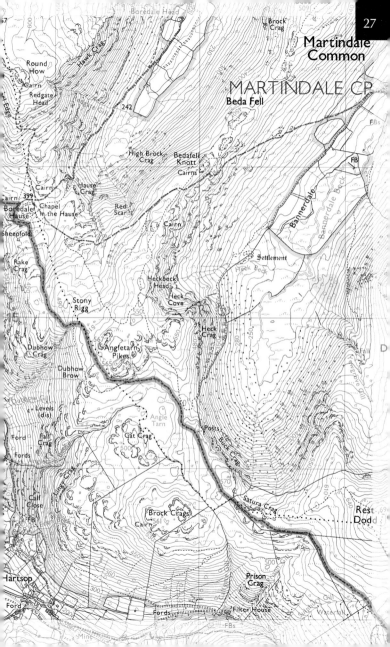

Heck Crag

Deer Forest

Sheepfold

Posts

Buck Crag

Satura Crag

Rest Dodd

Cairns

696

515

Kidsty Gill

ock Crags

61

Crags

Prison Crag

Filter House

FBs

Hayeswater Gill

ords

Sulphury Gill

Waterfall

Wall Gill

Rampsgill H

The Knott

739

Cairn

792

Cairn

Head of Rigg ind

Straits of Riggindale

Twopenny Crag

nes (s)

Adits

FB

Hayeswater

Short St

Gray Crag

698

Cairn

699

Pasture Bottom

Sheepfold

Cairn

High Street

Raven Crag

Cairn

828

Cairn

Racecourse Hill

Redcrag Tarn

Raven Howe

Long Grain

Bason Crag

Whelter Bottom

Bent Howe

Cairn

Low Raise

Whelter Crags

Bield

Whelter Knotts

High Raise

Bield

Cairns
802

East Grain

Waterfall

Hanging Stones

Birks Crag

Castle Crag

Waterfall

Scar

Waterfall

Lady's Seat

Kidsty Pike

Black Crag

Ford

Kidsty Howes

Band End

Flakehowe Crag

Gate Crag

Bowderthwaite Bridge

FBs

Sheepfold

Riggindale Beck

FB

Rigindale Crag

Rigindale

Hugh's Cave

Bield

Eagle Crag

Heron Crag

Swine Crag

Caspel Gate

Rough Crag

Dudderwick

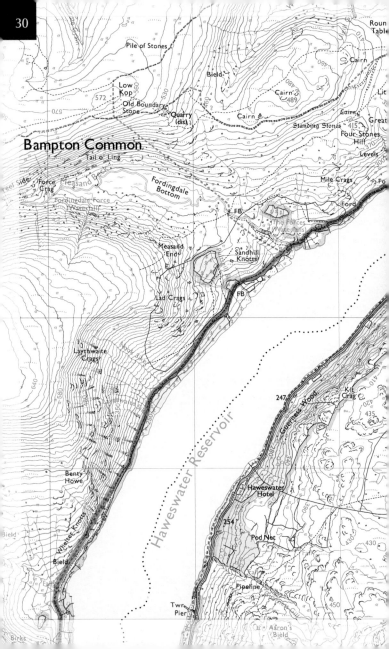

Roun
Table

Pile of Stones

Bield

Cairn

Lit

Low
Kop

560

Cairn
489

Standing Stones

415

Great

Old Boundary
Stone

550

Quarry
(dis)

Cairn

Four Stones
Hill

572

570

Cairn

Levels

Bampton Common

Tail o' Ling

Mile Crags

Fo

Steel Side

Force
Crag

Measand Beck

Fordingdale
Bottom

Ford

Fordingdale Force
(Waterfall)

FB

The Forces
(Waterfalls)

Measand
End

Sandhill
Knotts

Lad Crags

FB

Laythwaite
Crags

640

580

350

Guerness Wood

247

Kit
Crag

420

435

Haweswater Reservoir

Benty
Howe

Haweswater
Hotel

Whelter Knotts

254

Pod Net

430

Bield

450

Birks

Pipeline

Twr
Pier

Aaron's
Bield

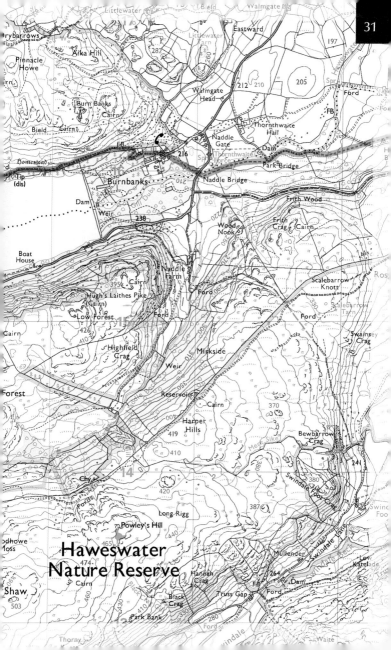

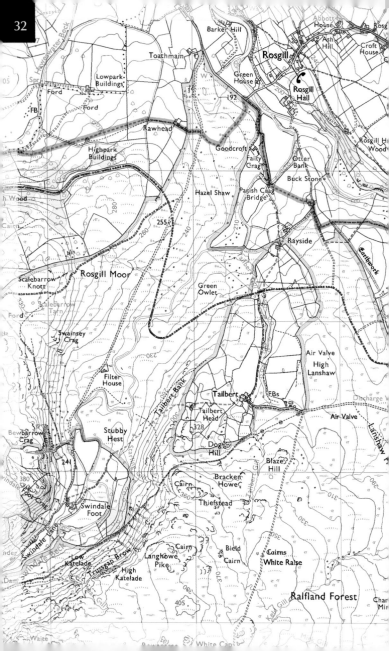

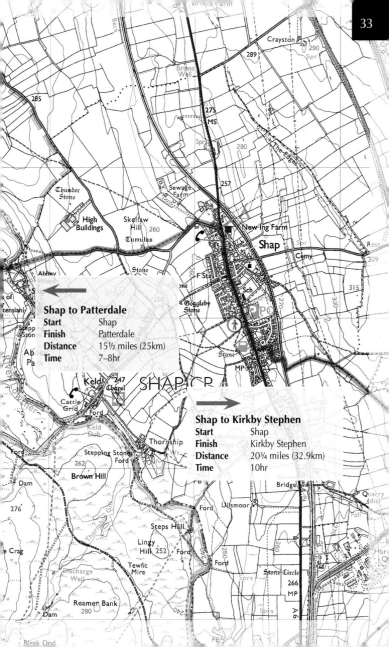

Shap to Patterdale

Start	Shap
Finish	Patterdale
Distance	15½ miles (25km)
Time	7–8hr

Shap to Kirkby Stephen

Start	Shap
Finish	Kirkby Stephen
Distance	20¾ miles (32.9km)
Time	10hr

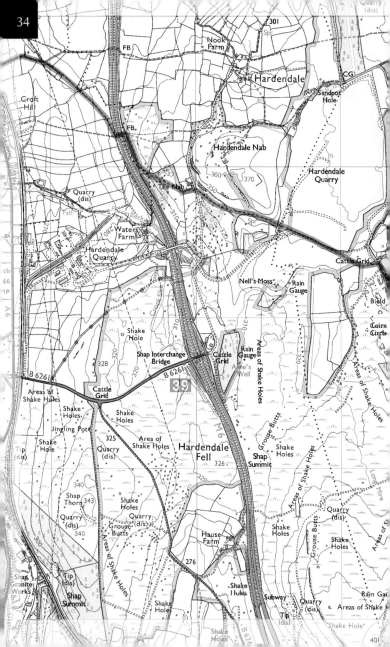

Cairns
High Pike
Cairn

Cairn
Great Asby Scar
National Nature Reserve

Cairn

Cairn

Cairn
Castle Folds
Settlement

412
Cairn

Cairn

Little
Kinmond

Cairn

Great
Kinmor

Dales High Way

Mitch
Sto

Sheepfold

Sunbiggin
Farm

Stony
Head

390

Sunbiggin

350

Raisbeck
Wood
320

Quarries
(dis)

Shake Hole

Quarry
(dis)
280

275

263

Spr

270

260

Acres

Keilsike
Well

275

270

250

Ford

Ingmoor
Moss

257

260

261

250

Tarn Moor

Raisbeck

240

Grimes
Moor

249

Grimesmoor
House

Grimesmoor
Bridge

Tarn Sike

Cattle Grid

68

Pinfold Bridge

255

Quarry
(dis)

Shake Hole

apestone
Bridge

Holme House

257

Kelleth Rigg

Sheep Dip

Cowdale Slack

Cairn

Cairn

Grange Scar

Asket Dub

Cattle Grid

Little Asby

St Leonard's Chapel (remains of

Earthwork

Sheepfold

323

Middle Busk

Lousy Brow

356

Little Asby Scar

308

Howes Well

Spear Pots

Cairn

339

Armaside Wood

Sheepfold

Seavy Dub

Mazon Wath

266

247

Cattle Grid

250

Ford

Fell Head

271

271

260

Sunbiggin Tarn

273

280

290

300

310

Black Rayseat

Rayseat

288

Grouse Butts

Mask Hill

Long Cairn

Rayseat Pike

Rayseat Sike

279

Great Ew

365

301

Ford

Grouse Butts

BS

Cattle Grid

Ewefell Mire

309

Resr

BS

284

Ravenstonedale Moor

Dales High Way

293

301

Cairn

Brackenber

Tip (dis)

Back Dub

Inta

Hard Rigg

Gracemoor

Spr

Riggs

Tunnel

206

Oxenbrow Wood

Sheepfold

BS

FB
Ford

Oxen Brow

244

198

Chapel Well

Beck Lane

240

Mill Banks

Smardale Viaduct

Smardale
220

Smardale Hall

School Lane

Smardale
224

235

236

Reservoir

Hazel Gill

Demesne Wood

Beck Wood

Flat

Smardale Demesne

Settlement

Tom Bank

Smardale Gill
National
Nature Reserve

Smardale Intake

WAITBY CP

Crag
Wood

Settlement

Witches
Stride

Pillow Mounds

Sheepfold

Limekiln
Hill

277

Little
Whitber

Gre.
Whitt

Smardale Fell

Sheepfolds
Near Black
Hill

Waitby Common

362

Tips
(dis)

Sheepfolds

The Riggs

Burnt Bottom

Crawl Rigg

Sheepfolds

315

Pillow Mounds

Wether Hill

Wyack Well
(Pond)

Quarries
(dis)

298

Sheepfold
Jervis Cross

Lingy
Intake

340

350

Slape Crag

Ash Fell Road

Sheepfold

Thorny
Pot Hole

our Hill

220

Rasett Hole

Waitby Scar

Shooting
Butts

High
Wood

BS

377
Tumulus

Rasett Hill

350

Quarry
(dis)
344

Ash Fell

KIRKBY STE

Quarries
(dis)

346

Wether Hill

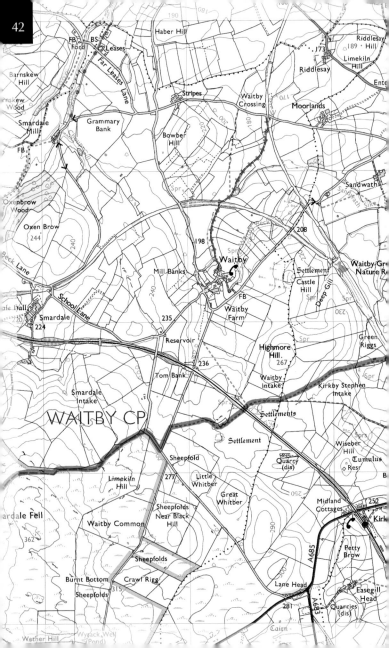

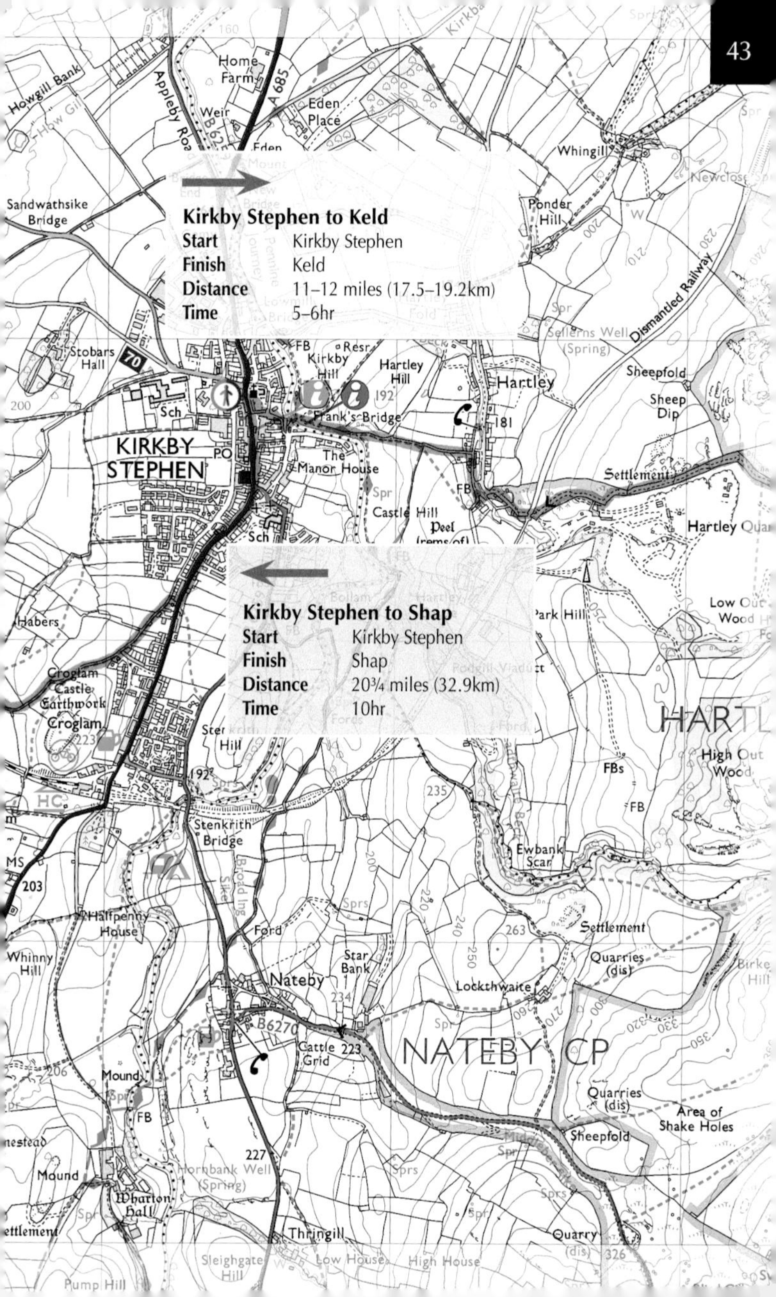

Kirkby Stephen to Keld

Start	Kirkby Stephen
Finish	Keld
Distance	11–12 miles (17.5–19.2km)
Time	5–6hr

Kirkby Stephen to Shap

Start	Kirkby Stephen
Finish	Shap
Distance	20¾ miles (32.9km)
Time	10hr

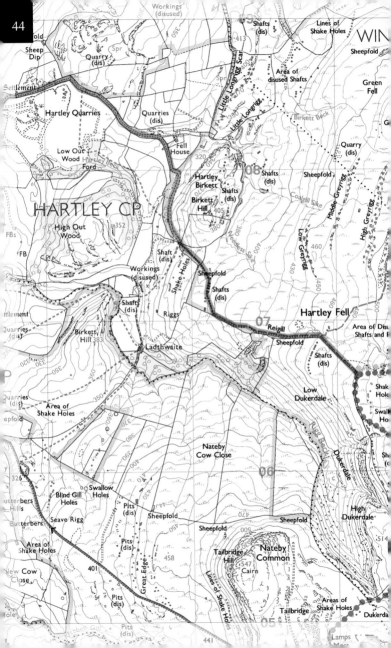

Workings (disused)

Shafts (dis)

Lines of Shake Holes

WIN

Sheepfold

Sheep Dip

Quarry (dis)

Spr

Settlement

Hartley Quarries

Quarries (dis)

Fell House

Low Out Wood

Hartley Beck Ford

Little Longrigg Scar

Little Longrigg

Birkett Beck

Area of disused Shafts

Green Fell

G

Quarry (dis)

Shafts (dis)

Sheepfold

Coalgill Sike

HARTLEY CP

High Out Wood

352

Hartley Birkett

Birkett Hill

405

Shafts (dis)

Middle Greyrigg

High Greyrigg

FBs

FB

Shaft (dis)

Shake Holes

Workings (disused)

Sheepfold

Shafts (dis)

460

430

450

Low Greyrigg

Needless Sike

400

Shafts (dis)

Riggs

Hartley Fell

07

Reigill

Area of Dis Shafts and F

ttlement

Shafts (dis)

Birkett Hill 383

Ladthwaite

Sheepfold

Shafts (dis)

Quarries (dis)

Area of Shake Holes

epfold

P

380

330

390

460

370

Low Dukerdale

Shak Hole

Swall Ho

Sh

Dukerdale

Red Beck

Nateby Cow Close

06

400

450

420

High Dukerdale

326

Blind Gill Holes

Swallow Holes

Pits (dis)

Sheepfold

Sheepfold

Sheepfold

utterbers Hills

Butterbers

Seave Rigg

Pits (dis)

Great Edge

458

Tailbridge Hill

547

Cairn

Nateby Common

Area of Shake Holes

New Cow Close

ole

401

Pits (dis)

Lines of Shake Holes

Areas of Shake Holes

Dukerda

Pits (dis)

441

Tailbridge

05

Lamps Moss

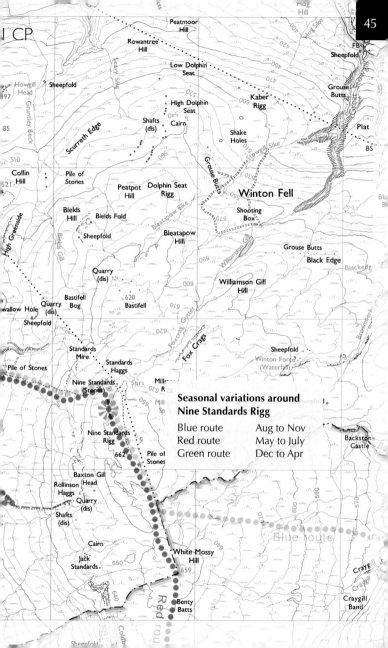

CP

Peatmoor Hill

Rowantree Hill

Hog Hill

FB

Sheepfold

Low Dolphin Seat

Sheepfold

Howgill Head

Sexty Sike

Kaber Rigg

Grouse Butts

High Dolphin Seat

Scurreth Edge

Shafts (dis)

Cairn

Plat

BS

Shake Holes

Stowgill Sike

Collin Hill

Grouse Butts

Pile of Stones

Peatpot Hill

Dolphin Seat Rigg

Winton Fell

Bields Hill

Bields Fold

Shooting Box

High Greenside

Sheepfold

Bleatapow Sike

Bleatapow Hill

Grouse Butts

Black Edge

Blackedg

Bields Gill

Williamson Gill Hill

Williamson Sike

Quarry (dis)

Swallow Hole

Quarry (dis)

Bastifell Bog

Bastifell

Foxcrag Gutter

Sheepfold

Sheepfold

Fox Crags

Brownbe

Winton Force (Waterfall)

Standards Mire

Mill R

Pile of Stones

Standards Haggs

Nine Standards (Stones)

Srs

Mill Sp

Seasonal variations around Nine Standards Rigg

Blue route   Aug to Nov
Red route   May to July
Green route   Dec to Apr

Nine Standards Rigg

Backstone Castle

662

Pile of Stones

Baxton Gill Head

Rollinson Haggs

Quarry (dis)

Blue route

Shafts (dis)

Cairn

White Mossy Hill

Jack Standards

659

Crayg

Craygill

Red rou

Benty Batts

Craygill Band

Sheepfold

Coldb

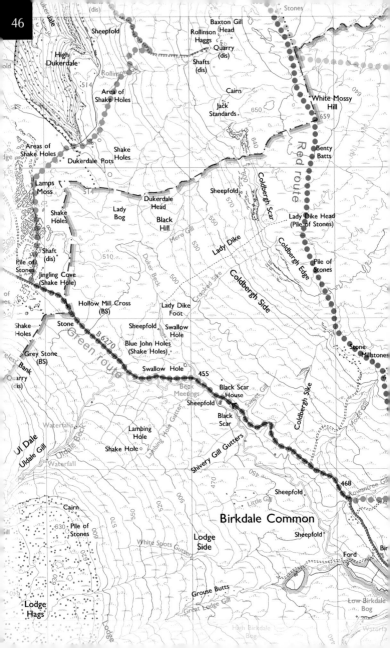

High Dukerdale

Sheepfold

Baxton Gill Head

Rollinson Haggs

Quarry (dis)

Shafts (dis)

White Mossy Hill
659

Rollinson Gill

Area of Shake Holes

514

Cairn

Jack Standards

650

640

Benty Batts

Areas of Shake Holes

Dukerdale Pots

Shake Holes

Lamps Moss

Shake Holes

Dukerdale Head

Sheepfold

570

Red route

514

Black Hill

Lady Bog

Coldbergh Scar

Lady Dike Head (Pile of Stones)

550

Mere Gill

Lady Dike

Coldbergh Edge

510

Shaft (dis)

530

Pile of Stones

Pile of Stones

Jingling Cave (Shake Hole)

500

Duker Beck

Coldbergh Side

Crooked Sike

Hollow Mill Cross (BS)

Lady Dike Foot

Shake Holes

Stone

Sheepfold

Swallow Hole

Coldbergh Sike

Green route

B6270

Blue John Holes (Shake Holes)

Sweet Gill

Grey Stone (BS)

Swallow Hole

455

Stone Millstones

Quarry (dis)

Beck Meetings

Black Scar House

Sheepfold

Ul Dale

Uldale Gill

Waterfalls

Ubdale Beck

Lambing Hole

Black Scar

Shake Hole

Shivery Gill Gutters

Waterfall

Lambing Hole Gutters

470

450

468

Rowantree Gill

Mere Gill

Cairn

630

Pile of Stones

600

White Spots Gutter

550

520

500

Little Gill

Birkdale Common

Sheepfold

Ford

Lodge Side

Sheepfold

Lodge Hags

Lodge

Grouse Butts

Great Lodge Gill

Low Birkdale Bog

High Birkdale Bog

640

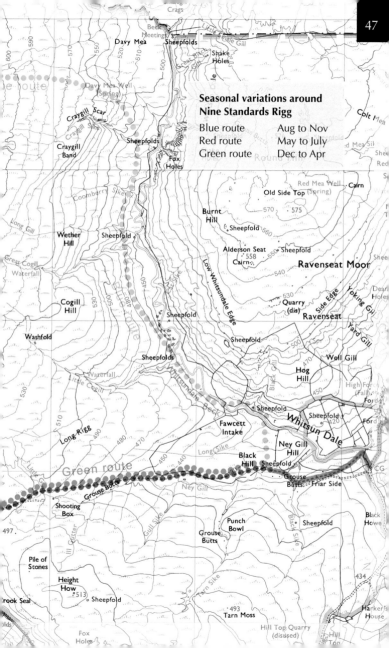

47

**Seasonal variations around
Nine Standards Rigg**

Blue route   Aug to Nov
Red route   May to July
Green route   Dec to Apr

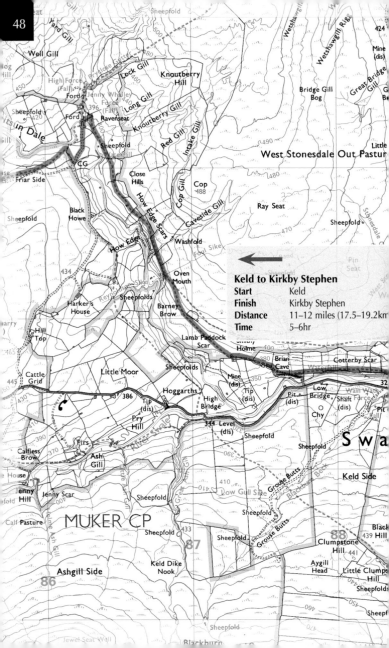

Keld to Kirkby Stephen
Start Keld
Finish Kirkby Stephen
Distance 11–12 miles (17.5–19.2km)
Time 5–6hr

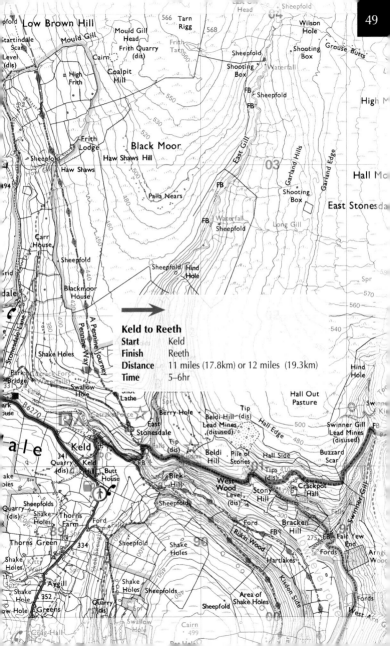

Keld to Reeth

Start	Keld
Finish	Reeth
Distance	11 miles (17.8km) or 12 miles (19.3km)
Time	5–6hr

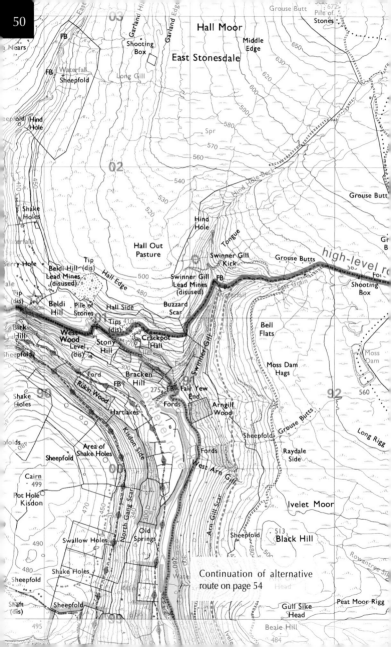

Hall Moor

East Stonesdale

Continuation of alternative
route on page 54

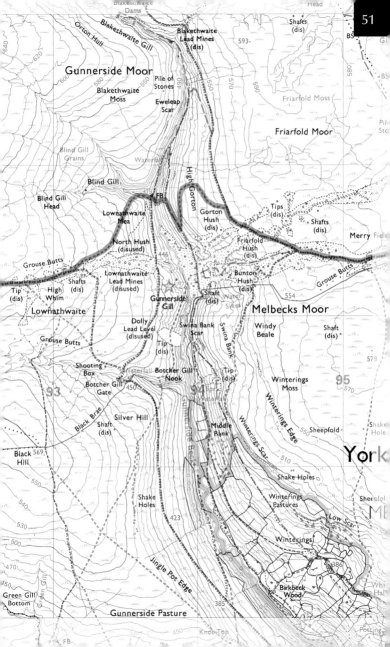

Blakethwaite
Dams

Orton Hull

Blakethwaite Gill

Blakethwaite
Lead Mines
(dis)

Shafts
(dis)

Head

593·

BS

Gunnerside Moor

Pile of
Stones

Blakethwaite
Moss

Eweleap
Scar

Friarfold Moss

Friarfold Moor

Blind Gill
Grains

Waterfall

Blind Gill

High Gorton

Gorton Hush
(dis)

Tips
(dis)

Shafts
(dis)

Blind Gill
Head

FB

Lownathwaite
Mea

Friarfold
Hush
(dis)

Merry Field

North Hush
(disused)

146

Bunton
Hush
(dis)

Grouse Butts

Grouse Butts

Shafts
(dis)

Lownathwaite
Lead Mines
(disused)

Shaft
(dis)

Water
Sike

554

Tip
(dis)

High
Whim

Lownathwaite

Gunnerside
Gill

Shaft
(dis)

Melbecks Moor

Windy
Beale

Shaft
(dis)

578

Dolly
Lead Level
(disused)

Swina Bank
Scar

Swina Bank

95

Grouse Butts

Tip
(dis)

570

Winterings
Moss

Shooting
Box

Waterfall

Botcher Gill
Nook

Tip
(dis)

93

Botcher Gill
Gate

450

94

Winterings
Edge

Gunnerside Beck

Black Brae

Shaft
(dis)

Silver Hill

Middle
Bank

Winterings Scar

Sheepfold

York

Black
Hill

569

510

Shake
Hole

550

Shake Holes

540

Shake
Holes

423

Winterings
Pastures

530

500

Winterings

Low Scar

Sheepfol
M

470

Jingle Pot Edge

Green Gill

450

386

Birkbeck
Wood

Whi
Hal

Green Gill
Bottom

385

Gunnerside Pasture

FB

Knot Top

Potting

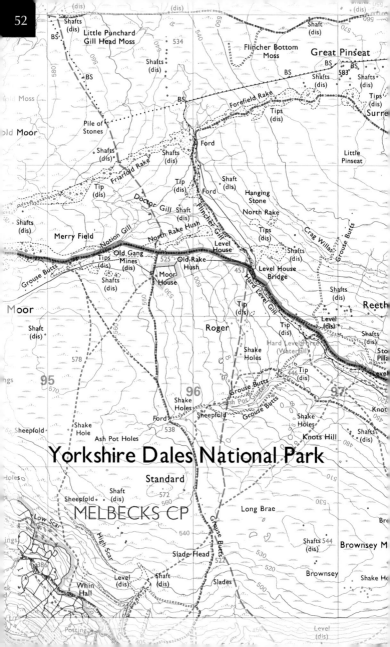

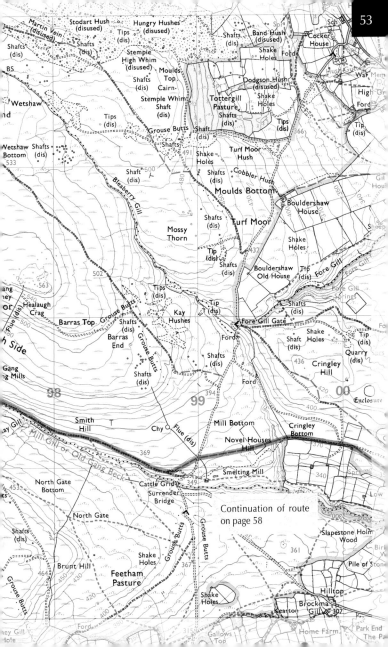

Stodart Hush (disused)
Hungry Hushes (disused)
Martin Vein (disused)
Shafts (dis)
BS
Wetshaw
nd
Wetshaw Bottom 533
Stempie High Whim (disused)
Shafts (dis)
Moulds Top
Stemple Whim Shaft (dis)
Tips (dis)
Grouse Butts
Shafts
491
Shaft (dis)
Shaft (dis)
500
Bleaberry Gill
Mossy Thorn
Shafts (dis)
502
563
ang
Healaugh Crag
Barras Top
Grouse Butts
Shafts (dis)
Barras End
or
h Side
Gang ey Mills
Grouse Butts
Shafts (dis)
Tips (dis)
Kay Hushes
Shafts (dis)
ay Gill
Smith Hill
Chy Flue (dis)
369
Mill Gill or Old Gang Beck
North Gate Bottom
453
ts
North Gate
Shafts (dis)
Brunt Hill
464
430
420
Feetham Pasture
Shake Holes
Grouse Butts
367
Band Hush (disused)
Shafts (dis)
Shake Holes
Cocker House
Ford
Sch
Hush Gill
War Mem
High Gr
Dodgson Hush (disused)
Tottergill Pasture
Shafts (dis)
Shake Holes
Tips (dis)
366
Ford
High
Tip (dis)
Turf Moor Hush
Shake Holes
Shafts (dis)
Cobbler Hush
Moulds Bottom
Bouldershaw House
Sheep
Shafts (dis)
Turf Moor
Shake Holes
Fore Gill
Gill Hou
Tip (dis)
Shafts (dis)
432
Bouldershaw Old House
Tip (dis)
Fore Gill Springs
Shafts (dis)
Fore Gill Gate
Shake Holes
Tip (dis)
Quarry
Ford
Shaft (dis)
Cringley Hill
Shafts (dis)
436
Enclosure
Ford
420
400
99
394
98
00
Mill Bottom
Novel Houses Hill
Cringley Bottom
370
340
Chy
Smelting Mill
349
361
Cattle Grid
Surrender Bridge
Low

Continuation of route on page 58

Slapestone Holm Wood
Pile of Stone
Birk
Hilltop
307
Ceanton
Brockma Gill
Shake Holes
Home Farm
Gallows Top
315
Park End
The Pa
ney Gill
ole
Ford

Continuation of route on page 51

Continuation of route on page 55

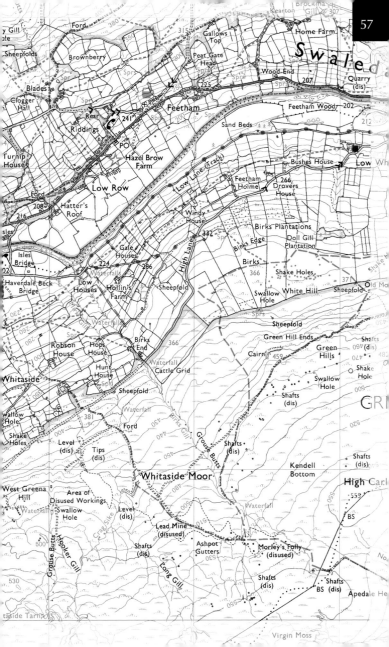

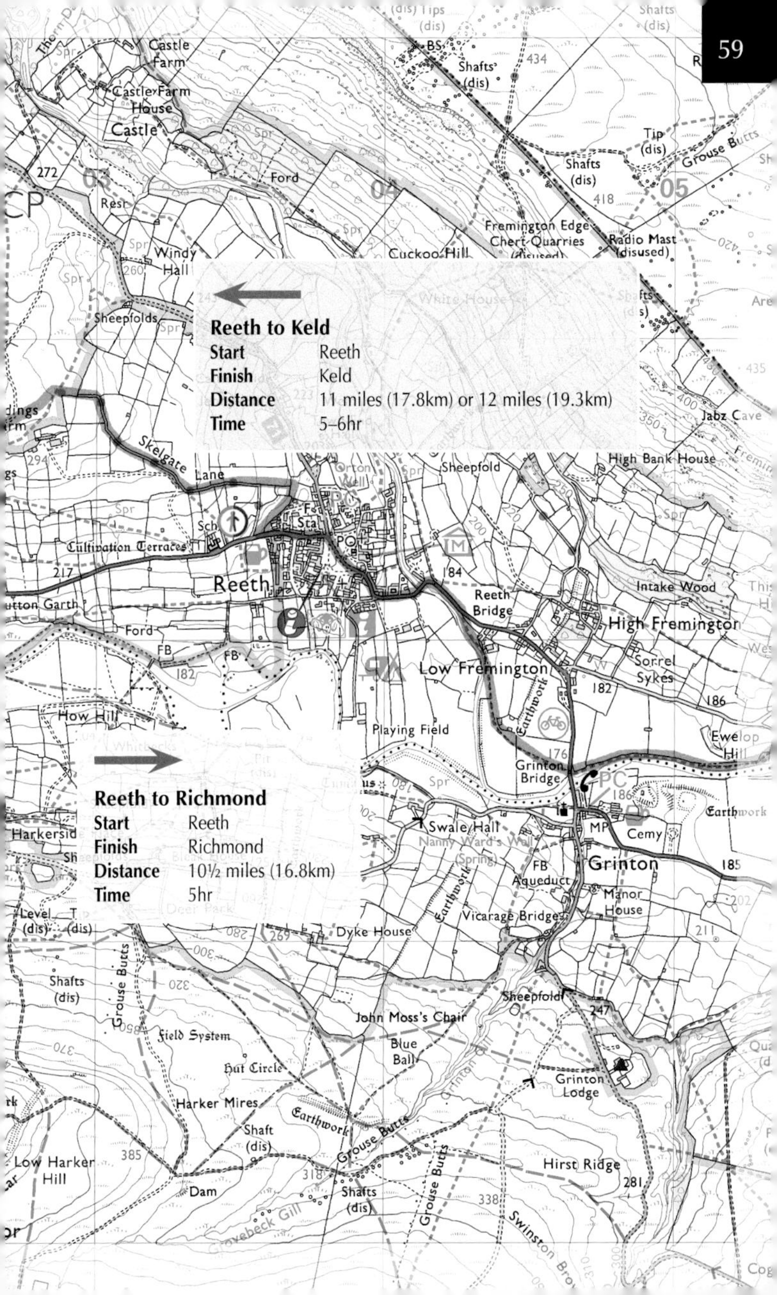

Reeth to Keld

Start	Reeth
Finish	Keld
Distance	11 miles (17.8km) or 12 miles (19.3km)
Time	5–6hr

Reeth to Richmond

Start	Reeth
Finish	Richmond
Distance	10½ miles (16.8km)
Time	5hr

Raygill Allotment

Ray Gill

Grouse Butts

Tip
(dis)

Marrick Moor

Shafts and Tips
(disused)

05

Copperthwaite Allotment

Tip
(dis)

Stelling Road

309

315

Helwith Road or

Shafts
(dis)

Fo

Shafts
(dis)

Radio Mast
(disused)

Shafts
(dis)

420

Shafts
(dis)

410

Area of Disused Shafts

400

Grouse Butts

Shafts
(dis)

Shafts
(dis)

327

Lower Stelling
Farm
324

435

Jabz Cave

430

400

386

Grouse Butts

309

Stelling

High Bank House

Fremington Edge

Intake Wood

Thistle
Hill

Sheepfold

High Fremington

West Hagg

Sorrel
Sykes

186

182

Ewelop
Hill

Grinton

Earthwork

Cemy

185

Manor
House

202

211

247

Quarry
(dis)

281

Ridge

Shaft
(dis)

Quarries
(disused)

Quarries
(disused)

Buska

Marrick Moor
House

New Close
Bank
324

Reels Head

Quarry
(dis)

Quarry
(dis)

Quarry
(dis)

314

The Hagg

224

Reels Head
Farm

Stony Bank
Plantation

Colt Park
Wood

Shafts
(dis)

Sheepfold

River Swale

Shafts
(dis)

Shafts
(dis)

334

333

Garnless
Scar

Garnless Wood

290

350

Ince Wood

Quarry
(dis)

Marrick
Barf

Shaft
(dis)

Garnless Scar
341

Cogden
Hall

Sheepfold

MP

175

B 6270

Pits
(dis)

Cogden
Wood

Stolerston
Stile

BS

BSs

202

Sprs

Remains of
Priory
(Benedictine Nuns)

MP

Mill Dam

Ford

Marrick
Priory

191

71

189

Steps
Wood

Wood
House

Earthwork

Pits
(dis)

338

Shaft
(dis)

BS

Shafts
(dis)

Stolerston
Wood

Hags Gill
Farm

220

188

Cogden Heugh

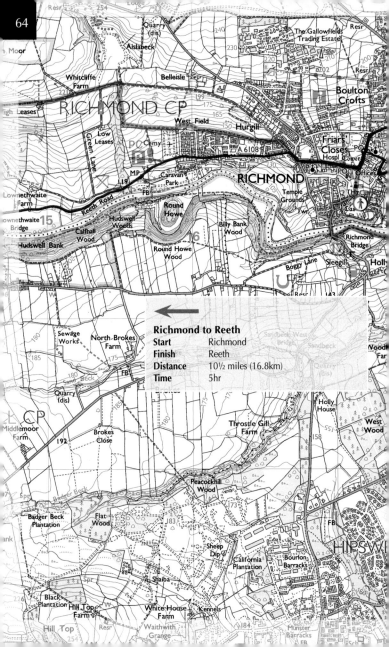

Richmond to Reeth

Start	Richmond
Finish	Reeth
Distance	10½ miles (16.8km)
Time	5hr

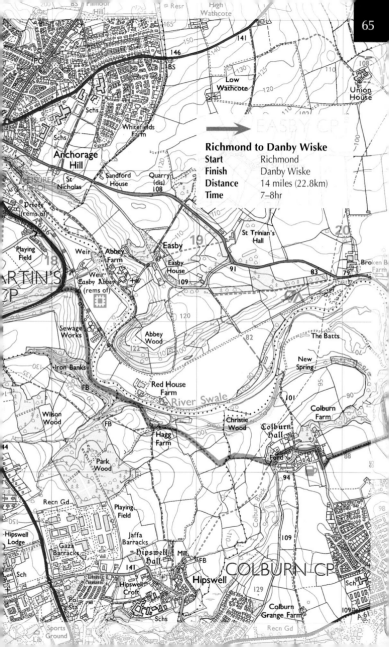

Richmond to Danby Wiske

Start	Richmond
Finish	Danby Wiske
Distance	14 miles (22.8km)
Time	7–8hr

BROMPTON-ON-SWALE
CP

Old Maids Farm
Park House
Broken Brae Farm
79
Mount Pleasant
Robin Hood Farm
The Batts
Brompton Lakes
Park Cottage
Weir
Mill
Primula Grange
Sch
Brompton Bridge
New Spring
Colburn Beck Wood
Colburn Farm
PO
Cemy
Crow Hole
Brompton-on-Swale
St Giles Farm
Thornbro

BROUGH WITH
ST GILES CP

Sewage Works
Colburn
Dismantled Railway
Ash House
Catterick Road
Brough With St Giles
Ash House Plantation
A 6136
N CP
Sch
PO
88
Home Farm
Walkerville
83
74
Brough
Balancing Pond
Sta
Colburn Sidings
Ford
Horse Park Wood
Brough Hall
Mill
85
Camp Plantation
87
Norway Wood
Plodmire Wood
109
108
ley
ill
Brough Lodge
97
Breckenbrough

23
24
25

Sand and Gravel Quarry

Rosey Hill

Settling Ponds

Elmfield Hall

Quarry

Banks Lane

Bec
Bri

Home
Farm PO

adilla

Hollow Banks

Howe Hill Lane

64

62

Howe Hill

Tancred Grange

Sch

B 6271

58

Cemy

Catterick Bridge

FB

Sand & Gravel Pit

Flat Lane

57

56

Bolt

P

Field House

55

Settling Pond

56

52

Back Lane

TARACTONIVM
ROMAN TOWN

Race Course

Leeming Lane

50

P

Sand & Gravel Pit

61

Bolton-on-Swale Lake

Ellerton Pa

Tel Ex

52

Dere Street
ROMAN ROAD
(course of)

War Meml

Quarry

Sch

51

Catterick

A 6055

Cemy

Sewage Works

Brough Beck

Manor House

Balancing Pond

Oran Lane

Marne Barracks

Sewage Works

h Beck

70

65

High Cowstand Bridge

63

Bainesse

Low Cowstand Farm

Cowstand Farm

A 6055

49

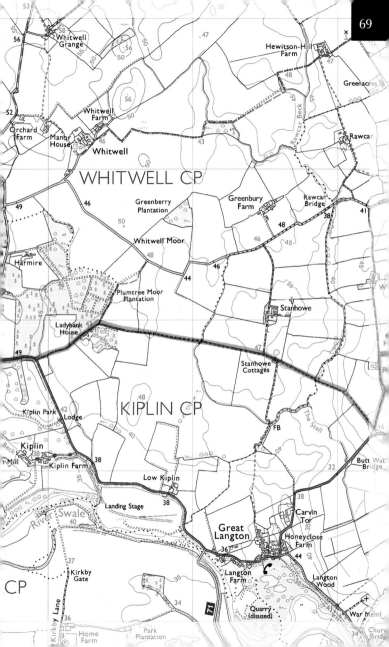

53
56 Whitwell Grange
58
50
50
.47
Hewitson-Hill Farm
×
47
48
Greenacres
52
Whitwell Farm
50
50
Orchard Farm
56
46
Rawcar Beck
Rawcar
Manor House
43
Whitwell
50
WHITWELL CP
49
46
Greenberry Plantation
Greenbury Farm
Rawcar Bridge
50
48
38
41
Whitwell Moor
46
45
48
Harmire
44
46
45
Plumtree Moor Plantation
Stanhowe
Ladybank House
43
49
47
Stanhowe Cottages
KIPLIN CP
The Stell
48
Kiplin Park
42
Lodge
40
FB
Kiplin
Butt Wat Bridge
32
38
Mill
Kiplin Farm
Low Kiplin
Carvin Tor
38
Landing Stage
38
Honeyclose Farm
River Swale
40
Great Langton
44
CP
37
Kirkby Gate
35
36
Langton Farm
Langton Wood
71
34
Quarry (disused)
War Meml
Kirkby Lane
36
Home Farm
Park Plantation
Church Bridge

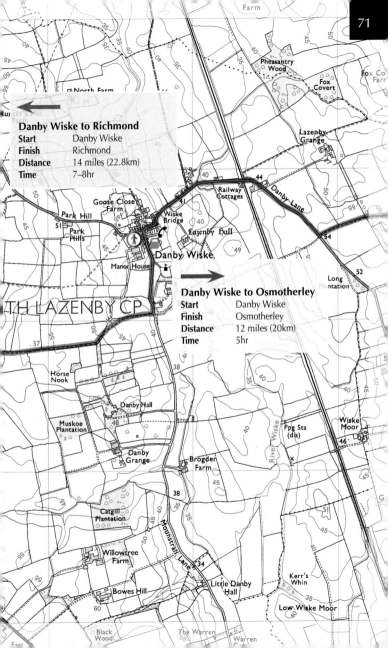

Danby Wiske to Richmond

Start   Danby Wiske
Finish   Richmond
Distance   14 miles (22.8km)
Time   7–8hr

Danby Wiske to Osmotherley

Start   Danby Wiske
Finish   Osmotherley
Distance   12 miles (20km)
Time   5hr

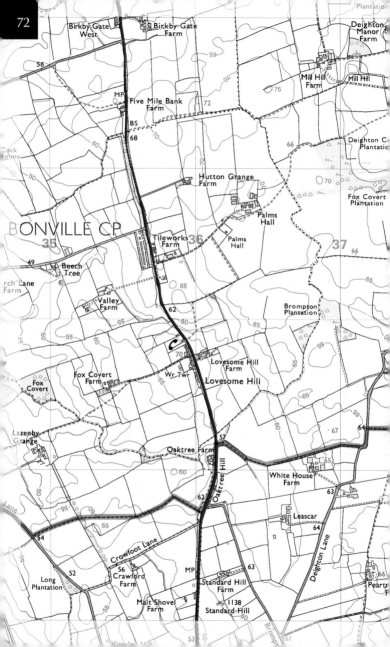

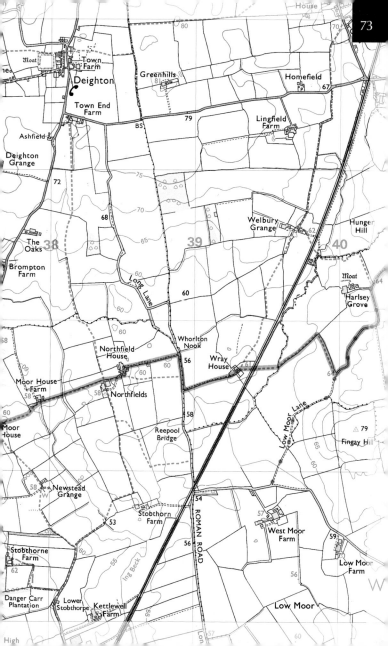

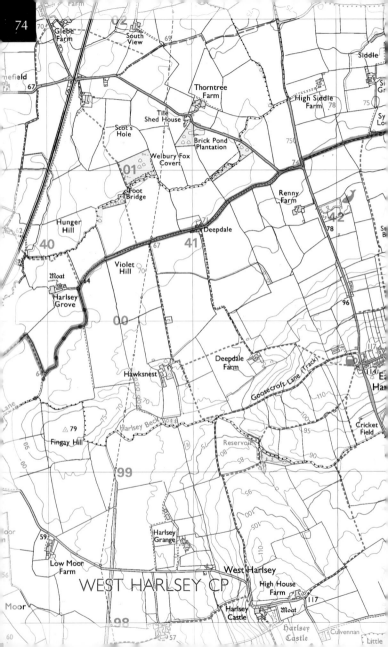

Fowgill

Fowgill Lane (Track)

Springfield
House

Salter
Bridge

Grinkle
Carr

Longlands

Ingleby
Arncliffe

Sch

MP
Sp

Pity Me
Wood

Larch
Plantation

Winchatt

Ingleby
Cross

Carr
Bridge

43

Baulk
Bridge
Farm

Somerset
House

Moat

Baulk
Bridge

44

Thornflatt
Farm

Thorntree
Farm

73

Wye
Carrs

Cock Bush
Hall Farm

Hall
Farm

Harlsey
Manor

Wyecarr
Plantation

Germany
Cottages

Park
House

Morton Grange
Farm

The Kell

The
Clumps

River Wiske

Carr Beck

A172

A19

Pond
Plantation

Cleveland Tontine
(Hotel)

HARLSEY CP

Little
Tontine

Jubilee
antation

Staddle
Bridge
House

Stony Lane

Mount Grace

Mount Lodge Fish Ponds
Farm

Mount Grace
Wood

Remains of
Mount Grace Priory
(Carthusian founded 1898)

Bruntcliffe
Farm

Mount Bank

Chapel Wood
Farm

Bruntcliffe
Bank

Siddle

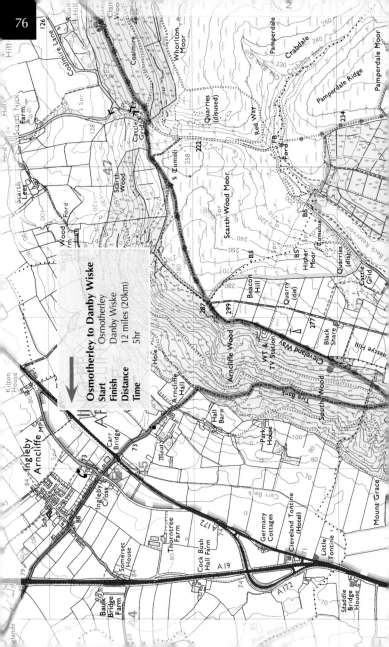

Osmotherley to Danby Wiske

Start	Osmotherley
Finish	Danby Wiske
Distance	12 miles (20km)
Time	5hr

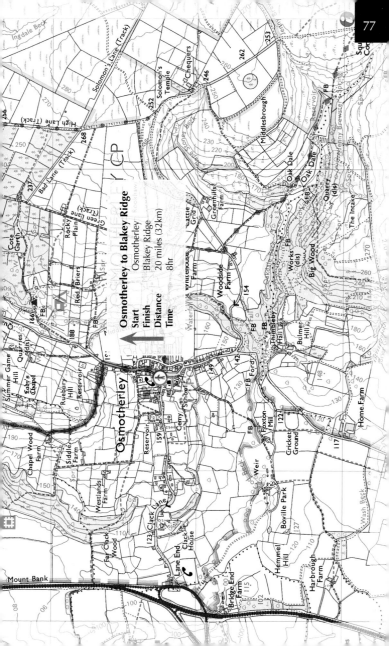

Osmotherley to Blakey Ridge

Start	Osmotherley
Finish	Blakey Ridge
Distance	20 miles (32km)
Time	8hr

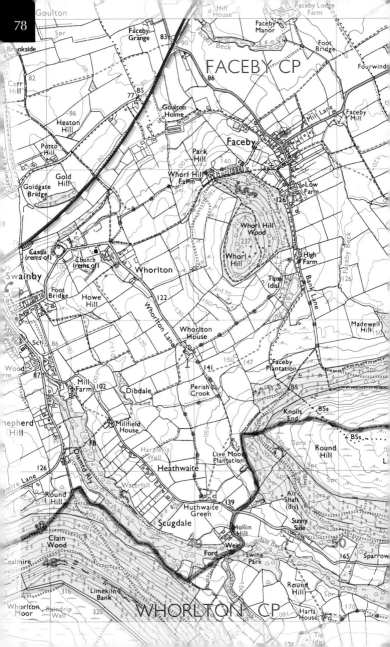

Alum House Lane

Busby Park

Resr

Underhill Cottage Farm

Underhill Farm

Resr

Manor Farm

Busby Wood

Busby Moor

Green Bank

Ash Tree Farm

FBs

FBs

Carlton Hall Wood

Tumulus

BS

BS

Tum

BS

Plane Tree Farm

Harry Wath Wood

Carlton Bank

Quarries (dis)

Quarry (dis)

Thwaites House

408 Cairn

Carlton Moor

Quarry (dis)

Bracken Hill

Tips (dis)

South F Farm

Great Bonny Cliff

Low Broom

Little Bonny Cliff

Cleveland Way

Faceby Bank

Thackdale

379

Staindale

Gold Hill

BS

BS

Cairn

BS

Holey Moor

Tip (dis)

Bilsdale West Moor

Raisdale

Whorlton Moor

Snotterdale Plantation

Raisdale Mill Plantation

Rakes Wood

Sprs

Brian's Pond

Sprs

Rakes Intake

Clough Gill Top

51

52

53

Delicate Hill

Stoney Wicks

Raikes Farm

BS

Pit (dis)

Barker's Crags

BS

Shotterdale

Scugdale Hall

Tip (dis)

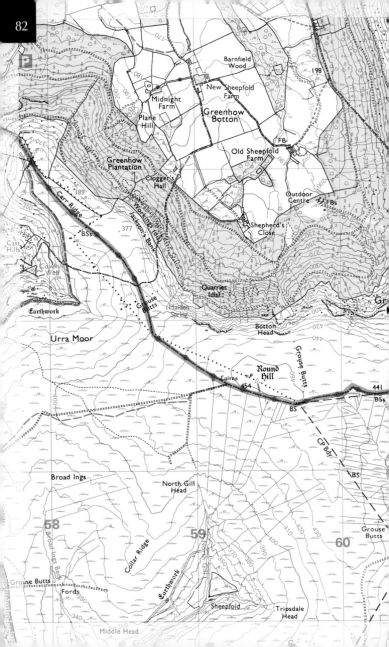

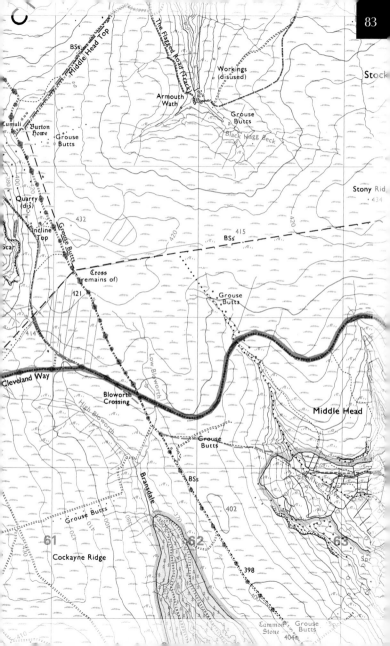

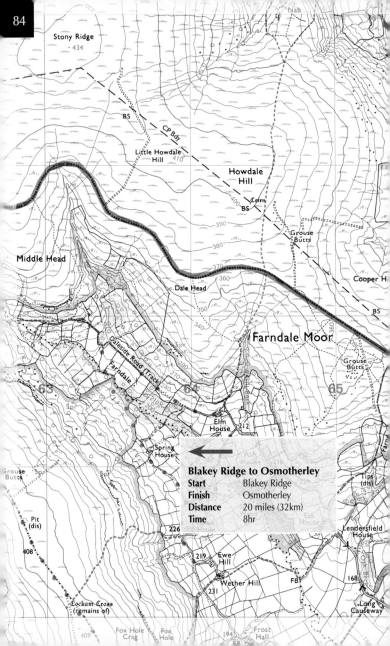

Blakey Ridge to Osmotherley
Start   Blakey Ridge
Finish   Osmotherley
Distance   20 miles (32km)
Time   8hr

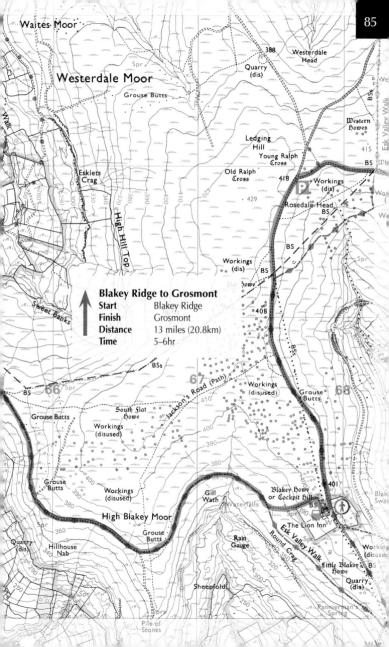

Waites Moor

Westerdale Moor

Grouse Butts

Walk

Esklets Crag

High Hill Top

Sweet Banks

388

Quarry (dis)

Westerdale Head

Western Howes

BS

Wo

Ledging Hill

Young Ralph Cross

Old Ralph Cross

415

·429

418

P

Workings (dis)

Rosedale Head

BS

BS

Wo

We

330

Workings (dis)

BS

Home

·408

BS

Spr

BSs

Blakey Ridge to Grosmont
Start   Blakey Ridge
Finish   Grosmont
Distance   13 miles (20.8km)
Time   5–6hr

67

Jackson's Road (Path)

Workings (disused)

Grouse Butts

68

BS

66

Spr

South Flat Howe

410

Grouse Butts

Workings (disused)

400

390

380

Grouse Butts

400

Workings (disused)

Grouse Butts

Gill Wath

Waterfalls

Blakey Howe or Cockpit Hill

·401

Esk Valley Walk

BS

Blak Swa

The Lion Inn

Workin (disuse

High Blakey Moor

Hillhouse Nab

Quarry (dis)

340

360

380

Spr

250

290

Round Crag

Rain Gauge

Sheepfold

Little Blakey Howe

Quarry (dis)

320

300

Ranniemann's Spring

250

Pile of Stones

Spr

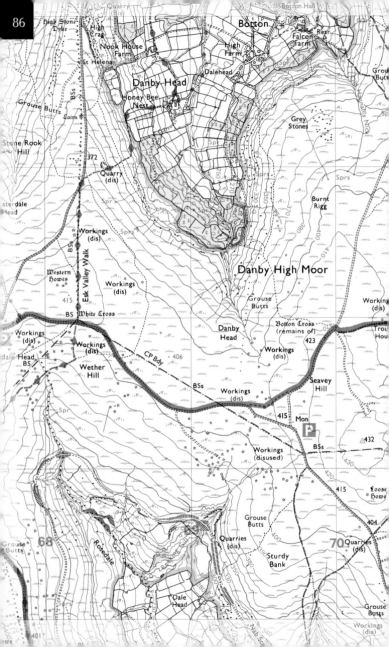

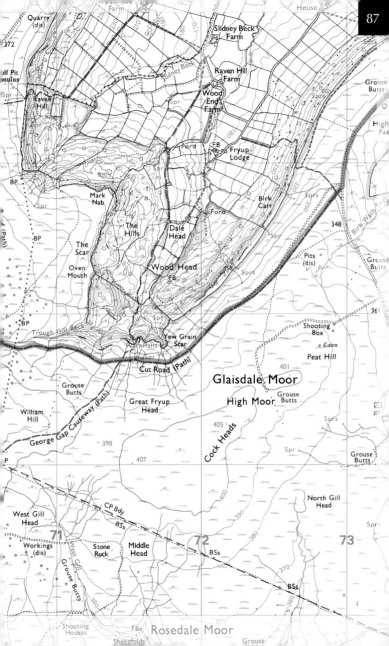

Quarry (dis)
372
olf Pit mulus
Raven Hill
BP
BP
The Scar
Oven Mouth
BP
Trough Gill Beck
Grouse Butts
William Hill
George Gap Causeway (Path)
P
West Gill Head
71
Workings (dis)

Slidney Beck Farm
Raven Hill Farm
Wood End Farm
Slidney Beck
Spr
Ford
FB
Fryup Lodge
Mark Nab
The Hills
Dale Head
Ford
Wood Head
FB
Yew Grain Scar
Waterfalls
Cut Road (Path)
Great Fryup Head
Stone Ruck
Middle Head
BSs
Cp Bdy
BSs

House
Grouse Butts
High Fa
Birk Carr
Birk With
348
Pits (dis)
Grouse Butts
36
Shooting Box
Cairn
Peat Hill
401
Glaisdale Moor
High Moor
Grouse Butts
405
Cock Heads
407
Spr
398
400
72
BSs
390
North Gill Head
73
Spr
Grouse Butts
BSs
360
Grouse Butts
Shooting Houses
Sheepfolds
FBs
Rosedale Moor
Grouse

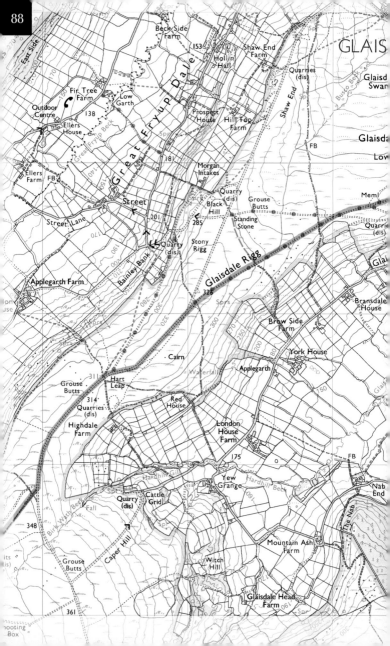

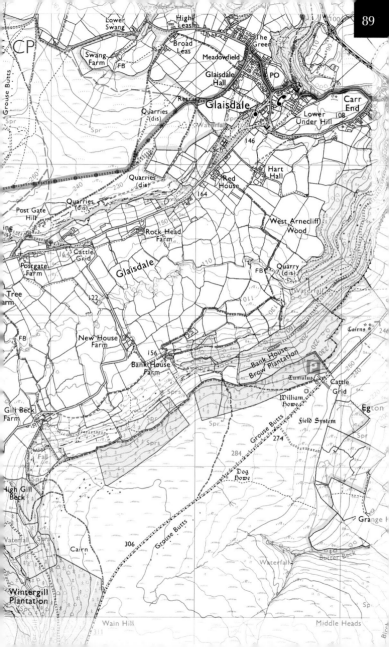

Grosmont to Robin Hood's Bay

Start	Grosmont
Finish	Robin Hood's Bay
Distance	15 miles (24km)
Time	6–7hr

Grosmont to Blakey Ridge

Start	Grosmont
Finish	Blakey Ridge
Distance	13 miles (20.8km)
Time	5–6hr

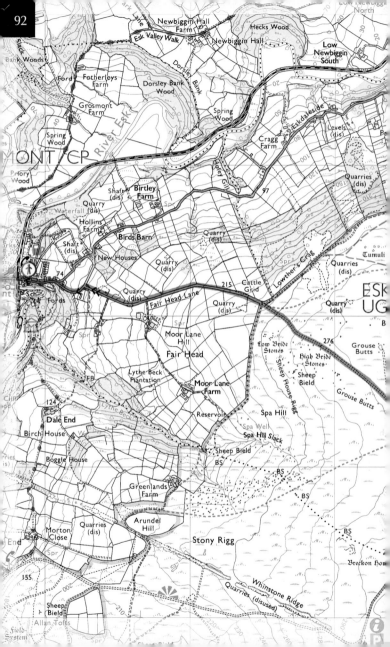

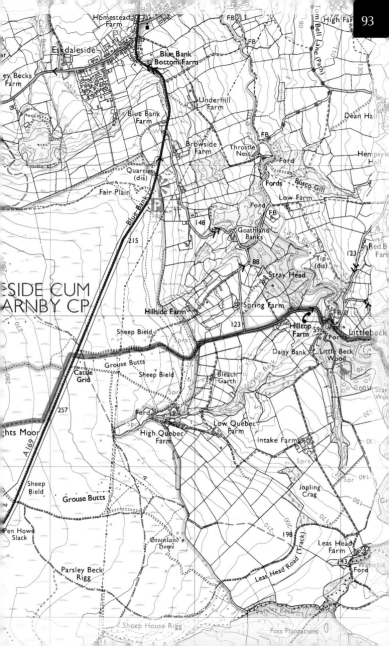

Catwick House Farm
Ford
Rigg Hall
Rigg Beck
Fern Farm
178

Normanby Hill Top
Hamilton
204
Skerry Hall
Tumulus
Kairn Dykes

Ford
Stony Gate Slack
Tumulus
200
Tumulus
220
White Moor Hill
Sheep Dip
FB
Quarries (dis)
Brow Top

Slack
Pit (dis)
Mossy Mere
Pit (dis)
Tumulus

Grouse Butts
Earthwork
213
Latter Gate Hills
Tumuli

Grouse Butts
Cross
Spr
Lodge Plantation
Graystone Hills
Robin Hood's Bay Road
Standing Stones Rigg
Spr
Partridge Hill Farm

A 171
B 1416
Nigh Middle Slke
197
Sneaton Corner
Tumulus
Standing Stones
190
150
Ramsdale
Waterfall
Spr
Oak Wood

Low Moor
Middle Rigg
200
Thorn Key Howes
Waterfall
Weir
Ford
Leith Rigg
Ramsdale Mill Farm
Carr Wood
FYLINGD

Grouse Butts
Far Middle Sike
Thorn Key Wath
Tumulus
Leith Rigg
Stevenson's Piece
Waterfall

Robin Hood's Bay Road (Path)
Mires Slack
Kirk Moor Plantation
Wind Hill
Chapel Garth
Quarries (dis)
Park Hill
177
182

Grey Heugh Head
Grey Heugh Slack
Foulsike Farm
190
198
St Ives Farm
Brock Hall Farm

206
Ford
178
Kirk Moor
Tumulus
Quarry (dis)
Kettle Well Cottage

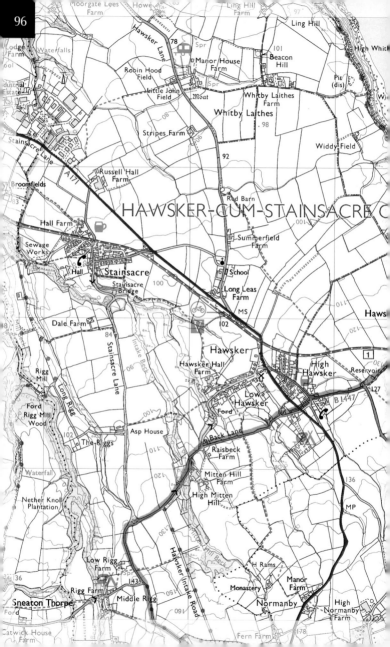

Maw Wyke
Hole
FB
we
Pursglove Stye
Batts
Oakham
Wood
Pursglove
Stye
Waterfalls
Northcliffe
Holiday
Park
108
Limekiln
Slack
White Stone
Hole
White
Horse
High Scar
Normanby Stye
Batts
Hilda's Howe
Far Jetticks
Pits
(dis)
Clock Case
Nab
Bottom
House
143
Bottom House Lane
Waterfall
Craze
Naze
Homerell
Hole
T'Awd Abba
Well
Rain Dale
Spring Farm
Cow & Calf
Raw Pasture
Castle
Chamber
Raw Pasture Lane
Bulmer St
163
Bulmer Ste
Hole
176
Smails Moor
Farm
Bay Ness
Ness Point
North Che
High Lane
Quarry
(dis)
Quarry
(dis)
193
Reservoir
Water
Ness Ruck
Green Hills

Robin Hood's Bay to Grosmont

Start	Robin Hood's Bay
Finish	Grosmont
Distance	15 miles (24km)
Time	6–7hr

52

LEGEND OF SYMBOLS
USED ON ORDNANCE SURVEY
1:25,000 (EXPLORER) MAPPING

Map data

ROADS AND PATHS — Not necessarily rights of way

M1 or A6(M)	Motorway
A 35	Dual carriageway
A30	Main road
B 3074	Secondary road
	Narrow road with passing places
	Road under construction
	Road generally more than 4 m wide
	Road generally less than 4 m wide
	Other road, drive or track, fenced and unfenced
	Gradient: steeper than 20% (1 in 5); 14% (1 in 7) to 20% (1 in 5)
Ferry	Ferry; Ferry P – passenger only
	Path

- Service Area
- Service Area
- **7** Junction Number
- **T1** Toll road junction

RAILWAYS

	Multiple track / Single track — standard gauge
	Narrow gauge or Light rapid transit system (LRTS) and station
	Road over; road under; level crossing
	Cutting; tunnel; embankment
	Station, open to passengers; siding

PUBLIC RIGHTS OF WAY

----------	Footpath
— — — —	Bridleway
+ + + + +	Byway open to all traffic
⊢ ⊢ ⊢ ⊢ ⊢	Restricted byway

The representation on this map of any other road, track or path is no evidence of the existence of a right of way

ARCHAEOLOGICAL AND HISTORICAL INFORMATION

⚜	Site of antiquity	VILLA	Roman	☆ ▦	Visible earthwork
⚔ 1066	Site of battle (with date)	𝕮𝖆𝖘𝖙𝖑𝖊	Non-Roman		

Information provided by English Heritage for England and the Royal Commissions on the Ancient and Historical Monuments for Scotland and Wales

HEIGHTS AND NATURAL FEATURES (continued)

Vertical face/cliff

75
60
50

Contours are at
5 or 10 metre
vertical intervals

Loose rock | Boulders | Outcrop | Scree

Water

Mud

Sand; sand and shingle

SELECTED TOURIST AND LEISURE INFORMATION

Building of historic interest			Nature reserve
Cadw			National Trust
Heritage centre HC			Other tourist feature
Camp site			Parking
Caravan site		P&R	Park and ride, all year
Camping and caravan site		P&R	Park and ride, seasonal
Castle / fort			Picnic site
Cathedral / Abbey			Preserved railway
Craft centre		PC	Public Convenience
Country park			Public house/s
Cycle trail			Recreation / leisure / sports centre
Mountain bike trail			Roman site (Hadrian's Wall only)
Cycle hire			Slipway
English Heritage			Telephone, emergency
Fishing			Telephone, public
Forestry Commission Visitor centre			Telephone, roadside assistance
Garden / arboretum			Theme / pleasure park
Golf course or links			Viewpoint
Historic Scotland		V	Visitor centre
Information centre, all year i			Walks / trails
Information centre, seasonal i			World Heritage site / area
Horse riding			Water activites
Museum			Boat trips
National Park Visitor Centre (park logo) e.g. Yorkshire Dales			Boat hire

(For complete legend and symbols, see any OS Explorer map).

OTHER PUBLIC ACCESS

• • •	Other routes with public access	The exact nature of the rights on these routes and the existence of any restrictions may be checked with the local highway authority. Alignments are based on the best information available
◆ ◆ ◆	Recreational route	
◆ ◆ ◆	🚶 National Trail (◊) Long Distance Route	
- - - - - - - - -	Permissive footpath ⎫	Footpaths and bridleways along which landowners have permitted public use but which are not rights of way. The agreement may be withdrawn
— — — — —	Permissive bridleway ⎭	
• • •	Traffic-free cycle route	
1 **1**	National cycle network route number – traffic free; on road	

ACCESS LAND

 Firing and test ranges in the area. Danger! Observe warning notices

Access permitted within managed controls, for example, local byelaws. Visit **www.access.mod.uk** for information

England and Wales

Access land boundary and tint

Access land in wooded area

 Access information point

Portrayal of access land on this map is intended as a guide to land which is normally available for access on foot, for example access land created under the Countryside and Rights of Way Act 2000, and land managed by the National Trust, Forestry Commission and Woodland Trust. Access for other activities may also exist. Some restrictions will apply; some land will be excluded from open access rights. The depiction of rights of access does not imply or express any warranty as to its accuracy or completeness. Observe local signs and follow the Countryside Code. Visit **www.countrysideaccess.gov.uk** for up-to-date information

BOUNDARIES

— + — +	National
— · — · —	County (England)
— — — —	Unitary Authority (UA), Metropolitan District (Met Dist), London Borough (LB) or District
	(Scotland & Wales are solely Unitary Authorities)
· · · · · · · ·	Civil Parish (CP) (England) or Community (C) (Wales)
▬▬ ▬▬	National Park boundary

VEGETATION

Limits of vegetation are defined by positioning of symbols

	Coniferous trees
	Non-coniferous trees
	Coppice
	Orchard
	Scrub
	Bracken, heath or rough grassland
	Marsh, reeds or saltings

HEIGHTS AND NATURAL FEATURES

52 · Ground survey height
284 · Air survey height

Surface heights are to the nearest metre above mean sea level. Where two heights are shown, the first height is to the base of the triangulation pillar and the second (in brackets) to the highest natural point of the hill

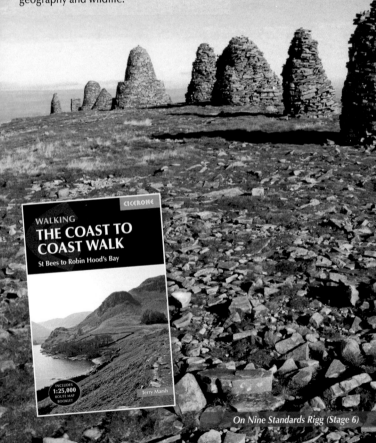

THE COAST TO COAST WALK

This map booklet accompanies the latest edition of Terry Marsh's guidebook to the Coast to Coast Walk, described principally from west to east (with summary route description east to west), between St Bees Head and Robin Hood's Bay. The guidebook features annotated 1:100,000 mapping alongside detailed step-by-step route description, with lots of planning advice and other information about local history, geography and wildlife.

CICERONE

WALKING
THE COAST TO COAST WALK
St Bees to Robin Hood's Bay

INCLUDES
1:25,000
ROUTE MAP
BOOKLET

Terry Marsh

On Nine Standards Rigg (Stage 6)

OTHER CICERONE TRAIL GUIDES

 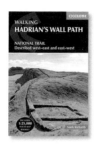 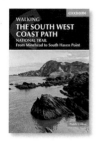

Cicerone National Trails Guides
The South West Coast Path
The South Downs Way
The North Downs Way
The Ridgeway National Trail
The Thames Path
The Cotswold Way
The Peddars Way and
    Norfolk Coast Path
The Cleveland Way and
    the Yorkshire Wolds Way
Cycling the Pennine Bridleway
The Pennine Way
Hadrian's Wall Path
The Pembrokeshire Coast Path
Offa's Dyke Path
Glyndŵr's Way
The Southern Upland Way
The Speyside Way
The West Highland Way
The Great Glen Way

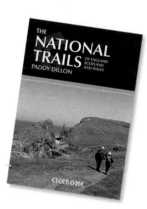

Visit our website for a full
list of Cicerone Trail Guides
www.cicerone.co.uk

CICERONE

Trust Cicerone to guide your next adventure, wherever it may be around the world...

Discover guides for hiking, mountain walking, backpacking, trekking, trail running, cycling and mountain biking, ski touring, climbing and scrambling in Britain, Europe and worldwide.

Connect with Cicerone online and find inspiration.

- buy books and ebooks
- articles, advice and trip reports
- podcasts and live events
- GPX files and updates
- regular newsletter

cicerone.co.uk